COMMON
AS MUCK!

COMMON AS MUCK!

ROY 'CHUBBY' BROWN

My Autobiography

TIME WARNER
BOOKS

First published in Great Britain in 2006 by Time Warner Books

Copyright © Royston Vasey 2006

A CIP catalogue record for this book
is available from the British Library.

Hardback ISBN-13: 978-0-316-02987-2
Hardback ISBN-10: 0-316-02987-4
C format ISBN-13: 978-0-316-03017-5
C format ISBN-10: 0-316-03017-1

Typeset in Baskerville by M Rules
Printed and bound in Great Britain by
Clays Ltd, St Ives plc

Time Warner Books
An imprint of
Little, Brown Book Group
Brettenham House
Lancaster Place
London WC2E 7EN

A member of the Hachette Livre Group of Companies

www.littlebrown.co.uk

Time Warner Books is a trademark of Time Warner Inc. or an affiliated
company. Used under licence by Little, Brown Book Group, which is not
affiliated with Time Warner Inc.

For Helen, Amy and Reece

CONTENTS

ACKNOWLEDGEMENTS

Boys and girls, throughout this book I have been honest and frank, but in my heart I feel that some of the participants need to be protected by a change of name. I thank them all for adding value and colour to my life. And, last but not least, thanks to you, the great British public (wherever you are), for taking me to your hearts . . .

If there's such a thing as reincarnation, can someone please tell me before I give it all away.

I have been a Jack the lad but it's better than getting no cards on Father's Day.

COMMON AS MUCK!

PROLOGUE

BLACKPOOL ROCK

'YER FAT BASTARD!'

Blackpool, July 2003. I'm on me home turf, the North Pier. It's a glorious day and I'm passing through the amusement arcade at the start of the quarter-mile walk along the boards to the theatre at the end of the pier. I'm enjoying the warm summer sun and looking forward to the evening ahead. The show doesn't start until seven-thirty and this is six o'clock, but I'm always in my dressing room early. It gives me time to soundcheck some songs and to rehearse a few new gags. Keith, my mate, is scuttling along beside me, carrying a Tesco shopping bag with a few cans of lager for before the show, when my good mood is shattered by a Glaswegian bellowing at full tilt.

Now, I know I'm a fat bastard without anyone telling me. After all, it's my catchphrase, one that, in less than two hours' time, more than 1,500 punters will be chanting as I come on stage. But some people go too far.

'Oi, you! Yes, you!' It's the Glaswegian again. '*You big fat cunt!*'

I turn around. There, in the dead area between the hot-dog

stall, the gift shop, the rock shop and the stall selling T-shirts with plastic tits on them, a lump of shite is sitting at a table. Nearby, there's a gang of lads who've got tickets to come and see me. They're standing at the bar, downing a few jars, getting blathered before the show and starting to take an interest in the rude fucker shouting his mouth off.

I can see he is what us Teessiders call a hacky get – a miserable, filthy waste of space. But he's a hacky get with a family, so I know to behave. There's his wife and his three little kids to consider. They're about nine, eight and six, I'd guess, and I don't want to upset them.

I haven't had a proper fight in more than ten years. I've learned to keep my hands to myself. I don't want to reawaken bad habits, so I ignore him and keep walking, my eyes fixed straight ahead.

'Oi! I'm talking to *you*, you big *fat* bastard,' the Glaswegian hollers again. I turn around and stare him down.

'Why don't you just grow up?' I say. And I keep walking.

'Ah, fuck off!' The Glaswegian is obviously not going to give up easily.

I stop walking and slowly turn around, my temper rising inside me like a kettle coming to the boil. From the way that he's carrying on, it's clear to me that he's got no respect for his wife or his kids. He's certainly got no respect for all the people around him. Every table in the bar is taken and they're all staring our way, wondering what's going on. I want to give the lanky lout a bat, show him that I might be fat and I might be old enough to be his grandfather, but that I won't be spoken to like that. But instead I ignore him and head for the door.

Just as I pass through the door he shouts again. '*Fuck you*, you fucking *fat cunt*.'

It's too much. 'I'm not putting up with this,' I mutter to Keith.

'You what?' Keith replies.

'I said that sackless nowt's taken a right fucking lend of me.' And I turn on my heels. 'I'm gonna have to ploat that cunt.'

I walk up to him. 'Have you got something to say to me?'

'Ahh, you're a big cunt!'

For a moment I don't know what to do. This kind of thing happens to me almost every day and it's a finely judged thing to get it right. Do I take offence or do I let it wash over me? After all, most of the time it's harmless. Just a couple of fans who don't know what to say and think it's okay to be rude. Because I swear and talk about tits, fannies and cocks on stage they think that they can insult me in the street. Like the little old lady who stopped me in my tracks on Blackpool South Pier fifteen years ago. She was in her early seventies and with a man I assumed was her husband. They looked like any other elderly couple, enjoying the sea air and taking in the Golden Mile.

'Eeeh,' she said. And she put her hand on my chest to stop me. 'Eeeh, you fat bastard.'

So I stopped walking. 'Yes?' I said, smiling.

'Eeeh, you fat bastard,' she said again. Then she giggled. 'Hee hee, you fucking fat bastard.' By now, the shock element had gone. I was looking at this elderly woman and thinking two things. First, that's a foul mouth you've got on you, especially for a woman of your age. And second, what are you going to say next? I know I'm a fat bastard. Right?

After the fifth or sixth 'fat bastard', I said: 'Now you've recognised me, what do you want?'

'Eeeh, I think you're fucking great, you fat bastard. Eeeh, you fucking fat bastard.'

I walked off, half in despair and half in frustration. What else could I do? If I had said owt, she would have thought I was the rude one. I couldn't win.

And it's not just old ladies. One evening, on the way to work, a little girl walked up to me. With blonde hair and blue eyes, she was no more than six or seven years old and absolutely gorgeous. If you ever wanted to paint a picture of a perfect little girl, she would have been it.

'Hello,' I said, smiling at her and glancing at her parents standing nearby.

'Hello,' she replied bashfully. 'You're a fat bastard, aren't you?'

'Am I?' I said.

'Yes,' she said. 'You're a big fat bastard.' And she looked around at her parents, who were smiling, beaming with pride at their daughter's cheek. What kind of parent tells their six-year-old child to go up to a complete stranger and insult them? If I had ever sworn in front of my father, he would have lifted me so high the weather would have changed by the time I got back down.

Now I can't tell people how to lead their lives and most of my fans are just great. But there's always the idiot who thinks it's fine to shout 'Hiya, Chubby, you big fat cunt' down a supermarket aisle when I'm doing my shopping. It makes me cringe with embarrassment as all the other shoppers stare at me. I can see what they're thinking: if he wasn't here, we wouldn't be hearing that. Or maybe they think that I'm the kind of person who sits in a restaurant and orders their food by saying to the waiter: 'I'll have the steak and chips, cunt face'. But I'm not and I never have been. And now, standing in the North Pier bar at Blackpool, I've had enough.

'If you are gonna say sommat to me, will you say it to me outside the bar, please?' I say.

The muscles in the Glaswegian's face tighten as I grab him by his T-shirt and wrap my fist around it. I pull him off his chair and drag him thirty feet to the door.

'I'll fucking kill you, you fat bastard,' he screams as I skid him across the sticky floor. 'I'll fucking glass you.'

'Yes, I know you will,' I say. The bar is silent. Everybody is watching. The customers in the gift shops stop in their tracks and come out of the shops to have a stare. People eating ice creams stand open-mouthed, watching what is going on.

'Now what are you gonna fucking say?' I snarl as we get outside and I pull him to his feet, pushing him across the boardwalk to the edge of the pier.

The Glaswegian is unsteady, so I see the swing of his fist coming towards me long before it's within range. I dodge the punch, turn him around and dig him once in the ribs. He goes down like a sack of shite, then jumps up.

'I'll fucking kill you!' he shouts as Keith grabs him. 'I'm gonna kill him. I'm gonna fucking kill the fat fucker,' he shouts, kicking Keith at the same time.

'You'll kill no fucker, else I'll throw you over the fucking side, you twat,' I shout. And I mean it. I want to give him a lacing, but Keith has him pinned down on the floor as three security guards come pounding down the pier and grab the lanky Glaswegian. With Keith and the bouncers between us, the Glaswegian tries to throw a few punches but he can't get near me.

'I wouldn't if I was you, mate,' Keith says. 'I wouldn't.'

The Glaswegian is carted away and I head for the theatre. An hour later, I'm on stage. The show's going well. It's always a buzz to play Blackpool and I'm more pumped up than usual, the adrenalin from the earlier aggro sharpening my timing and delivery. I leave the stage to a standing ovation and close the door to the dressing room. The first few minutes after any show are always the hardest. The silence after the noise and the adoration of the crowd is particularly lonely. Mulling over the performance, over-analysing the audience's response to new routines, I sip a cup of tea while the punters file out of the auditorium and into the night.

There's a knock at the door. Probably Richie, the tour manager, I think. Letting me know that some fans are waiting for an autograph at the stage door. Or maybe some friends have come backstage and want to say hello.

'Mr Vasey?' says a voice on the other side of the door. 'Could you please open the door.'

Two policemen are standing in the corridor. They charge me with common assault and require me to appear at the police station. The next morning I am arrested, fingerprinted, relieved of the contents of my pockets, my belt and my shoelaces, and led down to the cells.

The Glaswegian, the coppers tell me, is a heroin addict. He's in Blackpool at the council's expense for a weekend's rehabilitation with his children and wife, who had previously had a court order against him because of his violent behaviour. He provoked me and threw the first punch, yet *I* am being charged.

A month later I am in court. The police have dropped their charges, but I am fined two hundred pounds and ordered to pay seventy quid costs and eighty pounds compensation to the Glaswegian for ripping a T-shirt that looked like it cost no more than a fiver. I am recovering from recent throat-cancer operations and my wife is expecting our second child in the next fortnight, but that's not taken into account by the magistrates. My reputation goes before me and I have to face the consequences.

I am not particularly proud of what I did, so why do I mention it? Because it's what this book is about – what it's like to be Britain's rudest, crudest, most controversial comic, and what it's like to live with the consequences of that reputation. But most of all, it's about where that rudeness, crudity and appetite for controversy came from. I've come a long way since I grew up in the toughest of Middlesbrough's grimmest neighbourhoods, but Grangetown still runs through me like the lettering in a stick of Blackpool rock and I can't escape it. In the end, I suppose, it's about how you can take the lad out of Grangetown but you can't take Grangetown out of the lad. Grangetown is why I became Britain's foulest-mouthed comic. It drove me to escape a dead-end no-hope future. A hard life on its streets made me fearless. And if you come from where I did, it doesn't take much to change your opening line from 'Good evening, ladies and gentlemen. I'm the son of a bricklayer's labourer. My mother had to take any job when the war was on' to 'Good evening, ladies and gentlemen. My wife's got two cunts and I'm one of them.'

CHAPTER ONE

A PAIN IN THE NECK

JUST ONE SENTENCE can change your life for ever. The perfectly timed phrase, the gag that brings the house down just because of the way it's said, or a few simple words that trigger a gasp of shock. Like any comic, I know them well. But nothing had prepared me for the day I walked into a small, dark room cramped with veneered furniture in Stockton-on-Tees. My first thought was that with a bald patch and a thick beard, the man sitting in front of me looked like his head was on upside down, but this was not the time for silly jokes. The man was Dr Martin and the room was his office. He'd called me in to tell me something serious.

'Mr Vasey,' he said. 'I've got some bad news for you. You have throat cancer.'

The room spun as if I'd been hit. For once in my life I was speechless. There'd been no gentle warm-up, no light jabs to soften me up before delivering the bad news. The doctor had delivered a knockout with the first punch. It was cancer, he said. Plain and simple. Matter of fact. No warning. Just the truth. Maybe it was better that way. But to me cancer meant only one thing. A painful and imminent death. And, with it, the end of everything for which I had worked for many years. Decades of standing in smoky clubs and shouting into a microphone that I held to my stomach had finally taken its toll.

To add cruelty to injury, the cancer threatened to tear the very heart and soul out of me. The one thing that I'd always been able to rely upon was my voice. The gift of the gab was my greatest asset. It had rescued me from trouble, turned many crises into mere close scrapes and prevented skirmishes becoming fights. My voice had propelled me from back rooms above pubs, telling jokes to audiences of two or three uninterested punters, to adoring crowds of thousands at the Palladium and Dominion theatres in London or on the North and South Piers at Blackpool. My voice was my fortune, and now it was going to be snatched away.

The first warning sign had come five years earlier, when two nodules were removed from my vocal cords, a fairly common occurrence for any comic or singer. Now, in 2002, with a tour of Australia, New Zealand, Indonesia and America looming, I had a sore throat that never seemed to get better. Hoping that the nagging pain in my neck was no more than wear and tear, I'd gone to the doctor. The last thing I wanted was to arrive in Australia and find I couldn't speak.

'I don't like the look of your throat,' Dr Martin had said, shining a light into my gullet. 'I am going to have to do a biopsy.'

'How bad is it?' I asked.

'We won't know until we go further down. We are going to have to check down to your chest. Just a little investigation.'

Now, two weeks later, I was sitting in Dr Martin's stuffy little office, struggling to come to terms with the outcome of that 'little investigation'. And it had come as a complete surprise. There was no obvious cause. I didn't smoke and my days of heavy drinking were long behind me. I would have been no more surprised if he had hit me over the head with a baseball bat.

People say that when you're facing death, your life flashes before your eyes. And, at that moment, it did. My childhood in Grangetown and the early days playing in bands in Teesside pubs. My first attempts at comedy, then the years spent honing my act on the northern club circuit, working harder than Esther Rantzen's toothbrush, until I was ready for the big time and ready to become Britain's most controversial comic. There'd been good times and bad times, but when the kaleidoscope of images came to a rest all that was left was a clear vision of two people: my six-month-old son Reece and my wife, Helen. Sitting in that doctor's surgery, I thought back to an evening about six months earlier, just after Reece was born. Helen and I were at home, talking things over, when she looked at me seriously. 'You'll never marry me, will you?' she said.

We'd been together for five years. In that time Helen had transformed my life. But I'd been married before and . . . well . . . let's just say it wasn't a great success. No, that would be telling a lie. Let's say it was a complete fucking disaster.

'Well, I won't say never ever, you know,' I replied.

'No, you've been hurt too much to marry again,' she said and I could see the disappointment in her eyes.

'Now don't say never,' I said. 'Don't say never, because we might. We just might . . .' And that night I resolved to marry Helen.

A few months later, we were packing our cases for a holiday in Las Vegas. 'Take something nice to wear with you,' I suggested.

'Why?'

'Oh, you know, maybe there'll be a special occasion when we might need something smart.'

'Oh, right . . . right, I'll pack my best outfit,' Helen said innocently.

A few days later we were sitting in the bar of the Mirage hotel on the Las Vegas Strip, chatting to a couple who had just got married. 'How do you go about it?' I asked.

'Just go down to City Hall, queue up, give them your details, they give you a licence. Then you go to the church, hand in the licence and you'll be married in five minutes.'

'That easy?' I said. 'How much did it cost you?'

'Twenty-eight dollars. If you want a car it's thirty dollars. Fifty dollars if you want a ring and the car. And sixty-five dollars if you want to be married by Elvis Presley.' It sounded like Argos. A bit tacky, but at least it was quick and cheap.

Back in our suite, I took Helen in my arms. 'Do you want to get married?' I asked her.

'What, now?' she said, her eyes widening.

'Tomorrow.'

'Are you joking?'

'No.'

Helen took a step back to be able to look me straight in the eyes. 'You're not joking, are you?' she said.

'No.'

'Gosh.'

Helen hadn't said yes, but she didn't need to accept my proposal. I knew she wanted to get married and that I'd taken her so much by surprise that she didn't know what to say.

'We'll have a look tomorrow night,' I said.

'Right,' Helen said with a look of shocked surprise. 'We'll do that tomorrow, then.'

On 30 April 2001 we took a taxi down to City Hall and for two hours stood in a queue of gooey-eyed couples, each of them holding hands and grinning inanely. Inevitably, it got us talking. 'Ehh, what's he doing with her? Will you look at the face on him. She could do a lot better.' Or: 'He's old enough to be her grandfather.' And even: 'Is that two lesbians there, holding hands?'

Eventually we reached an office with a row of six desks. Behind one of the desks, a clerk asked us our names and our dates of birth. We signed an application form, paid the fee and that was it. We were licensed to get married.

Back at the hotel, I rang George Forster, my manager. 'We're getting married,' I said.

'You what?' George gasped. 'Getting married? Well, I couldn't think of a better woman, but what's she doing marrying a funny bugger like you?'

We chatted for a while, then George rang off. A short while later, the phone rang. It was George again. 'What time you getting married?' he said.

'Six o'clock.'

'Right. And where will you be before then?' I thought George was going to send some flowers for Helen.

'We'll be in the foyer until about quarter to six,' I said. 'We'll have a drink and then we'll get a taxi down to the little church. We're getting married at the Little White Wedding Chapel.'

'Oh, right. Well, good luck, then,' George said. 'I hope it goes well.'

Helen and I took our time getting dressed. I put on a white suit with a white silk shirt, a white tie and a white trilby. I thought I looked like a proper Mississippi gambler. And Helen, also in a white suit, looked a million dollars. On the dot of six o'clock, just as Helen and I were finishing our glasses of champagne in the foyer, a little bloke with silver hair and a moustache approached us.

'Chabby, innit?' he said in a thick cockney accent.

'Yeah?' I said, wondering what this little east Londoner was doing in the Mirage.

'My name's Dave,' he said.

'Er, hello Dave,' I said, still flummoxed.

'I'm Tom's driver.'

'Right . . . pleased to meet you.' I hadn't a clue who Tom might be.

'Tom sends his very best wishes.'

'Oh right, right,' I said, 'Tom who?'

'Tom Jones,' Dave said. 'I'm Tom Jones's driver.'

'What, *the* Tom Jones?'

'I've got a couple of tickets for the show,' Dave said, nodding. 'And I've got a limousine outside.'

Dave drove us to the Little White Wedding Chapel, where we were given the choice of being married by Elvis, Jerry Lee Lewis or Marilyn Monroe lookalikes. We thought it made a farce of marriage, so we chose the bog-standard wedding – a bloke in a dicky bow. We signed a register, walked into a little room and stood behind a black couple who were getting married before us. The woman must have been forty stone. She was so over-weight that she had to sit through the entire ceremony. The groom was as thin as a rake. From behind they looked like the number ten.

And then it was our turn. It was over before I'd blinked. In a couple of minutes we went from Roy and Helen to Mr and Mrs Vasey. We posed for a few photographs outside and paid ten dollars for a video. In all, it cost us less than a decent meal.

Then Dave whisked us in the limo to the MGM Grand Hotel and led us backstage, straight through to the green room. And there he was. Tom Jones. Standing there, sipping a drink, and looking like a proper superstar.

'Hello there, Chubby, how're you doin'?' he said. It was a shock. He had a lilting Welsh accent. I didn't expect him to talk like that. I thought that living in America might have rubbed out his accent, but he sounded just like a lad from the valleys.

'Congratulations to you both,' Tom said. And he gave Helen a big hug and a kiss. Helen is a massive Tom Jones fan and I could see she was on a different planet. And as for me? Well, I was gobsmacked. I was thinking I was going to wake up any moment. This is fucking ridiculous, I thought.

Tom opened a bottle of champagne and gestured to a buffet table piled high with a mountain of shrimps and enough roast beef to feed twenty people. 'I had this put on for you,' he said. 'Have something to eat, then I'll sort out a table for you at the show.' While we tucked into the buffet, Tom disappeared to prepare for his audience. A few minutes later one of his staff tapped me on the shoulder and led us through to the auditorium where a table was reserved for us centre stage, right at the front.

The lights dimmed, the band started up and Tom came on. I knew he was good, but this show was amazing. What a voice. And the band! The drummer was something else and the bass player was superb, really loose and funky. From the moment Tom started singing, everyone was on their feet. It was a magnificent show. When the curtain came down we were ushered back into the green room, where a new bottle of champagne had been opened. About a dozen young lasses, all top-class pussy, were milling around. Tom walked across the room towards Helen and me.

We chatted for a while, then Tom said: 'The first time I saw you was on a tour bus after a show in Munich. One of the crew put your tape on and I couldn't believe what I was hearing. I said: "Who the fuck is this?" Once I realised what you were all about, I was in hysterics. Since then, every year we've had your video on the tour bus. My son's a big fan as well.'

Tom told me how he'd had a phone call that afternoon from

his son Mark, who had been playing golf in Spain with my manager's son, Michael. Between them they'd hatched a plan to surprise Helen and me with a couple of tickets to Tom's show.

We chatted for a while, then Tom left, and Helen and I were left looking at each other, not quite believing what had happened to us.

'It's telling everybody, isn't it?' Helen said when we got back to our room. 'Who's going to believe that? Who in their right mind is . . .'

'If I tell the lads we spent our wedding day with Tom Jones,' I said, 'they'll go "Fuck off! Tom Jones my arse! More like fucking Tom Pepper!" They'll never believe it.'

I kicked off my shoes and Helen got straight on the phone to her mother, her sister and all her friends. 'Just run up the phone bill,' I said. 'Aye, go on.'

She was on the phone for about two hours. 'You'll never guess . . . Tom Jones . . . and he gave me a kiss . . . went to his show . . .' I could hear the excitement in her voice.

Tom invited us back to his hotel the next day but I thought it was time to make ourselves scarce. We were grateful for what we got and we'll never forget it. It's a memory Helen and I will always share, but I knew we had to recognise the rules. Don't get too familiar. Celebrities like Tom Jones, they've got fifty million in the bank and a whole different lifestyle to the rest of us. I'm not in that league, but I've learned that money creates big divisions. It's like the lottery winners who come off council estates and think they're going to keep the same friends. They're not. They'll move to bigger houses next to bank managers, surgeons and lawyers. They'll lose touch with most of their old friends. It's just human nature, a fact of life.

And there was one thing about which we'd been absolutely right. When we got home, many people wouldn't believe that we'd met Tom Jones and that he'd put on a wedding buffet for us. A few weeks later, I was talking to a chairman from one of the working men's clubs in Middlesbrough, a club I'd played dozens of times when I was starting out. Like many committee men, he was incapable of believing a word any act would say. He was one of the old school; he had no fingernails where he'd been scratching his way out of the coffin that morning and he couldn't pay anyone a compliment.

'I remember when I booked you for fifteen quid,' he said.

'Yeah,' I nodded. It was a familiar refrain, that peculiarly British habit of chopping down tall poppies. And club chairmen could be the worst offenders.

'How you getting on?' the chairman said.

'Oh, fine, thanks,' I said. 'I've just been to Vegas. We got married.'

'Aye.'

I pulled out a photograph. 'You know who that is, then?'

'Tom Jones,' the chairman said.

'Exactly.'

'Aye,' the chairman said, looking at me with all the suspicion of Quasimodo. 'Were you at Madame Tussaud's, then?'

'Madame Tussaud's?' I said. 'That's the real fucker, you daft old bastard. That's Tom Jones, one of the biggest stars in the fucking country.'

'Oh, right,' the club chairman said. 'Well, you didn't do very well when you last played our club.' And then he walked off.

Aye, I thought. Welcome to the big time.

Sitting in Dr Martin's surgery that afternoon, trying to come to terms with having cancer, it felt as if I'd come a long way since the days when I was at the total mercy of club chairmen. A lot of it had been fun, but just as much had been a hard and unpleasant struggle. Now, thanks to Helen, for the first time in my life I had true happiness. I was financially secure and the work was going well. The gags were flowing, the material was good and I was working on my music in my studio. I felt on top of my game and the future looked rosy. But right then it looked like everything for which I'd worked so hard and for so long was going to be taken away from me. I'd come a long way and suddenly it seemed all in vain.

●

On a Saturday afternoon, three months before the end of the Second World War in Europe, not far from a bomb crater that marked the site of what two years earlier had been a factory warehouse, a scream pierced the air and I took my first gasp of Grangetown's filthy air. Born on 3 February 1945, I first saw the light of day in the main bedroom of 78 Broadway, a two-up, two-down council house at the end of a terrace in the shadow of a steelworks that belched stinking fumes and dark smoke all day, every day, over the poorest and roughest of Middlesbrough's run-down suburbs. The milk bottles on our doorsteps were always covered in dust and you couldn't hang out your washing on the lines. The fumes from the coke ovens choked us and turned brass doorknobs blue. The air seemed to be permanently cold and damp. Even on a summer's day the sun would be blocked out by smoke and clouds of dust. And at night it would never really be dark because of the eternal glow of Dorman, Long & Co's steel furnaces and coke ovens at the end of the street. In fact, it was impossible to escape the steelworks. The streets were named after the pioneers of the steel industry, men such as Bessemer, Vickers and Laing. And if you looked beyond the streets to Middlesbrough in the west or Redcar on the coast in the east, steelworks, petrochemical plants and slag heaps stretched right across our horizon for twenty-eight miles along the south bank of the Tees.

Of all Middlesbrough's industrial suburbs, Grangetown was the most isolated. Boxed in by the massive ICI chemical works and the North Sea to the east, the steelworks to the north (and beyond the steelworks, by the foul Tees river) and the Cleveland Hills to the south, the only way out was through a tiny subway that cut under the railway tracks running all along Grangetown's western edge. More than 12,000 people lived in those enclosed few square miles, all of them working class, all living hand to mouth, and all white. I didn't see a black or Asian person until I was in my early twenties. And neither did anyone I knew. That was just the way things were back then.

Recently I went back to Grangetown and it's even more desolate now than when I was a kid. Back then, Grangetown was known as Cardboard City on account of the many rickety buildings and prefab constructions that dotted our neighbourhood, but Cardboard City is no longer. Most of the terraces have been demolished, leaving a grid of deserted streets running through derelict wasteland. Where once nearly 10,000 men worked in steel mills and coke factories, now the most prosperous industries are prostitution and drug dealing. Many streets have roadblocks to prevent joyriding and the street corners are dotted with tall poles with wire shrouds housing CCTV cameras that spy on the residents.

Grangetown has become an empty, soulless place in which to grow up, but it wasn't like that when I was a child. Maybe it was the brutal industrial environment, maybe it was the fact that most of us were descended from the thousands of Scottish, Irish and Welsh immigrants who came in search of work at the steelworks after Grangetown was established in 1881, or maybe it was the grinding hardship of a life with little chance of escape, but we were a tight bunch. Everyone knew everyone's business and we all led a common life. All the kids went to school together, all the dads worked at the steelworks and the mothers washed, cleaned and went to the bingo. The families were large – twelve kids in the McElroy family and the Harlems had nineteen – probably because nobody had owt and there was little for adults to do after work but go to the pub and get pissed or stay at home and fuck each other. *Everyone* had loads of kids – I used to think it was about survival – which made the Vaseys' small brood very strange by Grangetown standards. Just my mam, my auld fella, my sister Barbara, and me. Mam was one of the Grangetown Taylors, a well-known family with four girls – Ivy, Alice, Mabel and my mother, Amy – and three brothers: George, Bill and Herbert. George played the squeeze-box and Aunt Alice was such a good pianist that we used to say she could play fly shit. If a fly landed on a plate, we would joke, then my auntie Alice could pick a tune out of the black dots it left behind.

My mam was a real Hylda Baker, always getting things arse about face. 'Splash some Durex on them walls,' she'd say, meaning Dulux paint. She once announced that our neighbour Margaret had gone into hospital 'to get the contradictive pill'. Fortunately, Mam had a quick wit and could laugh at all her malapropisms. She also always needed to have the last word. When I was older and when my mam's legs started giving her trouble, I remember the doctor coming to the house.

'You've got arthritis, Amy,' he said. 'I think what we'll have to do is get you to do some exercise with your arthritis.'

'Well, what else can we do with arthritis?' Mam said.

By all accounts, my mother was a very attractive woman when she was younger. All I can remember from that time is that she wore a pinny and had a perm. I could see that I'd inherited her eyes, button nose and good teeth. However, when the photographs were brought out and shown, other people would make remarks. 'She stands very well, your mam,' they'd say and I'd wonder what they were getting at.

But my mam's beauty, wit and common sense had little effect on my father. A tall man with a thick lick of dark curly hair, parted down the middle and slashed back, Colin Vasey had only one true passion in his life. He was a good cricketer, he loved his tennis and snooker, and he liked to breed Alsatian dogs, which he sold to the police force, but all that paled in comparison to his devotion to the club. It was his life. He was a drinker and liked his booze, but even more than that he just loved being at the club. He went to work at half past seven in the morning, the clack of his nailed boots joining the echoing clatter of thousands of workmen making their way towards the belching chimney stacks of Dorman, Long, the steelworks at the end of our street. For eight hours a day, Dad toiled as a chart changer in the dark mill sheds. Each of the sheds was several miles long with a furnace at one end, out of which huge molten steel sheets would come tumbling. Dad would run along the steel every hour, changing the charts that recorded the temperature of the steel as it cooled, until the wail of the factory siren heralded his return at home at four-thirty p.m. He'd eat his tea silently in the kitchen, beside the fire grate where his underpants and socks would be hanging next to Mam's pies and cakes, then fall asleep in his chair. An hour later, he'd wake up and head upstairs to his domain: the bathroom. Dad was the only family member who got to soak in a proper bathtub. He'd use most of the hot water in the boiler tank, so Mam would fill pots and kettles to heat enough water for my sister and me to wash in the tin tub in the kitchen, with a brick underneath one end to make the water deeper where Barbara sat. After his bath we'd hear Dad upstairs, getting changed. Then there would be a rumble of footsteps as he thundered down the stairs and a bang as the front door slammed. Dad was off to the club in his suit and flat cap, his hair parted in the middle and slicked back with Brylcreem, a Woodbine wedged between his lips like a proper

Andy Capp. Come seven o'clock, that was his routine. Every day, including Christmas, New Year, our birthdays and holidays. He'd organise trips for pensioners and kids to the seaside. He'd book acts for the concert room and be a pillar of our local community, while my mam sat neglected at home. At half past eleven, Dad would reappear, always in a good mood, often singing and usually with a wrap of fish and chips, or a packet of crisps and some lemonade, or some other scran under his arm. We'd tuck into it before bed, so it's no wonder I'm a fat bastard. It's the way I was brought up.

And there was no shortage of places in Grangetown for my auld gadgie to go out drinking. Cardboard City had been a godless community for many of its early years. Without churches, the locals got used to congregating in the dozens of shebeens, pubs, clubs and dives that sprung up and became the heart of our neighbourhood. But by the time I was a kid there were four churches in a row in Bolckow Road, including the Methodist chapel, where Dad's twin sister Connie was a lay preacher and where I started in the choir as a young boy, loving Sunday school because, like many of the kids, it gave me an opportunity to take more money out of the collection tin than I put in it.

Dad had another sister, Ruby, but nobody talked owt about her. She was a schoolteacher who'd moved to Stokesley at the posh end of Middlesbrough and didn't want anything to do with us. It left just Connie, a spinster in love with a married policeman, to look after my grandparents. My grandfather, Thomas Vasey, was chalk to my father's cheese, a miserable old bastard who never said two words to me in all the time I knew him. He was such a grump that other people used to take bets on when they'd see him smile. He'd been a crane driver at Dorman, Long and seemed to me to spend most of his long retirement, until he died at ninety, sat in an old stiff-backed leather armchair, a spittoon beside him, placing bets on the horses and glowering at anyone who entered the room. In those days there were no legal bookmakers in Grangetown. Instead my grandad would use bookies' runners who stood on street corners, taking bets and paying out winnings. They always used to be short fellas in flat caps, with one eye permanently on the road in case a copper appeared. There were hundreds of them in them days, all over Middlesbrough and its surroundings. It was part and parcel of life.

And if you won something on the horses, you spent it straight away. There was no saving for a rainy day. No one in Grangetown saw a future beyond the steelworks, which meant you lived every day as if it was your last. You grabbed your pleasures when you could, so a win might mean a night getting blathered in the local dive or pub, which we called the claggy mat because your feet would stick to the floor. Or if you were that way inclined, you might head up to the black path that ran parallel to the steelworks, which was where all the prostitutes used to ply their trade. At times, particularly on a Friday night, there would be dozens of women up there, looking to pick up steelworkers walking home with their pay packets in their back pockets. As kids we used to point at them in the street. 'Eh, she's on the scut,' or 'She's on the batter,' we'd say. And we'd shout a few insults or throw a stone, and then run away.

Other than illegal bookmaking, prostitution and drunkenness, there was very little crime in Grangetown. Everyone in Middlesbrough knew that if you lived in Grangetown you had nowt. You could see it from the houses. No one had carpets down or curtains up – instead, we put cardboard on the windows – and at Christmas the most you hoped for in your stocking was an apple, an orange, some nuts, a colouring book and, if it was a good year, a little toy. That was it.

I'd like to be able to say I can remember happy times when

my auld fella, my mam, Barbara and I all did something together, such as going to the park or the seaside as a family, but I can't remember it ever happening. My parents couldn't even agree on what to call me. Dad had called me Royston, but Mam didn't like it. She said it was a snobbish, poncey name. Telling my auld fella that she was 'sick of people shortening it – either he's Royston or he's Roy', she went down to the registry office and had my name changed in the official register from Royston to Roy.

Given their many differences, it was perhaps unsurprising that few people ever saw my parents together outside the house. Funerals, maybe, but even that was unlikely as my father was one of the first people in Grangetown to turn his back on the church. It made him the black sheep of the family and maybe it played a part in the warfare between my parents. Theirs wasn't a passionate relationship; they just didn't get on. As soon as a row broke out between my mam and my dad, my sister and I would have to scat upstairs as fast as we could. Something would go flying and they'd start bawling at each other. Frying pans, ornaments, you name it, it became a missile. There was nothing in our house that wasn't chipped or broken.

My father once said something wrong as he was eating his tea at the kitchen table. Mam walked over, picked up his plate, opened the dustbin and threw it all out. The plate, the food she'd taken an hour to cook, everything. She had a wicked temper.

My mam's other affliction was that she was an epileptic at a time when there was no real treatment for it. Her fits were frequent. She once fell off the platform of the bus during a seizure and ended up in hospital. Another time she had a fit while cooking the tea and fell in the fire, burning the side of her face and her arm. And when I was a baby she had a fit while bathing me, trapping me in the bath. Fortunately, Aunt Alice was after a cup of sugar and found us. She pulled me out from underneath my mam, held me upside down and emptied me of water. If it hadn't been for Aunt Alice, I was frequently reminded, I wouldn't have lived to see my first birthday.

I've always suspected that my mother's epilepsy was triggered by the frequent beatings my father dealt out. In that, our home was no different to any other in Grangetown at that time. It was the way things were in those days: married couples settled their arguments with their fists and their feet. I'm not making any excuses for it, but on rough council estates where times are hard and there's not a lot of money about, people hit out when they don't get what they want and need. It's nowt to be proud of, but it goes on. Walking home along our street you'd often hear, 'Aaah! Fuck off!' and then a door would slam and you'd hear heavy footsteps pounding into the distance. Or a window would smash as something went flying.

Whether my mother's epilepsy was brought on by violence and depression, I'll never know. Although I've asked many doctors, I never got a proper answer, but no doubt it played a part in making my mother among the most negative and disillusioned people I've ever known.

So perhaps it was no surprise that Mam was well versed in catching the eye of other men. She was an attractive woman and there were loads of men after her. My auld fella once brought his foreman, Ted Bridge, home for tea. Ted was tall, wore a trilby and had a little moustache. Within weeks of Ted coming to our house, Mam was meeting him for walks and Dad was accusing her of doing the dirty.

In the midst of this domestic warfare, my sister and I tried to get on with our little lives. My mates and I would have clemmie fights against rival gangs of kids, hurling lumps of clay and mud at each other. Or we'd go down to the river and float on the water on big inner tubes that we found on a nearby rubbish dump. We were toughened against the cold and would spend hours drifting in the heavily polluted Tees. Once we ended up floating out to sea. The lifeboat had to come for us and I inevitably got a clout from my father when I got home.

I was always getting in trouble, which inevitably meant a hiding. On Sundays we were allowed to wear our best clothes and shoes, but God help us if we got them dirty. I'd gone down to the Veck, a little stream near our house, to throw match-sticks into the water and watch them race each other. Having got my shoes filthy and terrified of a beating, I hatched a plan. I'd take my vest off, use it to clean my shoes and throw it away. Convinced I'd pulled off my scam, I kept my head down all through tea that evening, praying that my dodge wouldn't be discovered. It worked until my mam, filling the tin tub in the kitchen, saw my sister and me getting undressed. 'Where's your vest?' she demanded.

'I didn't put one on this morning,' I said.

'That's not true,' my mam said. 'I put a vest on you this morning. Where is it?'

'I didn't have a vest on. Honest.'

My mam shouted: 'Colin!'

Dad was in the back kitchen and came through. 'What?' he said.

'I put a vest on him this morning and he hasn't got it on,' said Mam.

'Where's your vest, boy?'

This called for some quick thinking. I turned on the tears and through them I blubbered: 'These lads held me down and took it off me! These lads got me!'

'You lying little bastard!' my father screamed. The back of his hand lifted me clear off the ground. The next few blows took the skin off my arse. Then I was dispatched to bed without a bath.

As kids, we were left largely to our own devices. It meant we inevitably got up to no good, but it also meant we learned to fend for ourselves. If you had an old pram, pushchair or some worn-out tyres, you didn't bother taking them to the municipal dump. You just got rid of them on a strip of waste ground behind the King's Head. It was where the locals used to dump things. One day we found an old car. We played on it for ages, pretending to be cops or robbers in car chases. Over the next few days, the windows got broken and the doors were pulled off, but our games came to a sudden end when Leslie Dobson, a kid from my school, removed the cap from the petrol tank and threw a firework down the pipe. The car went up and Leslie passed me doing about thirty miles an hour. I think he ended up in hospital.

Next to the wasteland was a hut that sold fish and chips. The smell of fried food that drifted from that shop was a constant source of temptation to me, but I had no money so I'd run around all the houses in Grangetown, collecting old newspapers to exchange for chips. Most nights, there'd be a race between all the kids to be the fastest round the houses and get the most chips.

When I was about six, we moved from 78 Broadway to a brand new council estate. Our new home was at 30 Essex Avenue, a street in the far corner of Grangetown, next to the main road and the railway tracks, which carried coal to Dorman, Long. When a train was parked in the siding next to our house, my auld fella would hog me over the fence with a bucket to refill our coal bunker from the wagons. I'd be there for ages, passing buckets back to Dad and nicking coal for all our neighbours.

We'd steal anything we could get our hands on, but like most petty criminals we believed there was honour among thieves. Shops or businesses were fair game, but we wouldn't steal from each other because no fucker had owt. The exception was parents, who by the standards of us kids were loaded. On one occasion, I came home to find no one in the house and a pound note on the mantelpiece. I immediately snatched it and ran up to Baxter's, the local cake shop. Unsure of what to do with a whole pound, I spent it all on broken biscuits. They handed over a massive sack, enough to feed a cow. 'What do you want all these for?' Mr Baxter said.

'Er . . . we're having a party,' I replied. I hadn't realised I would get so many biscuits for a quid. I invited all my friends round and we sat in the back alley behind the shop, eating our way through the mountain of broken biscuits.

Meanwhile, my mother must have sent for my father and told him that a pound note was missing. I was lying in the alley, my stomach as full as a butcher's dog, when my auld gadgie appeared on his bike. As he pedalled down the alleyway, I saw him and jumped up. 'Come here, you little get!' he shouted.

I ran as fast as I could, so my father threw down his bike and chased after me. About fifty yards from the house, he caught up and lifted me right off the ground. 'Don't you lads ever come round to our house again,' he shouted at my mates as he gave me a bloody good hiding in the street. 'He'll never come out again!'

My sister, my mother and our next-door neighbour said that they could hear me screaming all the way home as my father dragged me along the street and into the house. There were twelve steps in our house and I didn't touch one of them, my father ran me up them to my bedroom that fast. 'You stay there now. Don't you move! If I hear one peep out of you, I will lace your arse!' he threatened and I never took another pound off my mother.

I did, however, dip into my mam's handbag when I thought I'd spotted some silver paper, the type that would normally be wrapped around a chocolate bar. I lifted it out and found just what I hoped for inside it. She won't miss a few squares, I thought, stuffing them into my mouth. And then I ate a few more. And some more.

Half an hour or so later, I was out in the street, playing cricket. I'd just bowled out someone and I was taking my turn with the bat in front of the lamp-post that we used as a wicket when I felt the need to blow off. What I thought would just be a silent, surreptitious fart turned into something much more unpleasant. All my mates looked shocked at the sight of a streak of shit running down my leg.

I ran home, straight past my mother in the kitchen, to the toilet at the back. I couldn't stop shitting. 'What's happened?' my mam asked.

'There's sommat wrong with my stomach,' I groaned.

'Have you eaten anything?'

'No . . . just a bit of chocolate.'

'Where did you get the chocolate from?'

'Er, your handbag.'

'You little swine,' my mam said. 'It's laxative.'

My family dined out on that story for years, laughing at how my thieving fingers had landed me in trouble yet again.

My mother used to say that I got my light-fingeredness from my father. It certainly seemed that, like him, I lived by my wits rather than my brains. If I liked the look of something, I just took it, and, like him, I had itchy feet – I couldn't wait to get out of the house every day. Because of our similarities, my mother was convinced that my auld gadgie spoiled me. She never let me forget the day when Dad won some money at the York races and returned home with a red wooden train under his arm. I was thrilled, but my mother went mad.

'You haven't brought Barbara anything back,' she screamed at my auld fella. Dad just shrugged, but I never lived it down.

Forty years later, my mother would still throw it in my face. 'A train set for you! And nothing for Barbara! What was your dad thinking of?'

It was a fair criticism. Dad always had time and a few spare bob for me, but little for my mother or sister. And I couldn't see any wrong in him at all. He seemed kind and generous. He always had time for people, especially down at the club, where I'd often wind up of an evening.

'Is Colin in?' I'd ask the doorman.

'Yes, son,' the doorman would say. 'Your father's in, all right.'

'Can I see him?' And Dad would come out. 'Dad, can I have some money for a bag of chips?'

His hand was in his pocket straight away. 'Here, that's all you're getting,' he'd say. 'Now, bugger off.'

When I was eight years old, the Queen came to open a new part of the ICI chemical plant in Grangetown. The smells from ICI used to take the wallpaper off our walls. 'What are they making in there?' we'd say. 'Dead rats?'

The Queen made her way from Middlesbrough to the Grangetown ICI plant along the main road that linked South Bank – or Slaggy Island, as we called our neighbouring suburb on account of the many piles of coal, coke and iron slag that surrounded it – to Grangetown. My mates and I climbed up to the main road, which ran along a viaduct in front of the house, and waved at the Queen as she drove past. Having come up from London, the Queen seemed so glamorous to us urchins and ragamuffins. We'd never been beyond Middlesbrough. Anyone who'd visited Redcar, five miles away on the coast, was thought of as exotic, so the day when the Queen passed through our little community was one I thought I'd always remember.

After the Queen's Daimler had passed by, I clambered down the bank to our house in Essex Avenue and walked into the kitchen. There, lying on the kitchen table, was another reason I'll never forget that day.

My mother had left home. The only explanation was a note saying she'd had enough. She couldn't live under the same roof as my father any more, it said. She had to go.

CHAPTER TWO

MOTHER LOVE

'I'VE GOT CANCER?' I said slowly. '*Cancer?* . . . Are you sure? Because I've been clean-living . . . I haven't smoked, you know . . .'

Dr Martin looked at me in the way I'm sure he's previously looked at hundreds of patients – that unique combination of professional sympathy and emotional detachment that medics have made their own. 'I'm afraid you have,' he said.

I felt as if I was never going to leave that dark, stuffy little room, with its surgical bed, its oxygen tank and its dipped blinds. I'd never suffered from claustrophobia, but when someone is sitting in front of you, telling you that you are dying, your body does strange things. And at that moment I felt like a prisoner. More than anything, I wanted to be outside that room, away from that man and his bad news. I felt like shouting out 'I know I'm going to die one day, but I just want a bit longer. I just want to see my kids grow up.' But instead I found myself saying 'Could you hold my glasses, please?' as the room started spinning ten to the dozen and I tried to look out of the window, where everything was a blur.

'He's coming round, sir.' It was a woman's voice, coming from somewhere above me. 'He's coming round.'

I opened my eyes to find myself lying on Dr Martin's surgical bed. There was a burning coldness on my head – a towel filled with ice. And in my mouth, a lump of ice. 'Your temperature went sky-high, dear,' the nurse said. 'Right through the roof. And then you fainted.'

I smiled weakly.

'You went down like a sack of coal . . . we had some trouble getting you up on here,' the nurse said, pointing at the bed. She explained that it took three nurses to lift me off the floor.

'Eh, I'm not surprised,' I said. 'The last time I looked, I weighed nineteen stone. Where did you hire the crane?'

The nurse giggled. At least I hadn't lost that skill. 'Roy, you know there is a lot we can do for you now,' the nurse said. 'You've had some bad news, but things can get better.'

The doctor said he would refer me to a specialist. He told me I might need chemotherapy, I might need a major operation and I might lose my voice box, but that it was early days and, at the moment, nothing could be said for sure.

I went outside and sat in the car. For ten minutes I stared through the windscreen, wondering what to do. I've always been pretty good at instinctively knowing the next move in any given situation. But this time I was baffled. If someone had told me that if I bungee jumped nude off a mountain it would cure my cancer, then I would have done it. Even if they'd told me that sleeping with Ann Widdecombe was the only cure, I'd have agreed there and then. But having cancer was a totally new experience and I hadn't a clue how to react. Should I get out the trumpet and start playing 'When The Saints Go Marching In' as if everything was okay? Or should I ring up the bank and say:

'I'm on my way round to pick my money up. I want to have a last bet on the horses'? I just didn't know.

So I rang Helen, who was in Lincolnshire, where her parents live. 'Are you sitting down?' I said. 'I've got some bad news.' I told her what the doctor had said. The phone went quiet. Then I heard sobbing.

'This can't be right' she said.

'Well, unfortunately it is,' I replied.

Helen was crying on one end of the phone; I was crying on the other end. When push came to shove, I was discovering, none of us are as brave as we think we are. After a while, we pulled ourselves together, said goodbye and I drove home to my house in North Yorkshire. Three hours later, Helen arrived. She'd dropped off Reece with her sister. They'd all been in tears. And then Helen had driven over to Teesside, weeping all the way. When she walked in the side door to the kitchen, I crumpled, falling into her arms.

'I wish it was me and not you,' Helen said. 'The kids need you.'

Typical Helen, I thought. Always thinking of others before herself. If only my mother had been made of the same stuff.

●

No one in my family ever explained to me why my mother left, but I got plenty of excuses. One neighbour's verdict was that 'all your mother ever wanted was to be taken out, but your dad would never do it.' This gossip insisted that if my auld fella had taken Mam to the Boy Scouts hut at the end of the street, where they held old-time dances on a Friday night, then she'd still be at home, cooking my dinners.

Jenny, who lived next door, never got over it. 'You were everything to her,' she said. 'It was such a shock when she walked out because she adored you. She never let you out of her sight.'

While the rest of the family never forgave my mother for leaving, my sister was more lenient, insisting that my father pushed Mam out of the house, even though my mother didn't want to go. Amidst all this, I tried to piece together my own understanding.

A few months after Mam left, life was starting to settle in down Essex Avenue when a letter landed on our doormat. Mam was in Pontefract, it said, working at the Bassett's Liquorice All-sorts factory and living with a man called Norman Trevethick. I'd been suspicious of Trevethick – the spelling of which my mother later described as 'thick on the end, but I'm not' – ever since he came to our house to repair the washing machine. I thought Trevethick was a slimeball and I was never able to work out what my mother saw in him. With his big round face and greasy hair, I thought he looked like a dirty old man, the kind of dirty old man that fixed the washer, then buggered off with it and me mam.

About a year after Mam left, my parents divorced. It made the front page of the local rag, the *Evening Gazette*. In those days nobody got stabbed or was left hanging in an alleyway, there was less crime generally and most marriages lasted, so a divorce was big news. But to me, living in a house where doors were slammed and ornaments were thrown, it seemed just a normal thing. My parents probably had their moments when they had a fuck on the carpet in front of the fire when my sister and I were out of the house, but otherwise it wasn't so much the good old days as just the days. In the end, only my mother and father knew why Mam left and they took it with them to their graves.

As a consequence, I have no childhood memories of my mother. And even today, more than fifty years later, I feel robbed. I used to see other kids coming home from school to their mothers cuddling them, giving them cakes and playing with them out in the garden. And I wanted that.

My father did a good job in Mam's absence. He looked after me, took me to football matches, held my hand and sat in the garden with me, talking things through, but he couldn't entirely replace a mother. Aunt Connie used to give us scones and buns, my friend John Clark's mum used to bake us cakes, and Jenny, who lived next door, kept an eye on my sister and me, but I pined for a mother's love. Without it, I simply became a nuisance. By the time I was nine, I was a complete pain in the arse who thought that if I wanted something all I had to do was steal it. 'If you can get owt for nowt, give us a shout,' I would say to my mates.

Every December, shortly before Christmas, my mates and I would walk through the underpass beneath the railway lines and into Slaggy Island, from where we'd take the trolleybus 'over the border' into Middlesbrough for a bit of shoplifting. We'd pinch presents for all our friends and family, who on Christmas Day couldn't understand how we managed to afford such nice presents and wondered why all of them had neither box nor guarantee.

'Ooh, that's lovely. That's beautiful, that,' they would say.

'Yeah, but it was so heavy I threw away the box,' I'd reply.

One year I got stopped just as I was leaving Hamilton's Music Store with four vinyl LPs up my jumper. The owner bundled me into the back of his car and took me to South Bank police station, where I was hauled into a room and told to 'shut up and wait' until a policeman was ready to see me. Thinking they might search me, I unzipped my anorak, pulled the four LPs out from underneath my jumper and stashed them behind the radiator. A few minutes later, the door swung open and a policeman walked in. 'We have reason to believe you've been shoplifting,' he said.

'Me?' I said. 'Not me.'

They searched me and, of course, found nothing. I was released and thought nothing more of it until about ten years later when my cousin Lee was going out with a girl called Dorothy. When I heard that Dorothy's mother was a cleaner at South Bank police station, I told her about my brief detainment when I was twelve.

'Well!' Dorothy's mother said. She looked at me and stood up. 'Well, I don't believe it. Do you know, I found them!'

'You never?' I said.

'Yes. You left them in one of the detective's rooms upstairs, didn't you? Was it you?'

'Yeah.'

'Well, they'd melted,' Dorothy's mum said. 'I found four LPs stuck together in a big lump.'

Most of my thieving was less risky. In those days, there was a threepenny deposit on lemonade and pop bottles. One of our favourite scams was to pinch empty bottles from the yard behind the local shop, take them into the shop and collect the deposit. We'd wait ten minutes for the shop owner to take them out the back and stack them neatly in a wooden crate, then we'd climb over the wall, pinch them all over again and claim the deposit a second time. On a good day, this never-ending con could net us a small fortune.

I even stole from Edmond Saul, my best friend at the time. Edmond was an only child and his dad and mam spoilt him wicked. His bedroom was rammed to the rafters with toys and I would go round to his house to stare at them with envy. More than anything, I coveted his massive army of little lead soldiers and cannons, all carefully painted in regimental colours. So each time I visited Edmond's house I'd pinch a soldier or two, or maybe a cannon. Over the months, his army got smaller, while my army was forever attracting new recruits. 'These are all right, aren't they?' Edmond said, surveying the troops in my bedroom one day. 'Where d'you get 'em?'

'Er . . . my dad saw yours, so he went out and bought them,' I said. Edmond never suspected a thing and I had no guilty conscience. When a thieving little bastard wants something, no thought is given to the consequences.

By the time I was ten, Mam had moved to Blackpool and taken my sister Barbara to live with her, leaving just my father and me in the house in Essex Avenue. I'd become a full-blown house-husband to my father and I was struggling to make ends meet. Thieving was the only way I'd get my hands on the things that other kids took for granted. And it was the only way of finding some kind of relief from domestic drudgery. I'd get home from school at a quarter to four and rush around the house, vacuuming and cleaning so it would be neat and tidy for my auld fella coming home. I'd put something on, a pie in the oven or beans on toast or maybe egg and chips. Jenny Robinson, next door, who was the closest thing I had to a mother, would come by with some vegetables, but mainly it was chips. Sausages and chips; egg and chips; bacon and chips; pie and chips; beans and chips – it always had chips on the end of it.

With Dad's tea in the oven, I'd run up to the end of the street and wait for him returning from work at four-thirty, when I'd see him in the distance, wobbling up Evans Road on his bike. When he reached the corner of Essex Avenue, I'd grab his hand and shout: 'Dad, Dad, Dad. Gizza tan.'

'Have you been a good lad?' he'd shout before pulling me on to the back of the bike for a ride.

'Yeah, I've been a good lad,' I'd say. Usually I hadn't.

While Dad was eating his tea, I'd go upstairs, make the beds and clean the bathroom. Then Dad would say 'Jenny's going down the launderette' or 'Jenny's going to wash the sheets' and

I'd fold up the washing and take it over to Jenny's house. I also kept the garden tidy, cutting the grass, trimming the edges and weeding the borders. I had my chores to do and I did them without moaning, otherwise I'd have got a backhander. For Dad, life went on as before. He still worked at Dorman, Long, he still went to the club and he still had someone to wash and cook for him. He'd replaced Mam with me.

Just as he had done with Mam, Dad would take me to the Lyric cinema – we called it the bughole because of all the bugs in the seats. Dad was a cowboy fan and we'd cheer whenever James Stewart, Roy Rogers or John Wayne came on the screen and we'd boo when the baddies appeared. In the summer he'd take me to Blackpool, where in those days the beaches were packed and the boarding houses were smart, with beautiful curtains and clean wallpaper.

And like my mam, I'd sit at home alone most evenings while Dad went to the club, waiting for him to come home with some scran. On New Year's Eve one year I was sat in the house at about half past eleven, shivering because there was two feet of snow outside and we didn't have any coal, and listening to everybody knocking on everybody else's door, exchanging bits of fruit cake, putting coal on the fire and singing Happy New Year, when there was a knock on the door. It was Jenny Robinson. 'I think you'd better come with us, Roy,' she said. 'It's your dad.'

Outside there were snowdrifts everywhere, so I put my wellington boots on and walked with Jenny and Harry Hardy, another neighbour, to the corner of Essex Avenue and Evans Road. There was our auld fella, singing at the top of his voice, lying in a foot of snow. He'd fallen over the fence, landed in a snowdrift and couldn't stop laughing. What a job we had to pick him up.

My auld fella's boozing was starting to catch up with him. He never had a day off work for illness, but he was suspended a few times for drinking. Dad would sneak out of the mill at twelve o'clock and run down to the pub for two or three pints. It wasn't allowed, but the Queen's Head, the Bottom House and the other pubs near the works gate were always packed at dinner time. They were so close that my dad and his mates could hear the wailing siren sounding the beginning of the afternoon shift and make it back inside before other men had returned to their workplace from the canteen.

Dad spent almost all his money on drink. He'd usually give me enough money to keep us in food, but beyond that I didn't have a penny to scratch my arse, so I was the scruffiest, most raggedy-arsed kid at my school, with one pair of shoes and trousers that were always ripped. My attendance record at Sir William Worsley, the local school, was poor, but when I did turn up I worked hard at being popular. I was good at geography and my best subject was art. At that time my ambition was to be a cartoonist.

'Stay back, Vasey,' my art teacher, Mr Nee, would often say at the end of a lesson.

'What, sir? I've done nowt wrong, sir?' I'd say.

'That's Robbie Hutchinson's. You drew that,' he'd say. 'That's Raymond Bassett's. You drew that. That's Billy Parfitt's. You drew that.'

I did it simply because I wanted to help out my mates. They couldn't draw, so they'd pass their papers over to me and I'd happily do it for them. But Mr Nee wasn't daft and I often got caught out.

It was the same in the playground. I was always the class clown. If someone said 'Let's jump through a glass window,' I would volunteer. I was always the one to whom they'd say: 'Go and kick that dog up the arse.' I always did it. I wanted to be popular, but it meant I was always the kid that got into trouble.

Like every school, Sir William Worsley had a pupil who was

known as the best fighter in the school. And there were other pupils who were recognised as the second-best and third-best fighters. You knew who to speak to and who to avoid. I plodded along quite merrily, having few fights, until I was about fourteen, when the kid who was apparently the third-best fighter stabbed a white plastic ball given to me by my father and with which I was playing in the playground. So I went over and kicked him. He fell to the floor, so I kicked him again and punched him. Amongst the lads, the buzz immediately went round. 'Royston, third-best fighter in the school, you know.'

Once I'd gained the reputation as the third-best fighter, every other hard nut in the school wanted to have a go at me. It was ridiculous. A couple of months later, I was in a science lesson. One of my classmates drew a funny face on a steamed-up window and wrote 'Goosey', the name of the second-best fighter in the school, below it.

Goosey walked over to me. 'You did that,' he said, pointing at the cartoon.

'I haven't done it,' I said.

'Yes, you did, you fucking cunt . . .' Goosey yelled, hitting me over the back of my head with a stick. By the time we got pulled apart, I'd given Goosey a black eye and broken his nose, so it was clear to everyone watching that I was winning the fight. 'Royston left Goosey keggy-eyed,' I heard the lads say in the playground. I moved up the rankings. I was now the second-best fighter in the school.

A short while later, as Dad was finishing his tea at home, he asked me a question. 'Are you a bully?' he said.

'I'm not a bully, no,' I replied

'They tell me you're a bully at school.'

'But Dad, I'm not.' It didn't matter. I'd been labelled a bully and in Grangetown the rule was 'guilty until proven innocent'. My father didn't believe me and that night gave me a right slapping with his belt. It didn't half hurt, but it did no good. I'd got used to living by my fists and I wasn't going to change. I didn't see myself as a bully. I thought I was the Robin Hood of my school, the lad the others could come to when they were getting bullied. 'Eh! Fucking leave him alone, all right?' I'd say. 'I'm telling you, leave him alone.' And I'd thump whoever was giving my mates a bashing. I thought I was doing the right thing, but I didn't realise I was gaining a reputation as a hard case to be avoided by decent kids and befriended by the troublemakers.

And at home I was chancing my arm more than ever. Finally realising just how scruffy I was, Dad gave me ten shillings to get some new shoes from Brown's, a shop opposite Grangetown police station. At school that day, I told Raymond Bassett, one of my new hard-nut mates, about the money burning a hole in my pocket.

'Your Dad's given ya ten bob and you're gonna spend it, are ya?' he said.

'Yeah.'

'You wanna keep that and we'll nick ya some shoes,' Raymond suggested.

'Eh, that's a fucking good idea.'

Outside the shop, I devised our plan of attack. 'You keep her talking,' I said, referring to an elderly shop assistant, 'and 'ave a skeg to make sure no bluebottle's coming and I'll pinch the shoes.'

We walked in and I chose a nice pair of brown winkle-pickers, really smart with very pointy toes. I tried them on, and when I'd made sure they fitted I bolted out of the shop. The shop assistant's screams of 'Stop! Stop! Stop that lad!' ringing in my ears, I ran straight into the path of a policeman coming out of the police station. I took off, running down the pavement as fast as my legs would carry me. Behind me, the copper took up the chase, so I circled my school, ducked down a side street and turned right. I looked round. The copper was out of sight, so I pulled off my new shoes and threw them in a dustbin on a nearby lamp-post. Thinking I'd got away with it because neither the policeman nor the shop assistant would know who I was, I ran home, where I put on some sandals. A little later, Raymond and the lads came round and we all had a laugh about it. 'Eeeeh, fucking hell, you sure shifted on that,' one of them said.

'Where did you put them?' Raymond asked.

'In a bin on a lamp-post at the end of Cheetham Street,' I said. 'C'mon, let's go back and get 'em.'

We headed back to Cheetham Street, stopping off on the way at the chip shop and the corner shop, where I spent Dad's ten shillings on some fish and chips, a bottle of lemonade and a packet of fags for my mates.

We found the shoes, covered in ash and rubbish but still OK, in the bin. I took them home, put them under the tap, cleaned them up a bit, gave them a good polish and put them on. They looked fantastic.

At half past four, Dad came in from work. 'Did you get some shoes?' he said.

'Yeah, Dad – look at them.'

'What the hell is them?'

'Winkle-pickers.'

'Well, you're not wearing them,' he said. 'They's going back in the morning. Bloody stupid shoes. You're swapping them.'

'But they're all the rage, Dad.'

'I don't care. You're taking them back in the morning.'

There was a knock at the door. Dad went to see who it was. 'Hello, Colin,' I heard.

'Hello, John, how are you?'

'Bit of bad news for you, Colin.' It was the copper. He told Dad what I'd done.

'Oi! Up them stairs now!' Dad shouted from the doorway. 'Go on, yer little bastard.'

I heard Dad talking to the copper. Then his footsteps on the stairs. 'Why do I put up with you, you thieving little bastard?' he demanded. 'Where is the money?'

'I spent it, Dad.'

'Spent it? Spent it! You'll get no more money off me – now get in that bedroom and don't come out. I've brought up a thief. A thug! A bloody vandal.'

A few days later I made my first appearance in a magistrates' court. I was fined twenty pounds for stealing the shoes, which annoyed Dad all the more because he had to pay the penalty. 'Little bastard, you're no good,' he screamed at me as he laced my arse with his belt yet again that night. 'You'll never be any good.'

Not long after that, I was sent to Medomsley Detention Centre for six weeks for throwing bricks and bottles and fighting while hanging around outside the Commercial, the roughest pub in South Bank. I'd become the black sheep of the family and visits from the bluebottles had become a frequent occurrence. Usually it was about something missing, often little more than oggy raiding – pinching apples – from the stall outside the greengrocer. They were small pickings, but to us pathetically petty thieves it seemed like gold bullion.

'The police are here,' my auld fella would announce with a weary tone. 'What have you done?'

'Nothing!' I would always say. 'I haven't done anything. I wasn't . . . it was . . .'

'It's always Mr Nobody, isn't it?' Dad would say. 'It's never you, is it?'

I was more frightened of my auld fella than I was of the filth, even if they took me down to the police station. Dad would have to come with me and promise the police that if they dropped the charges, he'd go home and give me a good hiding. I felt the back of my father's hand across my ears or his belt across my arse several times a week in those days. Or it would be his boot up my backside.

The more I got in trouble, the less I worried about it. I'd thieved so many times that it had become an everyday thing and I'd become immune to the threat of punishment. And as I became more blasé, I reasoned why pinch apples when I could rob a bank? With my mates, I climbed up church towers to remove lead from the roofs. We'd take it to Elsie Hines, a scrapyard in Slaggy Island. We all thought we were commandos or cat burglars, not petty thieves. To us, thieving seemed glamorous and exciting.

My greatest coup came one evening when I'd gone down to the Unity Club to see if my Dad would give me some money for some chips. When the doorman went in search of my auld fella, I noticed a big black bicycle with a light on it.

Fucking hell, I thought, that's a cracking bike.

So I took it. It was that large, I couldn't swing my leg over the crossbar, so I put my leg through the frame and pedalled it home like that.

Everyone had a wash-house at the back of their house, where they kept their mangle, a few spades, some tools and maybe a wheelbarrow. Digging around in the dark, I found some spanners in a toolbox and removed the bike's wheels, the seat and the light. Finding some paint, I sprayed the bike white and black. I was capped with it. Hey, I've got myself a proper bike, I thought.

At about quarter past eleven that night, my father came in.

'I was gonna come down and get some money for chips off you, Dad,' I said, 'but the man at the door said you were too busy.'

'Aye, some bastard's pinched Sergeant Carr's bike from outside the club tonight.' Sergeant Carr was our local bobby. And he was a right bastard.

Shit, I thought. That bike was now standing in our wash-house.

'If Sergeant Carr finds out who's took his bike,' Dad said, 'he'll get ten years in prison. He'll get the worst . . .'

My heart was thumping in my chest and my legs were wobbly as I went up to bed that night. Lying awake as rigid as a corpse, I waited until my auld fella went to sleep and started snoring. I knew that once he started, nothing would wake him. I went down to the wash-house, got the shovel out and carefully lifted up all Dad's prize cabbages in the back garden. Digging about a foot down, I buried the bike in the vegetable bed, covering it with soil and carefully placing the cabbages back in their precise rows on top of the bike. I was petrified Dad would find out.

Dad got up at half past seven the next morning and went to work, walking straight past the cabbage patch. He hadn't noticed a thing. Out in the garden, even I couldn't see any sign of the cabbages having been moved.

I never removed Sergeant Carr's bike from the vegetable bed. With the police often automatically assuming that I was behind any theft, Sergeant Carr was a frequent visitor to our house and I was always worried that he'd somehow stumble on his bike, maybe spotting its handlebars poking out of the cabbage patch.

'Your Roy broke into Roger's fruit shop last night. He was clearly seen,' Sergeant Carr insisted to my father on one of his many visits.

'Oh aye, was he?' Dad said.

'Yes, he was seen climbing the back-alley wall, breaking in the shop, and we've got a witness.'

'I don't think you have. If you did then Roy must have fucking long arms because he's sixty miles away camping. He was only talking to me on the phone last night.'

Sergeant Carr gave Dad a blank look.

'Our Roy is with the Grangetown Boys' Club. He's camping in Scorby.' It was near Scarborough. 'He's been there since Friday. So if somebody saw him in Grangetown, our Roy would have walked sixty miles. I think you better get your facts right.'

It was one of the few times the auld gadgie was really chuffed with me, although it was short-lived. Dad had paid seven and six for me to go away for the week with about a dozen other lads. We slept in a big tent beside a lake. Most days were spent rowing tubs on the lake, but one day one of the supervisors made a big target out of straw so that us lads could make spears to throw at it. When it come to my turn, I let go of my spear too early and it went straight through Edmond Saul's leg, so I returned home under a cloud and had to visit Edmond in hospital. Shortly after that, I was in even bigger trouble with my auld fella.

Every summer, Crow's Fair pitched up on a patch of waste-land at Slaggy Island, near where we'd catch the trolleybuses into Middlesbrough. I loved the smell of hot dogs and candy-floss, and I would go on all the rides with my mates. The waltzers had always been my favourite, but this year we were more interested in the tattooist's tent. After much egging-on, Robbie Hutchinson went in first for a tattoo and promptly passed out. Thinking I was the hardest, I went in last and made sure that I got the largest tattoo of the four of us, gritting my teeth and pretending it didn't hurt at all as the tattooist carved *True Love Jacqueline* and a red rose on my left arm. Jacqueline was a girl in my class. We hadn't even spoken; I just liked the look of her.

For the next few days, I kept my sleeves rolled down at home. After about five days, the scab fell off and the tattoo was revealed in all its glory. I was so proud. I thought I really looked the part. I dabbed a bit of Vaseline on it and rolled my sleeves up as I waltzed into school, swinging my jacket over my shoulder so that everyone could see it. I thought I was the hardest nut in Grangetown.

The next night, there was a letter waiting on the kitchen table when my auld fella got home. 'Can I have a look at your arms?' he said after reading it.

I rolled up my right sleeve. 'Nowt there,' I said. 'See?'

'And your other one.'

I rolled up my left sleeve.

'What's that?' Dad demanded.

'A transfer.'

'A transfer? What kind of *a transfer*?'

'It's just like a transfer, like.'

'Does it wash off?'

'Oh yeah.'

'Well, go and wash it off then.'

'Can I not leave it on for a couple of days?'

'No! Get it washed off now!'

I went upstairs, shitting myself. What am I going to say? I wondered. What am I going to do? I went back downstairs. 'Dad, it won't all come off 'cos it's like ink, you know.'

'Go and wash it off.'

'Er, I've got a confession to make . . .' I said. 'It's a tattoo.'

'*You stupid* . . . you bloody stupid . . . you've marked yourself for life!' Dad screamed. 'Where do you get your brains from? You really are as thick as shit. You stupid . . .' Once again, the day ended with me in trouble and my father's belt lacing my arse.

CHAPTER THREE

FIRST STEPS

NEWS OF MY CANCER spread around the comedy circuit like wildfire. Within days, I'd received hundreds of phone calls and emails. Letters arrived from America, Canada, South Africa, New Zealand, Australia and Hong Kong, from fans and from other comedians, all of them wishing me the best.

'I wish I could come and put my arms around you,' one of the letters said. It was from someone I'd never met, a fan in Canada. It touched me deeply, the thought of complete strangers wanting to see me fit and healthy back on stage. And closer to home, friends and relatives dropped by to wish me good luck. People I hadn't spoken to for years crawled out of the woodwork. And, best of all, I started to see my kids again. They began coming around the house every other day or so.

Amidst the gloom and my worries about my future, glimmers of hope emerged. If the cloud had a silver lining it was that for the first time in my life I felt that when I really needed support I got it. Everyone was there for me. I'd thought I was losing my family for the second time in my life, that they were too busy for me, that they were doing their own thing, forming their own lives with their children and my grandchildren. But as soon as they heard I was ill they all came around.

To be honest, all the sudden attention was a bit of a pain in the arse. I was forever opening the door to visitors at a time when I didn't want to strain my voice as I still had a few shows to do. The tour was off, but it was too short notice to cancel five imminent gigs. I was contracted to do them and I wanted to do them. Thinking it might be the last time I would ever work on stage, I put every last ounce of energy into preparing for those performances but, try as I might, my mind wasn't quite on the job. I wasn't as good as I would usually be. I knew it and by the final night, I pulled myself together. The last show was a barn-stormer.

As I walked off stage, the theatre packed to the rafters, the audience chanting 'You fat bastard, you fat bastard', the tears rolled down my cheeks. The stage had been my salvation, delivering me from a life of trouble and crime. Without it, I was little more than the urchin who'd caused so much trouble in Grangetown.

●

The only thing that slowed my mischief-making was a growing interest in girls and sex. Dad had been bringing women back to the house for a couple of years by then and by the time I was fourteen I'd got my first tantalising glimpse of a naked woman. I'd walked into Dad's bedroom to find one of his conquests standing in the middle of the room with absolutely nothing on. I'd never seen anything like it and I was shocked as much as I was fascinated. 'Get out, you mucky little bastard!' she shouted. I was confused. What had I done wrong?

'I saw my Dad's girlfriend's fanny last night!' I bragged at school the next day. All the lads were fascinated.

'Did you? What was it like?' they said.

'Oh, it looked like a big black spidery thing!' I said.

My own interest in women was taking time to develop, but like any adolescent I had a vivid fantasy life that made up for a lack of any real action. Anybody of my age knows about *Spick* and *Span*. They were little black and white magazines with pictures of ladies in their underwear. By today's standards they were quite harmless; you see more now in a home shopping catalogue. I was in my bedroom one afternoon, looking through *Spick* and *Span* and doing what any teenage boy would do in the circumstances. The next thing I knew, Dad was standing in my bedroom. 'Roy!' he shouted.

I jumped up. 'What?' I said.

'Your tea's ready, you mucky little bastard!'

I'd fallen asleep with my trousers down and my hand in my pants. It was obvious what I'd been up to and my father had caught me red-handed. I didn't dare go downstairs.

Compared with other lads in my class, I was a late starter. They were always bragging about what they were getting up to with girls. One day, Derek Harland, who was a couple of years younger than me, turned up at my house with two girls. 'These girls want fucking,' he said as I opened the door.

'Oh,' I said. 'Er . . . our Dad'll go mad.'

'I'll show you,' Derek said. He took Cynthia, a fat lass I knew from around Grangetown, and he fucked her on our stairs while me and this other girl I'd never met stood watching. I don't know whether Cynthia's friend expected me to follow Derek's lead. She certainly didn't come on to me and I was just not that way inclined. I was a little bit shy and naive when it came to girls. Although I had no qualms about pinching things, getting drunk or fighting in the street, I had scruples about the right way to treat women and that stopped me taking advantage. I was from a staunch Methodist family – Sunday school and things like that – and despite being the black sheep of the family I had stronger morals than many of the lads with whom I kicked around. I can't help thinking that the absence of my mother, and to some extent my sister, played a part in my attitudes towards girls when I was a teenager. Maybe it had made me scared of women; I certainly wasn't used to their company. Or maybe it made me put girls on a pedestal, as if they were something special and delicate that needed to be handled carefully because they were so rare in my life.

At that time I knocked around in a gang of about five or six lads. We all had nicknames. There was Sweaty, Namda, Baz, Carless, Panda and I was Spud. Spud Vasey. How any of us got those names I don't know. We were all in the same class and we had the same interests. We'd meet on a corner at five o'clock at night and wander the streets. When we were old enough, we joined the Boys' Club, where we'd play table tennis and do sports. I was good at basketball and a fast runner over a hundred yards. A hundred and one yards and I was fucked, but over one hundred yards I was good. I also got into painting, winning a local painting competition. I used to draw cartoon characters on the walls at home. Our bathroom had Mickey Mouse and Donald Duck. They were that good that my auld fella would say: 'You'll be a cartoonist one day.' But, like most things, I lost interest in it. I didn't have any idea of what I would do in the future. I just took each day as it came and never thought I'd amount to anything.

On Saturday evenings, the lads and I would go to a dance at Grangetown Boy Scouts hut. Local bands would play rock-and-roll and ballad standards of the day – 'Blue Moon' and 'A White Sports Coat and a Pink Carnation'. The girls wore pleated skirts and the lads stood around trying to look hard. We were all

Teddy boys, taking our lead from the *New Musical Express*, which had pictures of Lonnie Donegan, Alma Cogan, Frankie Vaughan and Mel Tormé. Cliff Richard was just coming through and I used to think I was just like him. I'd spend ages in front of the mirror in my bedroom, which I'd surrounded with pictures of Cliff, combing a DA into the back of my hair and teasing out a curl at the front. Barry Gerrard, who had the best quiff in Grangetown, used to give me tips on how to comb my hair. One evening, down at the Scout Hut, I thought I'd never looked better when Barry turned to me. 'What's that smell?' he said.

'What smell?' I said.

'I can smell something,' Barry said.

'What?'

'It's your hair,' Barry said. 'What's them bits in your hair?

'Them little bits?' I said. 'What?'

'It looks like little bits of bacon and egg.'

'You told me to get some lard and put it on my hair.'

'Not out of the fucking pan! Fresh stuff!' Barry said. The smell was overpowering.

When Sweaty, Namda, Baz, Carless, Panda and I weren't hanging out on street corners or going to dances, we'd pinch motorbikes and cars, dumping them when they ran out of petrol. We were no different from the joyriders that nowadays plague inner cities.

I met a lad called Terry who was particularly good at putting two wires together and starting up a car or bike. Between us, we decided to buy an old black Austin off an auld fella for eight pounds each. It wasn't taxed or insured, but Terry was what we called a sandscratcher – he lived in Redcar, on the coast – so we decided the best way to avoid the attention of the bluebottles was to fill up the tank and drive the Austin from Redcar to Warrenby, which had one long road that went along a breakwater to a pier head. There'd be no traffic there, we reasoned, just a few fishermen's huts.

We spent all day at Warrenby, taking it in turns to drive along the breakwater, until at about five o'clock we ran out of petrol. 'We'll leave it and take the can,' I said to Terry. 'We'll get the can filled and bring it back to the car in the morning.'

The next morning we walked to the garage, a good five miles from the breakwater, and filled the can. As we approached the breakwater we could see a group of men in the distance, but nowhere near where we'd left the car. Some of them were wearing peaked caps. 'What's happened there?' I said.

'I think it's the police,' Terry replied.

'Eh, we'd better just walk the other way. Maybe they've found the car and discovered it isn't taxed or insured.'

We made a detour around the sand dunes, then sat at a distance, watching and waiting. After about an hour the men dispersed. We walked up to a bloke wearing a hard hat.

'Hiya, mate!' I said.

'All right?' he replied.

'There's coppers there,' I said. 'What's happened?'

'Some fucking idiot's left a car on the railway track.'

'What yer mean?'

'The goods train hit it and pushed it two miles along the breakwater. It's a wreck.'

Fortunately, we'd not registered the car after buying it from the old man, so the only way they could trace it to us was if the auld fella could remember us. We knew he couldn't.

On one of the few days I was at school, a new girl was introduced to the class. 'Boys and girls, we have a new pupil today,' the teacher said as she walked in. 'Her name is Sandra Pallent.'

All the lads in the class immediately thought the same thing: Fucking hell, look at the tits on that. None of the girls in our class had breasts. Sandra most definitely did. I was soon besotted with her and fortunately Sandra took to me straight away. Within weeks, we were boyfriend and girlfriend.

Sandra was beautiful, easily the most attractive girl in our school. She looked like Olivia Newton-John, but with dark hair. She wore tight sweaters, which showed off her slim figure and large breasts perfectly. To start with, I was quite content with a little kiss and a feel of her tits through her jumper, but the pressure was on from my mates to go further. 'Have you felt her tits properly yet?' the lads would ask.

'No, I haven't,' I'd say. 'No, no.'

'What's wrong with you?' they'd say. 'You want to feel her tits. They're huge.'

But I wanted to take it slowly. We'd go for walks or to the cinema or we'd go round to someone's house to babysit. We were always kissing, but that was as far as we went, partly because I had a lot of respect for Sandra and partly because I didn't have a clue about proper sex.

We'd been going out for a few months when Sandra looked me straight in the eye. 'My mam goes to the bingo on Friday night at the Lyric,' she said, 'so we'll have sex then.'

I was petrified. I didn't have a clue what to do, so I swallowed my pride and asked the lads. 'How do you start?' I said. '*Where* you do start?'

'Oh, you put your tongue in her mouth and that'll get her going,' one of the lads told me.

Armed with this valuable information, I turned up at Sandra's terraced house on Friday night, a bag of nerves. As soon as her mother opened the door, I was convinced that I was being regarded with suspicion. Sandra's mum appeared to be watching my every move. Shortly before seven-thirty, when the bingo started, Sandra's mum disappeared out of the door and we were left alone at last.

'Would you like a sherry?' Sandra asked, opening her parents' drinks cabinet.

'Er . . . yeah,' I said, figuring I needed some Dutch courage.

'Shall we go upstairs?' Sandra said before I'd finished my sherry.

'Er, yeah,' I said. 'Why not?'

We had hardly set foot in the bedroom when there was a clicking sound as the door opened. I whipped round to find Sandra's mother, her auntie Pat and a policeman standing at the end of the bed.

'I think somebody's been caught red-handed, you mucky little get,' the policeman said. I was right. Sandra's mam *had* been suspicious of me. She'd gone straight to the police station, then picked up Auntie Pat on the way over. The policeman took me home and told my auld fella.

'Aaarrrggh, you dirty . . . what have I brought you up to do? Why . . .' Dad shouted what was becoming a familiar refrain.

'I didn't do anything!' I complained.

'You expect me to believe that?'

Sandra's mam was just as unbelieving and we were told to keep apart. They needn't have said it. Sandra and I were so shocked and embarrassed that we couldn't look at each other for a month.

The Sandra scandal had one welcome benefit. It took my mind off what was going on at home. Dad had met a woman and invited her to move in to our little house. I should have been happy for him, but after half a lifetime of just the two of us I felt invaded. We'd been a team for eight years. Now Dad was upsetting it all by bringing a woman into our home. And it got worse. Betty Allander, as my auld fella's woman was called, had five children – two of them twins – when we had only two bedrooms. I moved into the boxroom and the five kids, aged from fourteen to seven, took over my bedroom, pulling my toys out of my drawers, crayoning in my colouring books, snapping the heads off my tin soldiers, drawing moustaches on my Cliff Richard posters, ripping my other posters off the walls and damaging my carefully painted murals. I was livid and I've still not got over it.

My dad and Betty might have been lovebirds, but her kids and I were forever arguing and fighting. Jimmy, one of the twins, was such a little bastard that I tried to kill him. The cheeky recklin mouthed off to me so I pushed him into the washing machine and shut the door. That'll serve you right, you little twat, I thought as I tried to turn it on, but it wouldn't go. Jimmy's sister, Brenda, ran down to the pub and told me auld fella, who came home, dragged Jimmy out of the machine, shouted 'You nearly broke his neck!' at me and gave me the biggest hiding I'd ever known.

From the moment Betty and her kids moved in, I hated being at home. Even now, more than forty years later, I have no time for them. I once heard that Jimmy was bragging to somebody down the steelworks where he works: 'Oh, I'm Chubby Brown's stepbrother.' When I heard it, I had a simple reply: 'You tell him from me if he keeps saying that I'll come down and throw him off the fucking scaffolding. He's no stepbrother of mine.' The reason behind it was that I was possessive about my father – after all, my mum had buggered off and my sister had gone with her; I had no intention of losing my dad as well – and I expected him to be possessive of me.

It did, however, teach me that Dad had a bigger heart than I did. He couldn't have been that lonely he'd bring five kids into the house just to get at their mother's pussy. That took some doing. Nevertheless, it was something with which I could never get to grips, and from that moment on I was looking for a way to get out of that house.

*

I can't remember my last day at school. I was at school so infre-
quently – the school bobbies were rarely away from our house –
that I probably wasn't there when school broke up. I left with no
qualifications. I didn't even pass my eleven-plus. The lowest
class at my school was B2 and I was bottom of that. Thick as
two short planks, I had no prospects and no real future.

A few months before I left school, I'd started as a van boy,
assisting the driver of the Wilfred's bakery van every morning,
working from half past five in the morning until two in the
afternoon six days a week. It was easy work, the only exception
being the delivery to the nylon-stockings factory in Cargo Fleet
Lane, where the workforce of young girls delighted in embarrassing the driver and me as we dropped off their sandwiches
and buns. 'Show us your cock, boy,' they'd shout as I carried the
trays through the factory. I once went into the factory toilets. I'd
never seen anything like it. The walls were covered with graffiti
of crude boasts and erect penises being pushed into any orifice
you could imagine. The writing on the walls of men's toilets was
tame by comparison.

The bakery round paid decent pocket money, but I needed to
start earning a proper wage if I was going to get away from my
dad's overstuffed house and my irritating step-siblings. Scratting
around for odd jobs, I applied to be an engine driver at my
father's steel mill. They turned me down. I applied for jobs at
various factories, but they all rejected me, so I thought I'd join
the army. I had my mind set on being one of the guards dressed
in a red tunic and a busby outside Buckingham Palace. That
appealed. I went to the Royal Engineers and filled in some
forms. The sergeant handed them back to me. 'Your dad has to
sign them to say that you're old enough,' he said.

I was only fifteen, but my dad wasn't bothered. 'If you want
to join the army . . . you know . . .' he said. I could tell he just
wanted me out of the house. With my forms signed, I turned up

at the barracks a few days later. At eight o'clock that morning, there was a dozen of us sat on benches in an army careers office when a soldier with a clipboard marched into the room.

'Miller. Parfitt. Snowdon. Vasey . . .' the soldier read from a list on his clipboard. We trooped out of the office into a room where we were given a medical.

'Why do you want to join the army?' an officer asked me while I was being examined.

'Because I want to be a soldier,' I said. The officer didn't look very impressed with my answer. We were then ushered into a hall with two columns of desks and told to sit down.

'We want you to write an essay,' a soldier with a posh voice said. I didn't know what essay meant. Until then I'd never even heard the word.

'What do you mean?' I said.

'Well, a composition about your life. A story, give us a story.'

I still didn't know what he meant, so I didn't do it. I left that part of the paper blank and filled in the other parts, which asked again why I wanted to join the army as well as some personal details, such as my height and where I'd gone to school. The last question was 'Have you ever been in trouble with the police?' I wrote 'No.' It was an outright lie, but that was the least of my crimes.

The test finished at half past eleven. At ten to twelve, a soldier walked into the room. 'Vasey!' he shouted.

Fucking hell, I thought, I'm the only one who's passed. 'Yes, sir,' I said, getting to my feet.

'Come this way, please,' he said, leaving all the other lads in the room.

'I'm sorry . . .' he started, explaining that I had failed and that all the others had passed through to the next round.

'Oh, I really wanted to be a soldier,' I said.

'Why don't you come back in about a year's time and join the

Green Howards?' he said. All I could think was that if the Green Howards would have me after I'd failed, they must be right thick idiots.

A few days after failing the army recruitment test, I decided I'd had enough living under the same small roof as my father, his mistress and her five kids. Fifteen years old, fed up and unable to handle life at home any longer, I packed my belongings into two plastic carrier bags and hitch-hiked to Redcar, about five miles away on the North Sea coast. Apart from an occasional visit many years ago for a splodge in the sea with my dad, Redcar was as foreign and exotic to me as another country. Not knowing where to go or how to find somewhere to stay, that first night I climbed up on to a fishing boat that was dry-docked for the winter, laid up on bricks on the seafront. It was freezing. I hardly slept. The days weren't much better. I spent them walking through the town centre, pinching apples off fruit stalls and wondering if I would be picked up by the police. But nobody paid any attention to me. It was obvious my father hadn't even reported me missing. I'd caused that much trouble with his Betty and her children that he was clearly pleased to see me gone.

Several weeks into sleeping rough, I was trying to get warm enough to fall asleep one night when I heard a tapping sound outside the fishing boat. I lifted the canvas to find a copper staring straight at me. I was just as much a shock to him as he was to me. He nearly crapped himself. 'Hey! What are you . . . what do you think you're doing?' he said. 'Get out of there!'

The bluebottle dragged me to the local nick, where I gave him a sob story. 'How old are you?' the policeman asked. I told him I was fifteen. The next thing I knew, I was being pushed through the door of a home for wayward children at Westbourne Grove in Redcar. The couple who ran the home found me some clean clothes, gave me something to eat and a warm bed. I was one of four waifs they'd taken in who'd run away from home. 'As long as you get yourself a job and you behave properly,' the policeman said, 'you can stay here indefinitely.'

I got a job working for Calor Gas at Port Clarence on the Tees estuary. I'd been there for a few months when a gas tank blew up, killing a few men, so I moved on to a job at Pearson's driving a dumper truck. I didn't have a licence, but that didn't seem to bother Arthur Stairs, the foreman, as long as I drove it only on company property. My job was to transport concrete from large mixers to wherever it was needed on the site. It was good work, the pay wasn't bad and Arthur was a decent gadgie. 'Bring your bait, don't tell your mate,' he'd say when there was a chance of getting an extra shift. Or it was 'job and knock' when you'd finished your work early and could go home before the factory siren sounded. One day, I was delivering concrete to a deep hole in which some men were working. I tipped the front of the dumper to drop the concrete into the hole. The men then spread it with their shovels, but this time I got too close to the edge of the hole. As I pulled the lever to lift up the scoop of the dumper, I felt the dumper move beneath me. It teetered on the edge, then toppled into the hole, swiftly followed by me.

'Get out the way . . .' I shouted as I came crashing into the hole and the men below me dived for cover.

Just after I'd come to my senses at the bottom of the hole, Arthur turned up. 'Are you all right?' he shouted.

'Yeah,' I said.

'Well, you're fucking sacked!'

My P45 was in and out of my trousers more than my dick. The next week, I had three jobs in a day. At 8 a.m. I started with a sub-contractor cleaning out blast furnaces at Dorman, Long. Choking on the fumes after an hour, I collected my cards from the gaffer at 9.30 a.m. and walked over to the ICI plant next door, where I took a job with a firm doing the stone work on a chimney. By lunchtime I'd quit as I couldn't stand heights. After lunch I walked back to Dorman, Long and immediately got hired by Pearson's, a sub-contractor, as a labourer.

After that, I got a job at Shepherd's, a building company. For eight hours a day I toiled as a hod-carrier on the Lakes housing estate in Redcar. People say there's a dignity in the working life, but that was a load of rubbish. For six and a half days' work I got twelve pounds and each morning I had to get there an hour earlier than the bricklayers because I had to get the cement mixer started and carry the cement up onto the platforms before the brickies turned up. The bricklayers were on piece-work. The more bricks they laid the more money they got, but it didn't ever occur to them that it meant I had to carry more hods. None of them ever turned round to me, the hapless labourer, to say here's an extra fiver.

At the end of my shift I'd go back to the home in Westbourne Grove and write short poems. *The garden's full of flowers, the hive is full of bees*, one of my early monologues began. *The room is full of sound because the piano is full of keys. My head is full of emptiness, my throat is full of cough, this house is full of strangers, I wish they would all fuck off.*

I was fed up. Fed up with hod-carrying. Fed up with living in the hostel. Fed up with having no one that cared for me. And fed up with having no prospect of a better life. If I was going to get myself out of this mess, I needed to earn more money, so I got a job at Devonport's as a red-lead painter and then at Kellogg's, an American technical engineering firm, where I was taken on as an engineer's labourer. It was a grand title for a job that only entailed being a gofer – 'Go and get me this; go and get me that' – so when one of the foremen asked if anybody wanted to drive a van to take labourers from the works gate to the various locations on the site where work was being done, I volunteered.

No one asked if I had a licence and when you're fifteen years old you don't worry about it yourself. Every day I drove labourers around the site in a wrecked ambulance that was missing two doors. It was totally unroadworthy, but it didn't matter as long as the ambulance didn't leave Kellogg's property. One Thursday, about a month into the job, the lads asked me to drive them into Redcar. It was the Easter holiday weekend and they had double wages in their pockets. They were a rough lot, many of them Scottish, Welsh or Irish labourers who were looking forward to four days off work, but first they wanted a bellyful of beer to carry them through the long, hot afternoon. It was five miles from the site to the Clarendon, one of the roughest claggy mats in Redcar. I dropped off the lads. 'Roy, will you pick us up?' they shouted.

'Sure. I'll pick you up,' I said, not thinking for a moment about the consequences of driving on public roads without a licence or insurance. Three hours later, I returned. Turning the last corner before the Clarendon, I heard some voices yelling and some dogs barking. Then I saw where it was coming from. About a dozen of the lads I'd dropped off were involved in a massive street fight. The police were using dogs to try to control it, but they were getting nowhere. I pulled up. 'Get in the ambulance, you fucking arseholes!' I shouted. 'Just get in the ambulance.'

But the lads were too drunk to do anything but fight. A copper came over. 'What do you want?' he said.

'Er . . . I've come for the lads who work at . . .' I said.

'You're the driver of this vehicle?' the copper said.

'Yeah.'

'You've got bald tyres,' the copper said. 'There's no lights. And the doors are missing. What's it doing in the town?'

'Well, the lads asked me to come and get them as a favour.'

'A *favour*?'

'I've come from the Kellogg's site.'

'Is that why this van hasn't got a tax disc?'

'It's a site van,' I said. I still hadn't realised that I was in deep trouble.

'Where's your licence?' the copper said.

'I haven't got one,' I said.

'What are you doing, driving with no licence?'

'I just came to pick them up,' I said. I couldn't see any wrong in it. It seemed perfectly natural for me to do the lads a good turn by collecting them from the pub.

The policeman took me to Redcar police station. Downstairs the lads who'd been fighting were locked in the cells. Upstairs I was being questioned by the duty sergeant. 'Who started the fight?' he said.

'I haven't a clue. I'm just the driver.'

'Driver?' the sergeant said. I could see I'd have to go through the questions all over again. 'Of that vehicle? The one with bald tyres, a door hanging off and no tax?'

'Well, it's a site vehicle.'

'So what's it doing on the road in Redcar?'

'The lads asked me to pick them up.'

'And you just did it?'

The sergeant left the room. It was clear that the police didn't quite know what to do about me. I could see they were scratching their heads. The sergeant returned. 'You might as well go but don't touch that vehicle,' he said. 'Leave it where it is – you'll be hearing from us.'

I went back to the site and told one of the gaffers what had happened. 'Oh, fucking hell,' he said. 'No.'

On the Tuesday morning after the Easter weekend I reported at work, expecting to pick the lads up and ferry them around the site as usual. The gadgie called me into his office. 'There's your cards and there's your P45,' he said. 'You're finished.'

I was fired. For doing my workmates a favour. I still couldn't comprehend what I'd done wrong.

'You've got two weeks' wages to come,' the gadgie said. 'That will be in the post for you, unless you want to come back to collect it.'

I returned the next day for my money. While I was waiting for it, I got talking to a lad who said he was in the merchant navy. He'd been all over the world. 'Why don't you apply?' he said.

'Aye, I will,' I said.

I made my mind up that quickly and that easily. It was a simple decision and it was staring me in the face. I had nothing to offer Teesside and it had nothing to offer me. I just wanted to get away, see somewhere else and do something with my life. I'd wanted to join the army for similar reasons, but that hadn't worked out. As an alternative, the merchant navy appeared to tick all the boxes. My mother, father and sister had deserted me. Sandra had turned her back on me and one job after another had slipped through my fingers. If Teesside didn't want me, I'd find my luck elsewhere.

CHAPTER FOUR

AWAY FROM IT ALL

'IN YOUR CASE,' Mr White said, 'I think we can beat this.'

I'd got over the initial shock of having cancer and I was now sitting in the office of a small bespectacled man with neat hair, parted precisely to the right. A week or so earlier, Dr Martin had uttered a few words – 'Mr Vasey. I've got some bad news for you. You have throat cancer' – that had changed my life for ever. Now another few words were again changing my life. I'd assumed that cancer was a death sentence, but Mr White, a specialist cancer surgeon, was telling me otherwise. That one sentence of hope left me feeling like a million dollars.

'You know my voice is my life,' I said. 'Without my voice I can't earn a living.'

'I understand that,' Mr White said. The words seemed to hang in the air. The Royal Infirmary in Middlesbrough was the kind of building in which voices echo along corridors and where everything you say seems more loaded. Fifteen minutes earlier, Helen and I had walked in through the big heavy doors, our footsteps tip-tapping through chambers, along corridors with big marble pillars and up an old-fashioned staircase with a wooden banister to Mr White's office. Outside, it was just like any other hospital, with people milling in the car park, killing time and smoking cigarettes, making me want to shout at them that they were all brainless arseholes. 'Can't you see what's happened to me?' I wanted to say. 'Don't you realise what you're doing to yourself?' But I didn't. I just got on with the business of dealing with my cancer.

'How bad will it be?' I asked Mr White.

'That's something I can't tell you because we don't know yet,' he said. 'All I know is what I need to do to deal with this cancer immediately. We'll cut it away and see what remains. After that we will give you therapy. Hopefully, with good physio, you'll retain your voice. It will never be the same. You will never be able to sing . . .'

'Well, that's good,' I interrupted, 'because I couldn't sing before.'

'You've already taken the best steps you could to recovery,' Mr White said.

'Oh? What were they?'

'You've never smoked and you don't drink heavily. It makes a big difference.'

We talked through the procedure and then Mr White ushered me out into a corridor lined with photographs of ear, nose and throat cancers. I tried not to look – I've always been squeamish – but I couldn't stop myself glancing at the pictures. It took me back to when I joined the merchant service and the first thing they did when we had passed all our tests was to show us a film of men and women with syphilis, gonorrhoea and other venereal diseases. They were frightening pictures. Knobs and fannies that looked like lepers' dinners. Rotten flesh swollen with pus and infection. More than forty years had passed since I joined the merchant navy and saw those pictures, yet here in the cancer ward of an ear, nose and throat hospital they were using very similar pictures of throats and noses to show the effects of contracting cancer.

●

I was sixteen and a half years old when I turned up at a dock in Middlesbrough with dreams of life on the open sea. Having passed the entrance test for the merchant navy, I was sent to Sharpness, a training school for about two hundred and fifty boys on the river Severn. For six weeks I learned how to read a compass, tie knots and survive at sea. It was the first time I had buckled down to anything in my life, partly because I wanted to change my life and partly because they had a simple way of dealing with any trouble. If you had an argument with another boy at the training school, you put your name on a noticeboard. The following Friday night, the two of you, kitted out in massive sixteen- or eighteen-ounce gloves, would meet in the school's boxing ring. For three three-minute rounds you had to box your tormentor, no matter who they were. But because the gloves were so huge there was little chance of hurting each other.

Inevitably, I soon had an argument with a lad. I was serving food in the canteen and he took an extra roast potato. 'It's two each, mate,' I said.

'Who you fucking talking to?' he replied.

'You. And it's two potatoes for everyone.'

'Right. In the ring Friday,' he said.

'Any fucking time, boy!' I replied. On Friday I climbed into the ring, expecting a quick fight with the lad, who was a little bit smaller than me. Even wearing heavily padded gloves, he knocked ten colours of shit out of me. At the end of the second round I realised I was in trouble. When the bell rang and my opponent ran to the centre of the ring for the third and final round, I picked up the stool before the trainer had time to move in. I ran over to the lad and hit him over the head with it. Blood poured down his cheek, the fight was stopped and I was disqualified. The next day I had to go in front of the Captain.

'He was an Amateur Boxing Association champion,' the Captain said. 'You didn't stand a chance. I'm going to put you in jankers, but it won't go on your record.' For the next few days I scrubbed out toilets, peeled spuds and dug the gardens. But I wasn't barred from joining the merchant navy. I'd got away with a warning.

At the end of the training period, they gave us our papers. They showed us the VD film in the hope that it would stop us getting into port in Africa and going with a prostitute just because it was a shilling a fuck, then told us to head down to the British Shipping Federation Office if we wanted to work. Within days I was on the *McCauley*, casting off from Billingham Reach in Middlesbrough bound for Mozambique (then called Portuguese East Africa) with a cargo of black salt. The first thing the captain said when I arrived on board was: 'We've got too many deckhands. Who wants to go in the kitchen?'

Eh, that's a good idea, I immediately thought. At least I'd be in the warm there.

To feed a crew of twenty-eight there was a chef, a second chef and me. I peeled vegetables, scraped pans and worked my arse off as a general dogsbody. I was used to it: no change from the mind-numbing work I'd been doing at factories or on building sites. The only difference was that I was now at sea. After my training, I thought I knew everything I needed to know about crewing a ship. But there was one thing they couldn't teach us: how to deal with seasickness. For the entire twenty-one-day voyage to East Africa I couldn't stand upright, I couldn't eat and I coughed blood. Most of the time, I gritted my teeth and tried not to think about how bad I felt, but there were times when the chef used to say: 'Oh for fuck's sake, go and lie down.' As long as I was lying down, I felt all right. As soon as I got up, I felt ill. I'd never felt so bad in my life.

And in spite of the camaraderie with the other crew members, I found life at sea to be lonely. I spent most of each day on my own, either working in the galley or lying on my bunk. Sometimes I would stand for hours on deck, gazing at the ocean. There was a lot of time for thinking and I spent hours wondering what I was doing with my life. I was too young to have any easy answers, but I had a sense that things weren't going quite to plan. I would sit and draw and write down little lines or compose poems. But writing poetry is like songwriting – you don't know if they're any good unless you try them out on someone – and if I had told one of the lads on board that I was writing poetry, at best I would have been called a 'big soft fucking shit'. At worst I would have had my head kicked in.

By the end of my first voyage, I'd worked up to second chef and become a dab hand in the kitchen, particularly at Yorkshire puddings. As soon as we docked, I took the trolleybus from Smith's Docks back to Grangetown. I saw Sandra and picked things up with her. I was paid only two pounds, ten shillings a week, but I'd saved most of it. During a fortnight's shore leave, I spent it all on Sandra. I bought her handbags, clothes, shoes, perfume, anything she wanted. I'd lost touch with my family and many of my friends in Redcar, so I spent every moment I could with Sandra. I'd fallen in love with her.

Shortly before my time ashore was over, I went down to the Federation Office. 'We've got another job for you,' they said. 'The *King Malcolm*. It's sailing from Smith's Docks to Cape Town, Port Elizabeth, East London, Dar es Salaam, Mombasa and back through the Suez Canal. It's nine months. Do you want it?'

'What's my job?' I said.

'In the kitchens. Or Purser's second officer.' That meant waiting on the officers. It sounded an easy number. 'I'll go with the
Purser as second officer,' I said.

That night, I smuggled Sandra on board. I showed her
around and then took her back to my cabin where no policeman, mother or Aunt Pat could disturb the proceedings.

We sailed the next morning, carrying mixed cargo and ore to
South Africa. I was in the pantry one day when a couple of lads
approached me. 'Can you get us a couple of tins of lager?' they
said. Lager was rationed to two tins a day, which came out of
our wages. I couldn't see why they shouldn't have more. And
anyway, we were all Middlesbrough lads who believed in stick-
ing together, so during the next meal I went into one of the big
fridges where the lager was kept. I put a tin in the bottom of a
jug and filled it with milk.

'The lads just want some milk,' I said to the Purser before
taking it to the table where the lads were sitting. 'Don't forget,
lads,' I said as I dropped it off, 'keep a sip for me.'

The scam worked for weeks until one day the Purser stopped
me. 'Where are you taking that milk?' he said.

'The lads just asked me for some extra milk,' I said.

'Well, I'll have a glass,' he said.

'I'll get you one, boss.'

'*No*. I'll have a glass now. Out of *that* jug.' He held his glass
out. I poured some milk, then the tin fell out. 'What's that?' he
said, as if he didn't know. Somebody had obviously grassed on
me.

Sent in front of the Captain, I was severely reprimanded for
theft and my papers were stamped. Three stamps and I'd be
thrown out of the merchant navy. As usual, I couldn't see what
I'd done wrong. The lager wasn't for me. It was for someone
else, but I'd taken the blame.

After we dropped off our cargo at Cape Town, we took on some massive boxes that were strapped down on the main deck. It was fairly obvious what was inside the boxes. Ostrich heads poked out of one of them. They contained animals – monkeys, zebras, lions, ostriches and others – for Whipsnade Zoo. A rota was drawn up for the job of feeding them. When it came to my turn, I held up a bucket to the ostrich box. Nothing happened for a few seconds. Then an ostrich head darted out so fast and so hard that it dented the bucket. If the ostrich had targeted me, it would have killed me on the spot.

Meanwhile, in the kitchen, one of the chefs had taken a fancy to me, always putting his arm round me and trying to feel my arse. I warned him a couple of times. 'I'm not a poofter, you know,' I said. 'Will your take your fucking hand . . .'

'Oh, I think you're gorgeous', he said.

Every time I walked in the kitchen he'd try to touch me, until I lost my temper and lamped him. He flew about two feet in the air and landed on his arse. Getting straight back on to his feet, he picked up a knife and ran at me. I sidestepped him, then dodged his second lunge at me with the knife, lifting my arm up to protect my face. The knife slipped between the two bones in my lower arm, the tip coming out the other side. The head chef and a kitchen hand grabbed the gay chef as blood poured everywhere. The Captain had him locked in his cabin and sent for the Royal Navy to take him away. Meanwhile, I lost so much blood that I got the shakes. A few hours later, a frigate came alongside and took us both on board. The gay chef was bound for England, where he was charged with violent conduct, but first they took me to Malta where I was dropped off at the hospital. They patched me up and gave me a blood test. I had malaria. By the time I'd recovered, the *King Malcolm* was almost home.

My next trip took me west to Florida and Mexico. On the

return voyage, we detoured into the Mediterranean and stopped at a port in Algeria for two days. Called Bône then, it has now been renamed Annaba. Algeria was in the midst of a vicious war to win its independence from France. Buildings were being bombed and people were getting shot or kidnapped every day. We were told not to go ashore, but a boatful of young Teesside lads desperate for a drink and female company was unlikely to heed the Captain's orders. Billy Loadwick, a lad I knew from Middlesbrough, Ray Blenkinsop, another Teessider, and about ten other lads decided to go ashore.

The uniformed watchman at the bottom of the gangplank was a local. If we were going to get ashore, we'd have to find some way of getting past him. Realising that money was unimportant to him, I offered him my shirt to let us through and tell us where to find the nearest decent bar. He immediately gave in.

In the blistering late-afternoon heat, we crept down the gangplank onto dry land, crossed some railway lines, sneaked through a massive paper mill and emerged on a bush road. Everybody was dark-skinned and most of the buildings looked like mud huts. We walked for a couple of miles, sweating like pigs, until we came to a small village with a shop and a couple of bars with swing doors like on the saloons I'd seen in Western movies with my auld fella.

We walked into the first saloon and Billy walked up to the bar. 'We are from England,' he said. 'You speak English?'

'Little, little,' the barman said.

'Drink?' Billy said. 'Money . . . er . . . English, you know? No francs. No Algerian money.' Not having any foreign currency, Billy was trying to find out if we could buy a drink with some pounds.

'Your watch,' the barman said, pointing at Billy's wrist. Billy took it off and passed it over the counter. The barman gave us a round of drinks. Then Ray handed over his watch. Before long, the barman had five watches on his arm and we were on our way to getting gloriously blathered. After weeks at sea, stumbling upon that bar was like passing through the gates of heaven. Cigarette smoke, alcohol, sweat and cheap perfume made a heady cocktail after the stench of engine oil, and it was a relief to be away from the constant thrum of the ship's engines. I looked around. The bar was little more than a dusty-floored room, with a curtain along one wall, through which some of the lads periodically disappeared. I assumed they were going to the toilet.

I was lapping it up, savouring the atmosphere and wishing the evening would go on for ever when a siren sounded briefly. Then: *Bang!* There was an explosion outside and the doors to the bar flew off their hinges. 'Fucking hell!' Billy shouted. 'What the fuck was that?'

'Keep down,' the barman shouted. Terrified, we all dropped to the floor, one or two hands cautiously rising through the swirling dust to feel along the tops of the tables for our drinks. Fortunately, we were drinking out of bottles, so there was no chance of dust ruining our pints. We lay on the floor for a short while, waiting for the commotion outside to calm down. Then the barman opened the back door. 'You go, you go,' he shouted, beckoning us through the open door into the night.

Outside, the Algerian police and the French army were trying to round up some independence fighters. Bullets and fists were flying, so we ran as fast as we could back down a mud track towards the docks. Stumbling in the darkness, we kept running, too frightened to stop until we were safely aboard the ship. We ran up the gangplank, each carrying four or five bottles of beer from the bar, got aboard and collapsed, laughing with nerves. 'What a fucking carry-on,' Billy said just as two army trucks pulled up outside the ship and disgorged dozens of soldiers and police.

The soldiers formed a long line in front of the ship, brandishing their rifles. We sat on the deck trying to look innocent, watching the commotion on the dockside. A khaki-uniformed police squad marched up the gangplank. There was a few minutes' silence, then the Captain and the Purser came up on deck accompanied by several Algerian coppers wearing fezes like Tommy Cooper.

'*Un, deux, trois, quatre, cinq. . .*' one of the policemen said, pointing in turn at each member of the gang who'd been drinking in the bar.

'It appears, gentlemen, that you have disregarded my orders about nobody going ashore,' the Captain said. 'And you got yourself into a situation where you could have been killed.' A lengthy lecture followed. 'Several of you were seen in a bar,' the Captain continued. 'No, not a bar. A *brothel*.' I realised then that passing through the curtains at the bar led not to the toilet but to where the hookers were working. 'All of you who were in the bar take one step forward,' the Captain said.

About ten of us stepped forward. Once again, my papers were stamped. I now had two stamps. One more stamp and I'd be facing a dishonourable discharge.

By the time I got back to Middlesbrough, I'd decided that I'd had enough of the merchant navy. But what to do instead? Sandra Pallent, my girlfriend from school, provided the answer.

I'd been writing to Sandra the whole time I'd been at sea and met up with her as soon as I was back in Grangetown. One evening she laid her cards on the table. 'If you go back to sea,' she said, 'I am finishing with you.'

I loved Sandra. I thought she was wonderful, but I didn't want to go back to labouring on building sites and at factories. 'What am I going to do?' I said.

'You've been waiting on tables, you've been working in the kitchen as a second cook and bottle-washer, haven't you?'

'Yeah.'

'Well, come to Scarborough and you can do just the same, but on dry land. I'll get you a job at the Southlands Hotel where I've been working.'

I discovered that I was a good waiter. And at seven pounds a week the money was much better than at sea. I had more tables than any other waiter, my cutlery always gleamed, my dumb waiter was party polished and I'd soon trained myself in silver service. Sandra didn't like it. She was a waitress and I was encroaching on her patch. And to make matters worse, I was popular with the other staff. Sandra and I were always arguing. Sandra would accuse me of fancying the other waitresses. And sometimes she was right. I was seventeen and surrounded by young lasses. It was difficult not to fancy at least some of them.

As usual, our relationship was on and off like a whore's drawers. Sandra started going out with a lad she'd met who was working at another hotel. And I'd taken a fancy to a stunning girl who did the washing-up in the Southlands' kitchens. But the other relationships never lasted. Sandra and I always ended up getting back together.

I got in with a couple of Scottish lads who were also working at the hotel. One night they took me aside. 'Will you keep a lookout?' they said. 'We're going to break into a shop down the road.'

'Course I will,' I said. As usual, I didn't give a moment's thought to the possible consequences.

In the early hours of the morning, we met outside the gift shop, a shabby place with buckets, spades and a row of toy watches in the window. There was nothing of value in it except for the contents of the till. The two lads disappeared around the back of the shop while I stood on a corner that gave me a clear view along two streets. The lads had been gone only a few minutes when the alarm went off. Within seconds, the shop was surrounded by police and I was running as fast as my legs would carry me. I looked behind me. Two coppers were chasing me. We all got caught. Less than a week later I was in Armley jail in Leeds, having been convicted at Scarborough Magistrates Court of breaking and entering.

For a seventeen-year-old lad, Armley, one of the toughest prisons in the country, was a frightening wake-up call. Surrounded by convicted rapists, murderers, drug addicts and downright head cases, I didn't dare look at anybody in case they took it the wrong way. I was meant to be at Armley for only a short time, until I had to appear in court again for my sentencing, but it dragged on for three months.

Six weeks after I was locked away a letter arrived at Armley. It was from Sandra. 'Dear Roy,' it said, 'I've met somebody else. We love each other . . . I know this is going to hurt but I never know where I am with you . . . I might never see you again, so it seems best if we end it now.'

I was devastated, but determined not to give up. I wrote to Sandra every day, but she never wrote back. When I wasn't writing letters, I'd sit in my cell, counting the bricks on the walls and gazing at the picture of Sandra I'd stuck up above my bed. Shortly before I was sentenced, another letter arrived. It was from Sandra's mam. 'Sandra doesn't live here any more, Roy,' it said, 'so just forget it now.' By then, one of the other convicts had stolen my picture of Sandra. I'd been upset and angry when I first noticed it had gone. Now I thought they'd done me a favour.

A few days later I was back in court for sentencing. In those days they were allowed to refer to your previous record. It took them more than forty minutes to read out the list of my petty criminal acts, from stealing bottles of milk off doorsteps to six weeks in Medomsley Detention Centre.

'The spot has become a boil,' the magistrate said. 'And now

it needs to be lanced. I am sentencing you to two years' Borstal training.'

The two Scottish lads, whose idea the burglary had been, had clean records and got off with suspended sentences. While they walked out of the courtroom with relieved expressions, I was carted by the police down to the cells. Two hours later, I was pushed onto a prison van to return to Armley. As the Black Maria stopped at the traffic lights in Scarborough, I looked out of the window. Sitting in a Wimpy Bar, drinking cups of tea with their girlfriends, were the two Scottish lads. One of them was kissing his girlfriend passionately. A big smile creased the other lad's face as if he didn't have a care in the world. It had been their idea and they'd got off. I was taking the rap. They were with their girlfriends, while mine had jilted me for another lad. It broke my fucking heart.

CHAPTER FIVE

BORSTAL BOY

EVERY DAY THE same questions dominated most of my waking hours. What am I going to do if they remove my vocal cords? Will I ever talk again? Will I ever get back on stage? Should I open a little café? What else could I do? Should I get a job in a pub, playing a piano? Or should I get a drumming job with a band, just to get a few bob in? All sorts of things went through my mind, but one thought was bigger than all the others. What would be worse – to die or never to speak again?

And then I pulled myself together. I thought back to what I'd been through to reach my late fifties and, compared with some of that, fighting cancer was nothing. I'd been through tougher times on my own, with no money and no family to support me. Now I had my wife's love and care to support me and enough money to afford the expertise of the best cancer specialists in the country. I'd been through a lot worse.

●

I spent three months in Armley jail, waiting to be assigned to a Borstal. From Armley they sent me to Leicester jail and from Leicester to Wormwood Scrubs, where a Prison Commissioner would decide to which Borstal I should be sent. The Scrubs, a huge overcrowded Victorian prison on marshy wasteland in west London, felt utterly alien. They put all the lads awaiting Borstal allocation in Scrubs Block B, a foul, filthy place where the air buzzed with the stench of urine and dirty, sweaty adolescents. The cells were disgusting, the blankets and laundry were soiled and stained, and cockroaches crawled everywhere. Most of the inmates were Londoners who raised their eyebrows when they heard my Teesside accent. I knew to keep my head down if I wanted to avoid trouble.

As soon as I arrived, I was given jobs to do – cleaning out the toilets, scrubbing landings, washing down the stairs or feeding the animals on the farm. I'd been in the Scrubs about a month when a screw came up to me with a malicious smirk on his face. 'You're cleaning out the lifers,' he said.

Accompanied by two guards, I was taken to the high-security area of the prison, a group of six or seven steel-clad buildings fenced off in its own compound. Some of the inmates had been in prison for fifteen or twenty years and were now deemed sufficiently safe for day release. These murderers, bank robbers and serious criminals were let out after breakfast to work as painters, decorators or labourers. They had to be back in their cells by half past five. My job was to clean out their cells, often while they were in them. I'd always thought I was the toughest teenager in Grangetown, but I was petrified by these bona fide hard nuts. One of them had been an associate of the Kray Twins. Another was dubbed Frankie the Axe Murderer by the inmates, who would speak of him only in whispers.

I was cleaning out one of the lifers' cells one day when a short, bald fella who looked like a butcher came up to me. 'What you doin' here, son?' he said.

'I'm going to Borstal,' I said.

'What happened?'

I thought it best to exaggerate my crime. 'Oh, I robbed a shop,' I said casually.

'Did ya?'

'Yeah,' I said, puffing out my chest and trying not to show my nerves. 'Three of us broke into a shop.'

'Oh right, a shop.' he said. 'D'you wanna drink?'

'Yes, please,' I said, not knowing if it was best to be polite or stand-offish. The lifers had much better facilities than the rest of the convicts. This one put the kettle on.

'What did you do, then?' I said.

'I got rid of the wife.'

'Oh, right,' I said, hoping that my false bravado didn't show through. I looked at the fella. He was only about five foot, four inches tall. I couldn't imagine him being strong enough to kill anyone.

'Have you been in here a long time?' I said.

'Eighteen years.'

'Was it worth it?'

'Was what worth it?'

'Killing your wife.'

'Well . . .' he said, speaking very slowly as if I was stupid. It was very menacing. 'At the time, I was a pig farmer in Norfolk and I come home and I catch my wife in bed with my brother. So I killed the pair of them.'

'Oh.' I felt very naive. 'Was it in all the papers?'

'National news it was. But they never found no bodies.'

'Why not?'

'I fed 'em to the pigs. They ate the bones an' all.'

I couldn't quite believe what I was hearing. I never thought that as a young lad I would be mixing with these characters. I wasn't a gladiator, but I'd been thrown in with the lions.

After a few months at the Scrubs, the prison authorities assigned me to Guy's Marsh, a Borstal at Shaftesbury in Dorset. As soon as I arrived, I was given a cold shower, my hair was shaved into a very short back and sides, and I was handed a Borstal uniform of short trousers, itchy underwear, a rough shirt and socks that didn't fit. Only the socks and underwear were regularly changed: we got clean ones once a week, after the weekly shower.

Because I had a relatively minor record – burglary, theft and street fighting were pipsqueak offences compared with some of the crimes committed by Borstal-bound lads – I had been sent to a liberal open Borstal. Nevertheless, anywhere that cooped up several hundred lads, all with little regard for law and order, was going to have trouble. Mixing with them, I was bound to argue, fight and get into trouble. And I soon did.

Borstal was a strange mixture of strict discipline, corporal punishment, manual labour, handcuffs, leg-irons and physical education. The aim was to instil discipline by making us keep to a rigid timetable. It was early to bed, early to rise, regular meal-times and regular toilet breaks. Everything went by the clock. By six a.m. we'd be on the parade ground, running on the spot, the screws slapping our legs if we didn't lift our knees until our thighs were parallel to the ground. Mornings were spent doing our chores – scrubbing, polishing, cleaning – interspersed with classes or several circuits of the parade ground. Most afternoons there would be some kind of physical activity, then more classes in the evening until at eight o'clock we were banged up for the night.

I was playing football for my house one day and scored a goal against a house that nobody ever beat. You just didn't. They were the hardest cases of all, mostly cockneys.

In the shower after the match, I was washing off the mud when the curtain was pulled back. 'Awight, ya fackin' cunt,' a voice said through the steam and spray. I could make out three or four lads, but it might have been more. The first kick landed. I was naked and alone. They were wearing boots. Another kick. Then a punch. I swung out into the mist, but failed to connect. 'Ya fackin' wan' it?' one of them shouted and the kicks and punches rained in on me.

I don't know how much later it was stopped. They'd gone when I came to my senses. I was in a right state. I'd cracked my ribs and I looked a mess, but I knew there was one rule when you got beaten up like that. Don't grass.

That evening, one of the screws stopped me in a corridor. 'Who did it?' he said.

'I just fell in the shower,' I replied.

'Nobody falls in the shower,' he said. 'Nobody looks like this . . .' He was right. My face looked as if it had burst open. My mouth was swollen, bruised and bloody, although I'd managed to keep my teeth. I've always been dead jammy with my teeth.

By the time it had all calmed down and I had recovered, I knew exactly who had beaten me up. So I took them out one by one. I spotted the first one – Marriot – in his billet one day. I walked in and shut the door. 'Right,' I said, 'just me and you. Now.'

He went for me, but I was too fast. I didn't half smack him. I hit him about forty times before he hit the floor.

The second one was a mixed-race lad from east London. I was in the kitchen pouring custard on the jam roly-poly when he came along. 'I see you've beat Marriot up,' he sniggered. 'I'm gonna get you for that. You are gonna get so—'

So I whacked him over the head with a ladle. He screamed as burning custard dripped down the side of his face. The screws were on us in the blinking of an eye, sparing no punches as they pinned us down. Kicking wildly and screaming at the top of my lungs, I was hauled out of the dining room with a couple of screws on each limb. Outside the dining room they beat me until I was limp, then dragged me along the corridor and threw me into a cell. Within days I was at Portland, Britain's toughest Borstal, a place reserved for lads considered exceptionally diffi-cult nuts to crack.

Situated next to Verne prison and built on the Isle of Portland, a peninsula off the coast of Dorset that juts about four miles into the English Channel and which is battered by winter storms, Portland Borstal was worlds apart from Shaftesbury. At the time it was a top-security institution. I was now mixing with teenage murderers, rapists and young armed robbers. The lad in the next cell to me had poisoned his grandmother.

The first thing I learned – and I learned it very quickly, else I wouldn't have survived – is that when you enter a place like Portland Borstal you can't just be yourself. It's absolutely impos-sible. You shed your personal identity the moment you walk in through those heavy gates. And in that instant you adopt one of the Borstal archetypes or face the painful consequences. You had to be a poof or a hard case or a gang member or a grass. That was it. You had to fall into one of those personas. So I was in a gang. It meant I had other gang members to look after me and I looked after them. Once in a gang, nobody would come near you.

The other thing you learned double quick was that every day you would see, hear and experience things that you would never mention outside Borstal. Things happened that were kept strictly within the walls of the institution. I'm not proud of what I saw or experienced in Portland, but it all happened. I saw lads in there getting gang-raped. I saw bullies mentally torment or physically abuse their victims until they were fit only for a strait-jacket. There was a gay bloke on our landing who was quite happy to wank off whoever wanted it. I saw him do it to just about every lad on our landing, gay or straight. They were all very happy to be serviced.

Prison and Borstal are always glamorised on television or in films, but it was nowt like *Porridge* or any of those programmes. There were no friendly cell mates who helped each other out. I mixed with a bunch of complete arseholes who would talk about getting out and robbing post offices or killing people. They weren't sorry for what they'd done and Borstal wasn't going to make them change their ways. All it did was delay the time until they committed their next crime.

The Portland regime and routine were much tougher than at Shaftesbury. Our cells were inspected daily. We had to polish our boots, buff the floor and make sure the sheets on our beds were as taut as a painter's canvas. We even scrubbed and dusted the pointing between the bricks in the walls. Everything had to be perfect. If not, you'd be thrown in E Wing, which meant non-stop punishment and running around the assault course with a log on your back at five o'clock in the morning.

The usual routine was rise at six-thirty to slop out, clean, wash and polish. Then we had to stand to attention outside our cells with our uniform pulled tight and our closely shaved hair brushed. A screw would shout 'Right turn!' and we'd all march down for breakfast, which was palatable but paltry. We'd take the meagre breakfast back to our cells and be locked in to eat it and get on with our work. We used to sew mailbags or count seeds into envelopes for gardening companies. Some of us were allowed out of the cells to shovel coal into the boilers or to tend the vegetable gardens. At dinner time we'd put on our shorts and vests, run around the yard for twenty minutes, then walk for the rest of the hour, after which there'd be classes in the afternoon. After school it was back to sewing bags or metalwork until we were locked up in our cells at four o'clock. We'd put on our muck – our overalls – and queue up for our tea, which we ate in our cells or in a mess hall. Usually, we'd be banged up at six o'clock, but occasionally we'd be given an hour's recreation from six until seven o'clock, during which we could watch television, read a book, or play snooker, table tennis, cards or darts. Lights were always out by eight-thirty, when I would just lie in my cell, talking to the blokes I was locked in with or counting the bricks just to keep myself sane. I'd start at one end of one of the walls and keep going until I'd counted every single brick in my cell. It gave me a tiny sense of achievement that wasn't part of the prison regime.

On arriving at Portland, I was assigned to Nelson House and shown to my cell. I'd been in my cell for only a few minutes when a message was passed on to me, the first contact with anyone on my landing. 'Barney Mulraney wants a word,' it said.

As soon as I got a chance I made contact with Barney. 'You from Middlesbrough?' he said. I recognised him from Teesside and nodded. 'Any trouble you come and see me,' he said.

The rule of a Borstal like Portland was simple: kill or be killed. You had to play the part. It meant never letting your guard slip, night or day. Having Barney on my side was more valuable than anything else in that place. Status among the inmates usually depended on the seriousness of the crime that had put you in Borstal. Barney was inside for beating up a rent man and stealing his bag. It wasn't on a par with murder or armed robbery, but Barney was so rough it didn't matter. Everybody was frightened of him and he saved me from all sorts of trouble that I might not have survived without him as my guardian angel. I know he still lives in Middlesbrough because a friend saw him recently. 'Tell Spud he still owes me,' was all Barney said.

But Barney had a rival, a lad called Godson who was just as much a hard case. He was always winding me up, trying to bait me into fighting him. One day we were on parade in the yard and Godson was having a go, pushing and digging me in the back. He bent down to fasten his shoelaces, so I booted him in the mouth. He fell to the ground, clutching at his throat. The screws came running. We all stood to attention while we watched the screws trying to help Godson breathe. My kick had made him swallow his tongue.

'Step forward the lad who kicked him, or punched him,' the Governor said.

Nobody moved. I'd done it so quick that nobody knew it was me. And anyway, you didn't grass in Borstal.

'Well, one of you must have done it,' the Governor said. 'Come on.'

Again, nobody stepped forward. And no one looked around. Every pair of eyes on that exercise ground was pointed forwards. So they took Godson inside. I knew they'd try and get him to tell, but he didn't give in.

Godson never came near me again. The screws made us run around the yard fifty times. And I realised that if I didn't get my temper under control I would soon get myself into serious trouble. Not much later, I did.

Morgan, a screw who ruled my landing in Nelson House, had taken an instant dislike to me. He had a down on me and that was all there was to it. 'You're too big for your boots, Vasey,' he'd say. 'Nobody comes to Borstal and acts the way you do. Who do you think you are?'

Morgan never missed an opportunity to make my life a misery. 'Vasey, get yourself a bucket of cold water now!' he shouted at me one day. 'And bring your toothbrush!' It was coming up to recreation time and I was looking forward to watching television or playing snooker. I'd done nothing to provoke Morgan. He just fancied having a go. I wanted to tell him to get lost, but I did as I was told and turned up in front of him, bucket and toothbrush in hand.

'This landing is a fucking disgrace,' Morgan said. 'Now get down on your hands and knees.' He made me scrub chewing gum, mud and straw out of the cracks in the floor with my toothbrush in my hand. 'Vasey! Change that filthy water,' he shouted every ten yards or so. And I would trot off to the washroom to get a bucket of clean water before continuing my task.

The buzzer went, signalling the beginning of recreation time. I stood up.

'Where are you fucking going?' Morgan growled.

'It's recreation time, Mr Morgan.'

'Not for you it isn't,' he snapped. 'I want you to start again.'

I went to the washroom, cleaned out and refilled the bucket, and walked back to the beginning of the landing. I got down on my knees, dipped my toothbrush in the water and started scrubbing all over again. Morgan came over. Bending down until he was inches above my head, he shouted directly into my ear. 'And this time, I mean *clean*!' he screamed. '*Clean*, boy!'

I continued scrubbing. Just keep your head down, Roy, I told myself. Don't lose it. Don't do anything stupid. Keep your cool.

I'd scrubbed about ten yards of the landing when Morgan approached again. Expecting him to tell me to change the water, I was getting ready to stand up when Morgan kicked the bucket over, spilling water and muck all over the landing I'd just scrubbed clean for the second time. I completely lost it. My temper burst and my Grangetown instincts took over. Screaming at the top of my voice, I picked up the bucket and smacked Morgan over the head with it. There was a small amount of water left in the bucket. I threw it in his face, then flung the bucket with all my might at his open mouth. Morgan fell over, so I kicked him several times as he tried to crawl away from me along the landing. Seeing him reach for his whistle to call for reinforcements, I stopped kicking him in the kidneys and booted him as hard as I could in the face. Eventually more screws arrived and laid into me with their batons. By the time they'd finished with me I was in a straitjacket in solitary confinement.

For days I lay in my cell, trying to come to terms with my life. I'd had enough of fighting almost every day, but I couldn't see an alternative. When I wasn't contemplating the mess I'd created, I would spend hours screaming and shouting at the screws until my lungs ached and my throat was raw. I felt I'd lost everything. This is it, I thought: why don't I just kill myself? I'd always thought I was above suicide. Grangetown had taught me that I could always fight my way out of trouble and that if theft didn't work, violence would get me what I wanted. But now I was beginning to doubt it. And I didn't have an alternative. I simply didn't have the skills or the wisdom to find a different way to lead my life. I was ruled by my quick temper. I could take as much shit as anybody could dish out, but I had a button. And if someone pressed that button at the wrong time, then everything changed. I'd stop saying 'Hey, cut it out' and they'd have to take the consequences. It would be me or them. One of us had to win and one of us had to lose. The time for compromise and conciliation would be over.

Trapped in that cell, on my own for days on end, I realised for the first time that resorting to violence wasn't getting me anywhere. Trouble was, I didn't know what to do instead.

The fights continued after I was released from solitary confinement until the Governor sent for me. 'Vasey, you've been nothing but trouble since you came here,' he said. 'We've got to stop this. I'm going to make you my monitor. Every morning, as soon as you wake, you'll come to this office. The warden will bring you down. You'll eat alone here. Then you'll clean this office. You'll make the tea. You'll polish all the wood and the floor. You'll be working for me all day, every day. At four p.m., you'll go back to your cell and you'll stay there. That's what you'll do every day until you're released from this Borstal. You won't mix with the other boys. I am sick to death of you.'

I couldn't have cared less. I thought if you're going to stick pins in me, then stick pins in me. I'd given up thinking about myself as a person. I felt like a caged animal and I was happy to act like one, all my decisions made for me.

The other lads thought I was a lucky bastard, but they had no idea what it was like to be on my own all the time. My only human contact came from the screws or the letters that my sister had recently started to write to me. She'd moved back to Redcar, discovered I was in Borstal and hunted me down. Mam, her letters told me, had married Norman Trevethick and moved back to Teesside, so I wrote to Mam, asking her to visit me at Portland.

Mam came down to Dorset on the train. 'Can you tell me where Portland Borstal is?' she asked the ticket collector at Weymouth station.

'That's it on the hill,' he said, pointing at the prison and the Borstal. Mam passed out. She couldn't believe that her son was locked up in a building on a remote peninsula lashed by the sea.

'How did you end up in here?' she asked me when we met. It was the first time I'd seen her for more than ten years.

'Well . . .' I said, 'when nobody wants you . . .' I was trying to make Mam feel bad, but it didn't work. A few weeks later the Governor called me in to tell me that I was eligible for early release provided that someone would take responsibility for me during my parole. I wrote to my auld fella and to my mam, asking them to sanction my release and to take me in. Both wrote back to say they didn't want me and that I didn't have a home to go to. The Governor read my father's letter out to me.

'It says here,' he said, 'that your father thinks you're no good and that you're better off inside Portland than back at home. So we're stuck with you for another six months.' I'd never felt so rejected.

At the end of my two-year sentence I was released with about ten other boys. They gave us itchy tweed suits, put us in a van, drove us to Weymouth railway station, and gave each of us a train ticket and three shillings and sixpence. It had been two years since I had last held some money. I'll never forget the feeling of getting on that train, the money clutched in my hand as we made for the buffet car. We bought cups of tea and sat back to savour them in freedom. We'd passed Bournemouth before we spotted him sitting at the other end of the buffet car. It was Bruce Forsyth. 'Ask him for his autograph, go on, ask him for his autograph,' one of the lads said. So I did.

'I'm sorry to bother you, Mr Forsyth,' I said. 'Could I have your autograph, please?'

'Oh yes, of course,' he said, taking a pile of photographs out of his bag. While he signed some pictures of himself, he asked us what we'd been doing. I said we'd just been released from Borstal.

'Ooh,' he said. 'You are naughty boys!' We chatted for a while. He was on his way to the Palladium in London to rehearse for a show.

'Do us a favour, boys,' he said as we drew into Waterloo station in London, 'and behave yourselves in future. *Behave yourselves.*'

CHAPTER SIX

BEAT SURRENDER

TEN DAYS AFTER the cancer diagnosis, I was driving home after seeing Dr Martin for another consultation. Nothing had actually changed, but now that I knew I was ill, I felt as sick as a show-jumper with piles. As usual, Dr Martin was full of encouragement, but I was still convinced I was going to die. Why should I be any different from Roy Castle or Marti Caine, I reasoned. They couldn't beat cancer. So why should I get the break that they didn't? Why should a lad like me, from Grangetown and with a criminal record, deserve to live when other clean-living law-abiding folk hadn't? Surely, by escaping my past and making a name for myself, I'd already had more luck in a lifetime than anyone deserved. It didn't make sense, I thought. I was bound to die.

The car phone rang. 'Hello, is that Chubby?' said a very familiar voice that for a moment I just couldn't place.

'Yes, it's Chubby,' I said. 'Who's speaking?'

'It's Bob Monkhouse.' Fucking hell! I'd admired Bob all my life and now he was on the phone.

'Hello, Bob,' I said, feeling tongue-tied. Well, it's always difficult knowing what to say when you first speak to one of your heroes. 'You don't mind me saying this, but this is not a piss-take, is it? Because I know a few impressionists and you could be one of them.'

'No, it's me, Chubby,' Bob said. 'I'm sat here with Russ Abbott, on my veranda outside my house in Barbados, sipping a glass of wine, and I heard about what's happened to you and I just wondered how you got on today because I know you've been to see the doctor.'

I wasn't really taking in Bob's words. I couldn't. There was no space for them in my head. It was filled with just one thought. That's Bob Monkhouse – Bob fucking Monkhouse – and he's talking to me! I pulled the car into a lay-by. My eyes started to well up with tears. I couldn't believe it. Bob Monkhouse was talking to me from his home in Barbados.

'Bob,' I said. 'I'm sorry I've gone quiet. I am just gobsmacked that you rang me up.'

'And why not?' Bob said. 'We're fellow professionals, aren't we?'

'Well, we are, but I admire you that much, that I never thought . . .'

'Now listen,' Bob said, 'don't try and talk, son. Let me do the talking. I'm used to it.' And Bob went off on a routine, cracking joke after joke. Then he paused. 'You know I've just been through what you're going through,' he said. 'It's never easy, but you hold in there. It will get better. We'll fight this disease together.'

'Yes, I'd heard about you, Bob,' I said. 'I wish you the best of luck.'

'Well, don't worry. And don't believe everything you read in the papers,' Bob said. 'I never admitted on television I had cancer. I never said I was taking shark food to get rid of it. It's all baloney and I'm all right. Don't worry about me – I'm very well, sipping a lovely glass of wine, and the weather's gorgeous.'

'Well, it's blowing a gale here. It's awful,' I said. 'Rain's coming down in sheets.'

We chatted a bit longer and I thanked Bob for calling out of the blue. 'Well, all the best to you,' he said. 'Let me know how you get on and I'll write to you.'

I arrived home and Johnny Hammond, a Middlesbrough comedian, came over. Johnny's a great mate. 'You'll never guess who rang me,' I said. 'Bob Monkhouse.'

'Oh,' said Johnny, 'I've had quite a few calls asking for your number. Norman Wisdom was asking.'

'Oh, Johnny, fuck off!' I said. 'Pull the other one. You know it's got bells . . .' The phone rang. I got up and answered it. 'Hello . . . Hello?'

'It's Norman here.' I turned around to where Johnny was sitting on my sofa, a grin the width of a fat lass's knickers cracking his face.

'I know . . .' Johnny mouthed. 'He's ringing from the Isle of Man.'

We talked for about ten minutes. 'Norman . . .' I said, 'I'll never forget this phone call. Thank you.'

'Oh, right,' Norman said. 'Yes.' Norman hung up abruptly and I put the phone down. Twenty minutes later it rang again.

'Hello, is that Chubby?'

'Yes?'

'It's Norman here, Norman Wisdom.'

'You rang me a short while ago, Norman.'

'Oh, what a berk!' Norman said. And he put the phone down, leaving me shaking my head in disbelief. Bob Monkhouse and Norman Wisdom in one day.

●

I was soon back on Teesside, back with my mates and back in the King's Head, a claggy mat on a particularly run-down council estate. There was always fighting in the King's Head. Every night. It was that rough the Alsatian had sandals on and all the barmaid's tattoos were spelt wrong.

'Hey, I saw Sandra today,' Robbie shouted over the noise of the bar one night. I hadn't seen her for two and a half years.

'Did ya?' I said.

'Oh yeah, she looked gorgeous. She was with a blond-haired lad.'

'Oh, right. What's she doing here?'

'She's at her mother's,' Robbie said. 'Y'know, 17 Ann's Street.'

'Is that where she is?' Bolstered by seven pints of beer, I went up to Ann's Street. Approaching number 17, I noticed a van parked outside Sandra's mum's house. Inside the van, a bloke with blond hair was kissing a woman. Bloody hell, I thought. That's Sandra.

Buoyed by Dutch courage, I walked up to the van and banged on the window. Sandra jumped, turned around and stared at me. Her face went white when she realised exactly who was standing in the darkness. 'Go away!' she screamed. 'Go *away!*'

'I just want to talk to you,' I yelled.

'I don't want to talk to you. Go *away.*'

So I shook the van, rolling it back and forth, trying to turn it over. Sandra screamed and the man with her yelled at me. He was frightened, but he managed to start the engine. As the van lurched forward, I grabbed the side and jumped up onto it. With a crashing of gears, the van moved off, and accelerated. I fell off it. Sandra's mother was standing in the door to her house as the bluebottles turned up and I was dragged off to the police station. Sandra had moved out of my life again.

I spent a few months doing odd jobs in and around Middlesbrough until someone suggested there were better jobs to be had in Blackpool. With fond memories of the town from the summer that my father had taken me there for a holiday, I needed little encouragement to get out of Middlesbrough.

Walking along the seafront the day I arrived in Blackpool, I noticed some workmen loitering in a big blue shed and got talking to them. It turned out they were red-leading Blackpool tower. Fifteen minutes later, I had a job. Dressed in overalls, I got into a lift to the fourth floor, where we climbed onto some scaffolding. Three hundred feet above the Golden Mile wasn't a place for someone frightened of heights. 'You didn't last long,' the foreman said.

'I'll go on the pancrack,' I told the foreman, but when I got to the dole office they told me I wouldn't need to sign on. The Queen's Hotel needed a porter.

Every morning I would line up with the rest of the Queen's Hotel staff and hold my hands out so that the manager could inspect my nails. I had to wear a full uniform with a bow tie even though I was only carrying bags up to rooms. This wasn't for me, so I found work handing out mats for the slides at the Funhouse on the Pleasure Beach, the next in a succession of dead-end jobs, few of which lasted longer than a couple of weeks. I painted the Big Dipper; I worked for the council letting out deckchairs on the seafront; I grafted in chippies and hotels.

None of the jobs paid much, so most of the time I slept rough. In Queen's Square, opposite the North Pier, where I'd later play summer-theatre seasons, there was a gents' toilet with a green railing around it. I'd go down there when the pubs chucked me out, climb over the rail and break in. It was warmer than outside and I could sleep sitting on the loo. When the weather turned colder, I found rooms in run-down boarding houses or the YMCA.

One evening I met a fair-haired Scottish lad and an English lad, both drifters like me. 'Where are you stopping tonight?' the Scottish lad said.

'I'm thinking of the youth hostel near the bowling alley by the North Pier,' I said. It was two and six a night and they had hot water.

'If you fancy a change, do what we do,' he said.

'What's that?'

'Past the Savoy there's a big roundabout and on the other side is Pontins. Round the back, near the airport, there's a hole in the fence. You can get in there. Some of the chalets aren't taken. Look through the window and if there's no bags in it, you know nobody's staying there. Give the door a good push and it'll come away from the latch.'

'Eh, great,' I said.

It was worth the effort just to save two and six. The scam ran so well that we got to know some of the holidaymakers and would go back to their chalets for a party. Then I got caught by security. I told them I'd come about a job. They put me in charge of teaching kids to swim. But teaching swimming also involved tearing arse – a load of tiresome tasks such as sweeping up at the end of the day, collecting sunbeds and stacking towels. I'd had enough and was looking for a way out when the Scottish lad made a suggestion.

'Let's hot-wire a car,' he said.

We broke into an old Austin and set off, taking turns to drive along country roads with no particular destination in mind. We thought of ourselves as fugitives from society, but really we were just a trio of shitheads. Ending up near Oxford, penniless, tired and filthy after sleeping in the car for two nights, we came upon an old house in a country lane. We knocked at the door. There was no answer. We looked in the garage. No car there. So we smashed a back window and climbed into the kitchen, where an army uniform was hanging behind the door. Finding some food in the fridge, we cooked ourselves bacon and eggs, then ransacked the house looking for money. We found nothing of any value, but I loved every minute of it. I thought I was one of the Kray Twins, a proper gangster, when all we were attempting was petty burglary.

We left the house, needing to refuel the car. As we approached Oxford I noticed a middle-aged woman standing at a bus stop. 'Slow down and I'll open the window,' I said to the blond Scot, who was driving. 'I'll grab her handbag.' It worked a treat. We found a couple of pounds in the bottom of the bag, dumped the evidence, filled up the car with petrol and drove home.

Back in Blackpool, we spent what remained of our booty on three beds in a boarding house in Grassmere Road. The next morning, we drove the car to a nearby café for breakfast. After all our escapades, we were starving and the breakfast tasted great. We'd been in the café for about twenty minutes and I was just finishing a cup of tea when a copper walked in. 'Whose is that red car outside parked on the yellow line?' he said.

And like an idiot I opened my mouth without thinking. 'Oh, it's mine, mate,' I said.

'You better move it if you don't want a ticket,' the copper said, so I ambled outside.

A squad of bluebottles was waiting and the cuffs were on me straight away. The gang of three was soon in a police van bound for Oxford. After two days in the police-station cells we were in court. The woman we'd robbed had the make of the car, its licence-plate number and a full description of the three of us, down to the colour of our eyes and our hair. Served us right for robbing a local magistrate. We were sentenced to six months' imprisonment and I was sent to Bristol jail.

I'd left Borstal less than three months ago. Now I was in prison, but for some reason it didn't seem a big deal to me. I wasn't frightened. I wasn't even particularly bothered. Thinking that my most likely future was a life of crime, my reaction was simple and unsentimental. This will do for me, I thought. I'm going to be like this. I'll be an arsehole all my life.

Bristol nick was a comparatively cushy number. There was none of the football, cricket, swimming and rehabilitation of Borstal – prison is just about being locked away and left to rot – but I'd been in Wormwood Scrubs, Leicester and Armley jails. They were shithouses compared with Bristol. Full of lags who'd been there for twenty years or more, Bristol jail was like an old people's home.

My cell was painted green and white with two black heating pipes running along one wall. If I stood on them I could see out of the window. In the distance I could see the gate of a match-box factory. Beside it was a park with trees and people taking their dogs for walks. I used to watch them for hours, but I never wanted to join them. I had nothing on the outside, whereas my little cell felt like a safe haven from a world where nobody cared about me. And because nobody wanted me, it was very easy to be an arsehole. It was up to me to snap out of my destructive behaviour, but there was little chance of that if it made no difference to anyone else.

After three months with good behaviour I was released. I returned to Redcar where I rented a room in Westbourne Grove, a few doors along from the home for wayward kids. There were few jobs for someone with no qualifications and even fewer for someone with a Borstal and prison record. So I fell back on the occupation of hundreds of former convicts: a nightclub bouncer. Working the door at the Red Lion was an easy number. There was a disco at the back and a bar at the front. Most of the time it was quiet, but when the Redcar races were on a fight was a dead cert. Busloads of Geordies and Mackems would converge on Redcar from Newcastle, Gateshead and Sunderland, and they all hated each other.

One particular night after the races, I'd ejected some Geordies who had been throwing glasses and fighting with some Mackems in the disco. The Geordies stood outside waiting for the Mackems. 'Come out, come out . . .' they chanted to the Sunderland lads. 'We'll fuckin' have you . . .'

Inside the club, the rest of the bouncers and I decided we'd had enough. It was time to get the Geordies to move on. We steamed outside to find that the Mackems had followed behind us. Stuck between the two gangs, there was nothing to do but fight our way out. Six bouncers against thirty or forty pissed-up lads. It might not sound like a fair fight, but a couple of the bouncers were karate experts and weren't frightened of anyone. The rest of us knew how to take care of ourselves.

It was like a fight in a cowboy movie. Everyone piled in. Then the coppers turned up with dogs. I was swinging punches and dodging blows when a young copper came wading in and punched me.

'What the fucking hell are you doing?' I shouted at him.

He hit me again, so I loafed him, the worst thing I could have done. I was handcuffed and dragged to the police station two hundred yards down the street, where I was lined up in front of the duty sergeant. I could hear the drunken Geordies locked in the cells downstairs, screaming and shouting revenge on us. Upstairs, us doormen were waiting at the desk in the front office while the coppers tried to sort out what had happened. The copper who I'd head-butted was standing to one side, a big bruise on his brow. He came over to where I was standing with my hands behind my back.

'You!' he shouted inches from my face. 'You think you're fucking hard, don't you?'

'No, sir,' I said.

'Yes, you do. You stuck the head on me,' he said. 'I'll show you what head's all about.' The copper went to head-butt me, so I ducked. His forehead collided with the crown of my head. I heard a crack as he broke his nose, but hardly felt a thing myself. 'I'm gonna fuckin . . .' the young bluebottle shouted, blood pouring down his face as the sergeant stepped over.

'Whoa, whoa, whoa, cut it out before you lose it,' the sergeant said. Instead of getting a beating, I was charged with assaulting a police officer and sent down for three months to Durham jail.

Durham was as rough as prisons come. It was where they sent you when they thought you were scum. From the moment I stepped inside its walls, I was terrified. With a bunch of other new arrivals, I filed into a reception area. 'Left turn,' barked one of the screws. 'Stop! Now strip off. *Everything.*'

We put all our clothes and belongings in a cardboard box and stood naked in a windowed room like a conservatory but with a counter running down the middle. A screw wrote my name on my box of belongings and put it on a shelf. 'Right, through that door,' he bellowed.

'Name . . . address . . . distinguishing marks . . . tattoos . . . height . . .' one of the screws shouted. Then, hair clipped and dressed in prison uniforms, we were led to our cells. Like most of the prisoners at Durham, I was on my own.

I immediately realised that the only way to survive was not to cause any trouble. Durham prison was not a pretty place and the rules were simple: keep your nose clean; do as you're told; don't look at anybody; keep your eyes on the ground. All the inmates wore overalls, but some had big red and green patches sewn onto them. It meant that they were escapees or that they were inside for murder, violent conduct or killing children. Most of the time, these high-security prisoners were cordoned off from the rest of us and we'd see them only through the nettings. But every now and then, one of them would mix with the rest of us and send a shiver down my spine. They looked the part, just evil, to me. I didn't need to ask questions about why they were inside. I'd glance at them, then I'd look away in case they clocked me and decided to do something about it.

I spent only twelve weeks in Durham prison, but it was long enough for me to see sense. I realised there was nothing I could do about having a temper. No one plans to have a short fuse. There's no such thing as a premeditated loss of cool. Everyone's got a limit and if things aren't going right, you'll reach it at some point. It was just that the distance between me saying 'This is wrong' and me saying 'Fuck the consequences, I can't take this any more' was less than for other people. What got through to me in Durham prison was the realisation that there had to be a better life than bouncing in and out of jail. I felt I needed to do something, to create something with my life, and that if I didn't sort it out very soon, I'd miss the chance. As soon as I got home from Durham prison, I went to see my auld fella. 'Dad,' I said. 'I've had enough of being an arsehole.' And I promised him faithfully that I would never get in trouble again.

Determined to avoid employment that would land me in trouble when I got back to Redcar – such as working as a door-man – I took a job at the Dorman, Long steel yard. The social security provided a small flat above a hairdressing salon at 54 Coatham Road, a few hundred yards from the home for way-ward boys at Westbourne Grove. With my bait (as we called a packed lunch) in a box beside me, I'd take the bus to work every morning and do my hours. For the first time in a long while it felt like I could have a normal, stable, honest life. My fellow sandscratchers had always regarded me as a hooligan and never taken much of an interest in my welfare. But now they encouraged me to keep my nose clean. 'You know, Roy, there's more to life than what you've been through,' they'd say.

Around this time my sister Barbara moved back from Pontefract to Dormanstown, where she was living with her boyfriend. I bumped into her one day in the street in Redcar.

'Our mam's back in the area,' Barbara said. 'She's living at 48 Wilton Road.'

'Oh right,' I said. It meant nothing to me. I would have been more interested if Barbara had told me chips were half price that day.

'She wants to see you,' Barbara said.

'Hmm . . . maybe . . .' I conceded.

A few days later, I knocked on the door to the house where Mam was living with Norman Trevethick. Maybe I was expecting Mam to put her arms around me, but she didn't. Instead we sat down quite far apart on separate chairs on opposite sides of her front room.

'Hello,' I said.

'Hello,' said Mam. 'How are you?'

I told her a bit about what I was up to, but she felt like a stranger, a feeling I never really shook off for the rest of my life.

I think Mam wanted to wipe out the memory of all the things she'd done, but she'd deserted me so long ago and I'd heard too many relatives and friends badmouth her, saying things like 'your mother can't have loved you; anyone who walks out on a family must be hard as nails', to be able to forgive and forget. It was only when I was much older that I came to understand why a mother or father might walk away from their children if they were trapped in a violent marriage.

I didn't see much of my mother after that, but a few months later, I knocked on her door. 'Mam, I've been told to get out of my flat,' I said. 'I haven't got any money, but I'm starting a new job at ICI soon.'

'I'll ask Norman if you can live in the back bedroom,' she said.

A few days later I moved in with Mam and Norman, who, in an attempt to befriend me, gave me a motorbike.

Every Thursday I'd pay Mam some rent, but after a couple of months, I returned home on a Thursday with empty pockets.

'You all right?' Mam said, as I sat down to a plate of sausage, eggs and chips she'd just cooked. 'What was it like getting your second month's wages?'

'I haven't got any,' I said.

'What?' Mam snapped. She still had a terrible temper. 'Where's your money?'

'I went to the bookies and put it on a horse.'

'You haven't got a penny?'

'No.'

'You wasteful little shit!' Mam shouted. She picked up my dinner and threw it at me. I ducked. The plate hit the wall.

As Norman walked in from work, the sausage, egg and chips were running down the back kitchen wall. Thinking it was my fault, he yelled at me. 'Out! Get out! We don't want you here. You're no good. Get out!'

That was the last occasion I spent more than a couple of hours with my mam for at least another decade. I'd drop by her house once in a while, but a year could pass quite easily without us seeing each other and I never received the love and affection from her that other people take for granted from their mothers.

I moved into a bedsit and continued to do my job at ICI, where I spent most of each working day supplying a gang of welders with materials. Whenever we stopped for a chat or a cup of tea I would tap out a beat on the welding rods. I'd always had a good sense of rhythm and would tap my knees or the table or anything else within suitable range. 'Are you a drummer?' one of the welders said one day.

'No.'

'Well, you've got it,' he said. 'You ought to think about drumming.'

I didn't think any more of it until a few weeks later when, in the works canteen, I was tapping the table with my cutlery. 'What is it with you?' one of the lads said. 'You're always tapping.'

'Dunno . . . I just like it,' I said.

'Have you ever tried drumming?'

'Only when I was school. I played in Thornaby boys' band for a while.'

'What happened there, then?'

'It didn't last.' I shrugged. 'I was only in it for a while. They shut down the band.'

'You're a good drummer, you should take it up,' the lad said.

The welder and the lad were right. I really did enjoy tapping out beats. Maybe I should give drumming a go, I thought. So I visited my auld fella. His first reaction was that drums cost a lot of money, but he dug out the *Evening Gazette*, spotted an advertisement for a drum kit and took me round to a cottage near the seafront. An old bloke let us in and pointed at a kit in the corner of a back room. The bass drum had a rope around it and a picture of Jesus on the front.

'Dad, it's Salvation Army . . . ' I said. The auld fella just raised his eyebrows.

There was also a snare drum and a foot pedal with a big wooden hammer. It was a bit makeshift, but it would do. I lugged it back to my flat and began to practise.

Just along from the flat was a pub called the Station Hotel where a woman played standards on the piano in the lounge most evenings. Nancy Pinky was from Slaggy Island and she was the ugliest woman I'd ever seen. We used to say she had Wednesday eyes because they looked both ways to the weekend, but her worst problem was that she had terrible wind. Nancy would sit in the lounge, drinking pints of Guinness (which surely didn't help), and lifting her backside off the stool as she played the piano, farting all the while.

'*When you're smiling . . .*' she'd sing. Fart. '*When you're smiling . . .*' Pump. '*The whole world smiles with you.*' Fart.

The lounge was always packed, everyone laughing at Nancy while I would tap the beat on the bar. Some nights, an auld fella on the drums would accompany Nancy, but quite often he didn't turn up. At the end of one night I went up to Nancy.

'Where's the drummer?' I said.

'Oh, he can only make it now and again,' Nancy said. 'He's got a couple of other jobs.'

'I've got a set of drums,' I said. 'Can I play along with you?'

'There's no money in it,' she said, 'but I'll get you a pint.'

'That's all right.'

The next evening I set up my drums. The first song was a disaster. I was far too loud, the boom of my Salvation Army bass drum drowning out Nancy and the piano, but I soon got the hang of it and from then on I'd race home after work to be ready to join Nancy in the Station Hotel at seven o'clock. After a while, I'd saved enough money to trade in the Salvation Army kit for an old second-hand Rogers kit. It was falling to bits, but it was a proper kit with tom-toms and cymbals and it was good enough for me to accompany Nancy singing and farting at the piano. Playing at the Station Hotel several nights a week, I got friendly with some local sandscratchers. Barry Gardener, Billy Blackburn, Lol Gibbon and Marty Miller, whose family ran market stalls, were all good Redcar lads. 'Why don't you come on the market?' Marty said one day. 'You'll make more money than you do at the works.' Although I didn't have a licence, I was driving an old van with L-plates around Redcar. Marty assumed it meant I could drive his four-ton truck. 'Do you want to pick us up in the morning?' he said.

From then on I'd pull up outside Marty's house at half past five and knock on the door. Marty was a nightmare to get out of bed. I'd shout through the letter box, thump the door and bang on the windows. 'Marty! It's Roy! Get up!'

And from where Marty was slumbering with his girlfriend, I'd hear: 'I'll be with ya in a minute.' I'd sit on the doorstep, reading the paper and drinking tea from my flask, sometimes for half an hour. 'I don't know how you can be so fucking bright and cheerful this time of the morning,' Marty would say when he eventually emerged. 'I'll never get used to getting up this early.'

We'd drive to the wholesale market in Middlesbrough, stock up, head back to Redcar and arrange the fruit and veg on the stall. I'd polish the apples while Marty would go off to the pie shop and buy us all a saveloy sandwich, a thing of beauty of which I'd have two for breakfast with a bottle of cold milk.

I loved being a barrow boy. It wasn't so much about selling vegetables as the crack that could be had in the process. It would be so cold some mornings that I'd not be able to feel my toes, but that didn't matter because I'd made a discovery that would change my life. I'd always been the class clown, but the market was where I first realised that I really had the gift of the gab and that I could use it to make people laugh.

I would make up little poems up about the fruit that went down a treat with the women. 'It's a wonderful thing, is a strawberry,' I'd shout as a pretty woman walked past.

'It's so round and so red and so thick. If you're out for a lark and you're stood in the dark you can hold one and think it's a . . . *five pence a pound*! Five pence a pound!'

When apples were in season, I'd bellow: 'An apple a day keeps the doctor away, that's an old wives' tale which is true.

Eating two at a time, being a pig's not a crime, but you'll suffer when you're on the loo!'

But my favourite ploy was to see how rude I could be and still get away with it. I'd hold up a cucumber and, in a typical barrow boy's inaudible chant, shout out: 'Fanny crackers! Fanny crackers! Two for a shilling! Fanny crackers!' Women would come up to the stall and ask what I'd just said. 'Cucumbers,' I'd answer.

'No, you said something else,' they'd say.

'Oh, I said Christmas crackers.'

'Right, I see . . .' And having made them stop, I'd usually get them to buy some vegetables.

The tricks of a barrow boy's trade were never-ending. At Christmas, the profit was unbelievable. We would buy fifty sheets of wrapping paper for two shillings, then roll up ten sheets, put an elastic band around them and sell them as twelve for a shilling. We knew that no one would count them until they got home, by which time they would have forgotten whether they bought ten or twelve sheets and Marty's big leather bag would be stuffed with our takings.

Marty paid me well. I was on around fifty pounds a week and then I'd work on the door of a pub a couple of evenings a week, earning two pounds an hour. Drumming didn't earn me anything, but I was convinced that would come later and at last there was some stability in my life. It wasn't entirely without incident – I ended up in hospital after coming off the motorbike given to me by Norman Trevethick – but on the whole I was managing to stick to the straight and narrow, a massive change for me. The biggest turning point, however, came when there was a knock on the door of my flat one evening. I opened the door to find my cousin Derek Vasey standing there.

'Hiya, Roy,' he said. 'Can I come in?' Derek entered my little bedsit. 'Erm . . . somebody saw you playing the . . . erm . . . drums the other night in the . . . er . . . Station Hotel.'

'That's right, yeah,' I said.

Derek was very awkward. We'd not spoken for ages and I'd hardly recognised him. He was acting like he had come to collect a debt. 'Erm . . . our drummer . . . I've got a pop group . . .'

'Oh, have ya?'

'Yeah,' Derek said, 'we're . . . er . . . called The Pipeline and our drummer, Geoff Briggs, is going on holiday for a week. Will you stand in?'

I immediately agreed. I didn't know anything about Derek's group and I didn't know how to play drums beyond just accompanying a pianist, but this was too good a chance to turn down.

'We're at the Magnet Hotel at Grangetown. We play there every Saturday night,' Derek said.

'How am I going to get my kit there?'

'Maybe come on the bus?' Derek suggested. It wasn't very rock 'n' roll but it was a start. That Saturday I lined up with my drum kit beside all the shoppers at the bus stop, slipped my bass drum under the stairs when the double-decker arrived and sat with my tom-tom and my snare drum on my knee. I had no boxes for them or polythene bags to cover them. Just me and my drums on the way to a proper gig. I was thrilled.

There was no need for rehearsal before the gig. Every song was in a four-four beat. 'Johnny B. Goode', 'Let's Work Together' – everything was tap, tap, tap, tap. In that week, I played four gigs with The Pipeline, the last one at the British Legion across the border in Middlesbrough. As soon as Geoff arrived back from holiday, Derek fired him. 'We're going to take our Roy on,' he said.

'No, you're fucking not,' Geoff said. 'That's my job.'

'Yes, we fucking are. He's a much better drummer than you.'

I'd never had a drum lesson in my life, now I'd landed myself a job in a rock-and-roll act. Already, prison and Borstal seemed a very long way away.

After Geoff was fired, we immediately changed our name to Four Man Band. Derek and his brother Lee, who was only sixteen years old, were the heart and soul of the group. Our Dec was a really great bass player and Lee was just as accomplished on the guitar. They were fanatical, listening to music all the time and watching music programmes on television. Living in the same house, they could bounce ideas off each other and work on the music night and day. Funky jazz was their passion. Then there was Tony Morris, a classy singer who was just as good at belting out rock 'n' roll as barber-shop harmonies.

With Dec and Lee's ambitions, and Tony's talent, the Four Man Band was never going to be a comedy band, that was evident. They were serious musos and they saw the band as a stepping stone to greater things, but I was determined to exert my influence.

Within a few months, I'd bedded myself right into the band. It was the early 70s and we'd play all the songs we'd heard on the radio. The Beatles and the Rolling Stones, mainly. Tony Christie was building up quite a following, so I suggested to the band that we have a go at some of his tunes. I looked nowt like him and our Tony sounded nowt like him, but I thought we could win over the audience by changing around some of the words to his songs. Because I'd written them, I used to sing them.

'I Did What I Did For Maria', Christie's biggest hit at that time, I changed to: '*Sunrise, this is the last day that I'll ever see, Out in the yard her mother's waiting for me, Hey I did what I did full of beer, That's why I did what I did to Maria.*'

When I heard the audience laugh at my lyrics, I got an even bigger thrill than when they applauded my drumming. From the first evening that I came off the drums, stood at the microphone and made people laugh, I wanted more. There was no feeling like it. I was hooked.

On a good night, we'd earn about twenty pounds for two sets. After we'd hired the van, bought a bottle of lemonade, some fags and fish and chips on the way home, it left about two quid each for a night's work. Not a bad wage, but less than I could earn for a day on the market stall with Marty. Problem was, if I played all night I was too tired to work on the market all day. And if I worked for Marty all day, I was often too tired to play that evening. Something had to give, particularly as the debt collector was never far from my door.

We were playing the Magnet Hotel in Grangetown, a pub I'd watched being built while sitting outside the chip shop as a kid. As usual, we'd opened with 'Let's Work Together' by Canned Heat, 'Please Please Me' and another Beatles number. Then we sneaked in a couple of less familiar songs before moving onto the comedy songs. I was tapping away on the drums when Lee came over. 'Bloke on the door wants to speak to you,' he said.

I looked over towards the entrance. A man standing there looked familiar, but I couldn't place him. After we'd finished the first set, I went over.

'Mr Vasey?' he said.

'Yeah?'

'Roy, is it?'

'That's me.'

'I'm from Hamilton's Music Store in Middlesbrough,' he said.

'Oh yeah?'

'I've come for the drums.'

'They're my drums,' I said.

'Not any more they aren't. You haven't paid for your drums for six months. I've come to repossess them.'

It was the last thing I had expected. My dad was supposed to be paying the instalments on my kit, but the bastard hadn't kept

up to date. 'Could you not wait until we finish this second spot?'
I said.

' 'Fraid not,' the bailiff said. 'I can't wait.'

'I'll give you a tenner,' I said. I didn't have ten quid, neither
did the band, but I needed to buy time. The bailiff agreed.

'You're quite good, aren't you, you and the lads,' the bailiff
said as we went on for our second set. I smiled weakly. Then, as
soon as we finished our spot, I made a run for it, sneaking out
the back door without giving the bailiff his ten pounds and
waving the kit goodbye.

The loss of my drum kit made it obvious that we needed to
find a way to earn more money. And, in the short term, I
needed a new kit fast. Other drummers would lend me parts. I'd
have one person's bass drum, somebody's else's snare drum and
another drummer's tom-tom and cymbals.

We decided to play more evenings each week, but that made
it even more difficult to keep up my job on the market stall. In
desperation, I went to Marty and called it a day. Marty was
upset, but he took it well. 'Anyway,' he said, 'how're you getting
on?'

'The band's doing really well,' I said, 'although I could do
with a better kit of drums. In fact, I've not got any drums at all.
The ones I had before . . .' And I told Marty the story about the
bailiff from Hamilton's Music Shop.

Marty listened. Then – and I'll never forget this – he gave me
more than two hundred pounds to buy a new set. I didn't know
what to say. It was incredibly generous, but more than that,
since the day my mam left home, I'd not known anybody to put
themselves out for me like that.

I bought a lovely set of second-hand silver-and-pearl Premier
drums. It was a beautiful kit and I'll always be deeply indebted
to Marty for it. It took me years to pay the money back, but
really I still owe him to this day for his wonderful generosity.

On my prompting, the Four Man Band gradually incorpo-
rated more comedy, soon discovering that it was a sure way to
earn more money. We would walk on stage with a prop and
crack a joke. Our first attempts were amateurish – and muggins
on the kit was the daft-arse who had to try to get away with it –
but in time we improved and the comedy started to take over
from the music.

The more I moved to the front of the band, the more I was
gripped by stage fright. Some performers need a drink to go on
stage. Others throw up in the dressing-room sink. I always
needed a good dump. I tried all sorts of things to get around it,
but nothing worked. My bowels always had the last word.

I'd always take my shoes off to play the drums because I had
more control of the pedals in my socks. One night, we were
approaching the end of our set when our Dec looked down at
my feet. 'Where's your sock?' he said. One of them was missing.

I shrugged. 'There was no toilet paper.'

Dec, who knew my stage-fright symptoms, started laughing.
That set me off and the more we looked at each other, the
more we laughed. We were in fits of laughter, the tears rolling
down our cheeks as we tried to suppress our giggling in front of
the audience. In the end, we had to come off. We couldn't play
any longer, we were laughing so much.

Derek, Lee, Tony and I had been playing together for nearly
two years. We'd built up a good reputation and we were getting
decent work. We'd backed local stars, but Dec and Lee were
impatient. They wanted to play jazz. Their musical skills had
outrun the band and they wanted us to change direction. 'I'd
love to play jazz,' I said, 'but there's no money in it and we have
to earn a living.'

But Dec and Lee were adamant. It was jazz or nothing for
them. So the band split and we went our separate ways. I was
disappointed but thought it might be for the best. After all, a lot

had changed in the time I'd been playing with the Four Man Band. I'd started to settle down and, by my standards, I'd become respectable. I was a married man now. And I'd just started a family.

Isn't my sister beautiful?

Me filling my nappy –
my mam doesn't know . . . sssh

Daddy, who's nicked your hair? Hitler?

My dad. We buried him with a pint in his hand,
but we all loved him

Whitworth Road, Grangetown.

The good old days (my arse!)

My angelic face – what an actor

Dad and me at Blackpool. It cost two shillings to sit on a scooter and have your photo taken – then we pinched it . . .

I joined the navy so the world could see me

The Pipeline, Redcar, 1970:
George, Lee, me and Dec,
frightening the fish

The very first Alcock and
Brown: Mr Hall, Mr Cock
and Mr Brown. Sorry girls,
I was Mr Brown

ROY (Chubby) BROWN
P.T.O. →

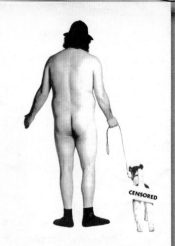

CENSORED

Early publicity
– arse about face
(John Herring)

FIRST BOOKING AS NUTS WAS AT DUMFRIES
LABOUR CLUB ON APRIL 30th 72
GREAT NIGHT.

ORIGANAL NUTS.

BEACON SOCIAL CLUB
Cabaret
Admission 10p

B2

B3

The Nut's

Lee Vasey, me and Dave Richards. The other two still dress like that!

I was so chuffed to be on at our local pubs, I kept a scrapbook

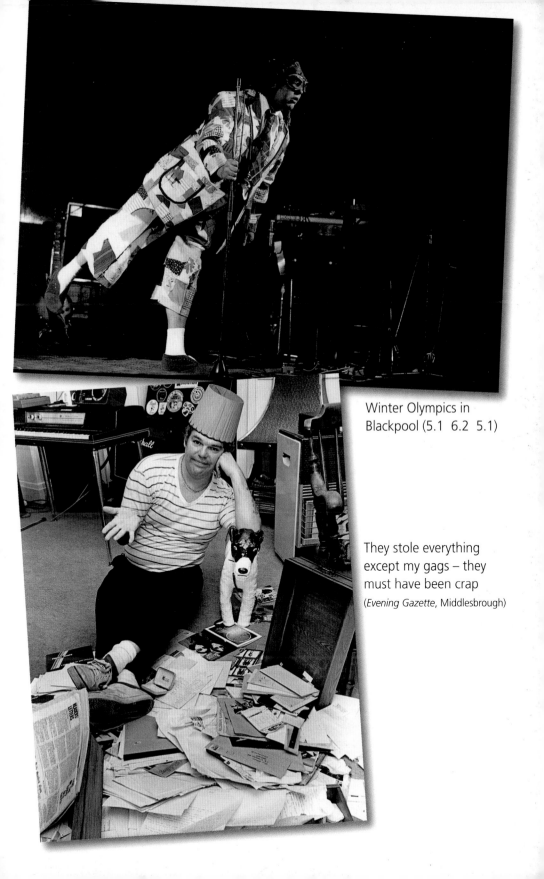

Winter Olympics in
Blackpool (5.1 6.2 5.1)

They stole everything
except my gags – they
must have been crap
(*Evening Gazette*, Middlesbrough)

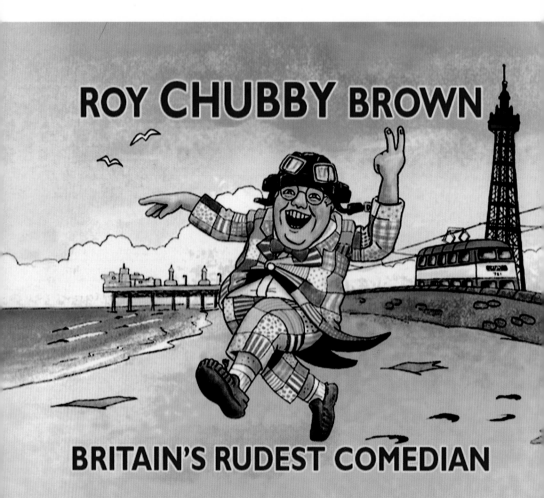

Notice I'm the only fucker on the beach

CHAPTER SEVEN

TROUBLE AND STRIFE

'YOU'LL BE ALL RIGHT, pet,' Helen said. 'Don't worry, you'll be fine. I've got faith in these people. You'll be great.' Sitting on our sofa at home, the night before my first cancer operation, I listened to Helen's reassuring words, looked at her in that strange way you do when you don't know if you're going to see someone you love again, and thought: I hope you're right. I *really* hope you're right.

I've always believed the world is full of lucky people and unlucky sods. There's little you can do about it. Some people attract bad fortune like flies to shit. I have friends who, try as they might, are just not lucky. Keith, my driver, is one. If he backs a horse, it always comes in second. If he buys a car, there's always something wrong with it. If he gets a new television, the aerial will snap off his roof. Every time I ask Keith to put my lottery ticket in, I never get a single number right. If I do it myself, I'll often get a tenner back, but never when Keith does it for me. *Never.*

Of course, we'd be lost without the unlucky sods. They make

me laugh and without them, us lucky ones would never realise how good we've got it.

Now Helen's always been lucky. When she says owt to me, I take it in. I pay attention and I believe it's going to come true. And Helen kept saying I'd survive. 'Don't worry,' she'd say. 'I feel lucky for you. You're going to be all right. They're not going to get rid of you.'

And I just said: 'I hope you're right.'

Mr White told me very little before the operation. While I sat in his office, cursing my sweaty palms and churning stomach, he calmly explained what he was going to do. There was something in his ordinariness – a little man with spectacles and dark hair parted to one side – that was very reassuring. He held up an X-ray image and, pointing at a dark area of my throat, described the procedure. That was enough detail for me. I'm squeamish at the best of times – I once punched a bloke on the nose and when he started bleeding, I passed out – and I took in very little of what Mr White told me.

But as Mr White went on, I realised he was making the operation sound like an everyday thing, like he was talking me through a holiday brochure or the plans for some building work on my house. And then I realised that's *exactly* what it was to him. Booking a holiday or having an extension built or having a cancer operation can all seem complicated, momentous things. But for the people who do it every day – travel agents or builders or surgeons – it's just another day at the office. And when I realised that, I felt strangely calm and the nervousness seeped away.

'When you came to see me about your throat,' Mr White said, 'what were you about to do?'

'I was going to Australia for a six-week tour,' I said.

'If you'd done that, we might have been talking about a completely different operation. You came to me at just the right time. Any later and it would have been a lot more difficult.'

'Right . . .' I could see what Mr White was getting at. I just hoped it didn't mean I'd used up all my luck.

'Now you've already had two investigatory operations,' Mr White said, 'and we're going to have to stop putting you to sleep for routine investigations because if we continue to do it, it will affect your brain.'

That put the shits right up me. Would it mean I wouldn't be able to remember my own name when I woke up?

'It means we'll have to try something else the next time we put a camera down your throat,' Mr White said. 'And it might be a bit uncomfortable.'

I got used to investigations without sedatives, but when it came to the operation to remove the cancer I was allowed a general anaesthetic. The nurses in the hospital were like angels. While I lay on my bed on the morning of the operation, my mind wandering all over the place, they gave me hope. Their actions and comforting words made me feel a million dollars. The problem was that I'd walked around the hospital and seen what could happen to me. There were cancer patients in the Royal Infirmary who'd had their throats removed. With big blue steam boxes beside their beds and tubes leading to their mouths, they were fighting to keep the germs at bay. I could see the fear in their eyes. They knew they'd have to learn to speak all over again. And I knew they were wondering if they could do it.

●

Judith Ann Armstrong first caught my eye in – where else? – a Redcar pub. It was shortly after I started drumming with the Four Man Band and I'd gone into the Clarendon. As was so often the case, a gang of lasses was sat near the jukebox. I recognised a couple of them – one was called Diana – but my attention was totally focused on Judith. Wearing a miniskirt and with short boyish hair, Judith looked a bit like Lulu. I heard her dirty laugh, saw the cheeky glint in her eye and immediately thought, 'Eh up, that's a pretty bewer!'

Supping my pint, I was keeping half an eye on Judith when a lad I knew only as China walked in. China was half-Italian and was said to be a bit of a bully, a reputation to which he immediately lived up by walking over to the group of lasses and giving Judith a clip across the top of her head.

'Eh, eh, fucking pack it in,' I interjected.

'Shut ya fuckin' mouth or I'll tear off ya face,' China replied. Thinking it best not to provoke any trouble, I turned my attention back to my pint and waited for China to go to the toilet. Then I followed him into the gents'.

'You'll rip my face off, will you?' I snarled as China stood at the urinal. 'Well, get on with it.'

China responded with a single word: 'Outside!'

As we passed through the front door, I smacked China on the back of his head. He went flying. He picked himself up and came at me, his fists a blurred whirr in front of him. I hit him once. On the chest with my fist. It lifted him a foot or two in the air. The punch wasn't hard enough to cause real damage, but it was hard enough to make him reconsider his next move. By the time he was back on his feet, China had changed his mind. 'Aye, we can talk about this,' he said.

'What's there to talk about?' I sneered. China paused for a second. He wasn't the brightest bulb in the room. I could almost hear the rusty cogs inside his head struggling to turn thoughts into action. Then he ran off.

I returned to the Clarry's lounge and sat down. Sitting on the far side of the jukebox from the group of lasses, I'd just got my breath back when Diana sat down at my table. 'Judith sent this over,' she said, holding out a pint of beer.

'Is she knocking about with China?'

'Yeah,' Diana said.

'He's an arsehole, isn't he?'

'Oh yeah.'

I went over to the lasses' table and got chatting. When they got up to leave, I asked Judith for a date. The next evening I took her to see a cowboy flick at the cinema. It was the beginning of a regular thing. I soon discovered that Judith was not only very easy on the eye but also easy to get along with. Having grown up in Bellingham, a small mining village near Hexham, she was like a character in a Catherine Cookson novel – a good honest worker, who kept herself spotlessly clean and could make curtains or clothes from potato sacks. Judith was a wonderful woman and within three months I'd decided she was the one for me. Standing in the bookie's one afternoon – there was none of that getting-down-on-one-knee rubbish in Redcar in those days – I popped the question: 'Do you want to get married?'

'Aye, all right then,' Judith said. 'We'll get married on Saturday in two weeks.'

Shortly before eleven o'clock on the morning of 12 August 1967, Judith and I rolled up outside the registry office at Guisborough, up in the Cleveland Hills. Having moved on from being a Teddy boy, I was dressed in a mod suit. Judith wore a light blue silk suit and hat. There was a short ceremony, then we headed back to Redcar to sit with twenty mates in the Clarendon, the scene of our first meeting, and to tuck in to sandwiches and beer. Most of the afternoon was spent running back and forth between the Clarry and Garveys, the local bookmakers. Not that I had any luck. My middle name that afternoon should have been Second. By late afternoon, we were all paralytic from the drink and getting radgy because none of us had won anything on the horses. Petty disagreements were turning into arguments and it wasn't long before I caught sight of a lad swinging a fist in my direction. By grabbing George, a youngster with a gammy arm who collected glasses in the Clarendon, I avoided the lad's fist. Instead it hit George, who was carrying a tray of drinks, full on in the mouth. The drinks flew everywhere and I was barred from the Clarendon for three months. Not what I wanted on my wedding day.

We moved onto the Berkeley, a bar with a late licence in Redcar's bowling alley. We had a few more drinks, then the music struck up on the jukebox. It was an old Chuck Berry number. '*It was a teenage wedding and the old folks wished them well . . .*' Everyone got up to dance with Judith and me. Towards the end of the song, I jumped up from the dance floor onto the stage, ran across it and leaped the gap to the grand piano. Landing on my knees, I slid across the piano's lid, straight through a plate glass window and into the car park, a drop of about ten feet. I landed on the tarmac with a crunch, ripping my mod suit and scraping the skin off my knees. Up at the window, the entire wedding party was watching in fits of laughter. Beside me, a copper was standing with a dog and van.

'What the fucking hell do you think you are doing?' the blue-bottle said. I couldn't think of an answer. I was arrested and carted off to the cop shop, where I was charged with being drunk and disorderly.

Judith turned up. With tears rolling down her face, she pleaded with the duty sergeant to let me go. 'I know he's had a lot to drink, but it's our wedding night,' she said.

'Just get rid of him,' the sergeant said, and I was allowed to go home to our flat at Newcomer Terrace on the seafront.

Within a few days of us getting married, Judith announced that she was four weeks pregnant. I was delighted, but I didn't feel ready to be a father. We were given a council house at 36 Cedar Grove in Redcar and on 17 April 1968 Richard was born at Teesborough Maternity Hospital.

Judith was a fantastic mother and immediately adapted to looking after a child, but I didn't handle it at all well. I was too immature to be a father. And having found a woman to love me and stand by me fifteen years after my mother deserted me, I struggled to accept a competitor for my wife's attentions.

Richard was a bonny little baby and I did all the fatherly things, although I drew the line at changing nappies. I took him for walks in the pram and played with him on the beach. I loved little Richard and I loved looking after him, but I'd come to a point in my life at which I had to decide who I wanted to be. Richard's birth had coincided with my first steps in show business, behind the drums with the Four Man Band, and it had presented me with a difficult choice. Did I want to try to improve my life? Or did I want to see how it panned out if I didn't make any changes? For too long I'd allowed myself to be shaped by events.

When I looked back at my early life, I realised I'd often blamed circumstances for getting me into trouble. The truth is that I courted trouble. Not because I was a born trouble-maker, but maybe because I'd lost my mother and because I had a father whose only reaction to any mischief was to tan my arse. I'd grown up with no real idea of what was right or wrong. I rarely considered the consequences of my actions and I had no notion of what was sensible and what was stupid. In short, I'd become an ignorant, clueless arsehole – stealing, fighting, drinking and fucking whatever and with whomever I could get my hands on – and I'd already paid a price for it.

But now, with a young son and a newly-wed wife, I had the opportunity to change my life. I could play the dutiful husband

and the devoted father, but that would mean being trapped forever in the destiny I had so far carved out for myself – a future
of no-hope jobs that in the past had always led me to boredom,
frustration and petty crime. Or I could grab hold of the one
thing that had given me a glimpse of a better future – show
business.

From that first gig with the Four Man Band at the Magnet
Hotel, I'd known that I'd found something at which I was good
and which offered me an alternative to a life of crime. Was I
going to be a loving, hands-on father? Or did I want to be an
entertainer? I'd already discovered that the adoration I got from
the audience was far greater than anything I could get from my
wife and a little baby. It sounds callous, but that's just the way it
was. Any entertainer would say the same. You can't wait to get
back on that stage. That's why I still do it today. It's a drug – just
like heroin, only more addictive. And, like a drug, being on
stage was to become the biggest thing in my life, something for
which I would neglect everything in my path. So, faced with
deciding between the stage and my new family, the choice
wasn't difficult.

It didn't occur to me then, but with hindsight I now realise
that I was following in my father's footsteps. I did exactly what
my father did to my mother. I neglected Judith and devoted
myself to the clubs instead. Judy and I had our ups and downs
but, like my father, I made sure I still provided for the family.
Shortly after Richard was born, I realised I needed to earn
more money than playing with the band could provide. I'd given
up working on the market stall with Marty, so I went back to
hod-carrying. Lugging bricks or cement five and a half days a
week, I worked from Monday morning until Saturday
lunchtime for twelve pounds and ten shillings. Out of that, I
gave Judy ten pounds, leaving me two pounds and ten shillings
to go out on a Friday with the lads, have a bet on the horses on

Saturday afternoon and then take Judy out on the Saturday evening.

It was barely enough to scrape by, but we managed. Judy's mam and dad would give us bits of furniture that I'd repair and polish or paint white. And I resorted to my old tricks to get my hands on things we needed.

I'd moved on from hod-carrying on building sites to mixing up vermiculite fireproof plaster for the pipe-laggers at ICI when I decided I needed a shed. Knowing I couldn't afford a new one, I took a mate called Billy down to ICI where I'd spotted a garden shed being used to store cement sacks. We dismantled it, put it on the back of a truck and headed for the main gate.

'What you doing?' the gateman asked.

'We're working for Pearson's,' I bluffed. 'We've got to deliver this shed.'

When the gateman went into his little office to check, I jumped out of our pick-up truck, pulled the gate open, let Billy drive through the gate, jumped back in the van and raced off. We'd got halfway round the first roundabout outside ICI when a security van caught up with us. A guard forced us to pull over. 'You're nicking this shed,' he said.

'I'm not,' I replied.

'Yes, you are. You're nicking it,' he said. 'Now, go and put it back and we'll forget about it. If you don't, I'll prosecute you.' So we drove back and re-erected the shed, but I wasn't going to abandon my quest for a shed that easily.

I found an old fifteen-hundredweight furniture van at a scrapyard and bought it for ten pounds. The scrapyard owner took the back of the van off the chassis and delivered it to our home where, with inches to spare, I squeezed it through the space between our house and the neighbouring house into our garden. It was enormous – so long and so high that it blocked out the light from our neighbour's garden. Our neighbours complained to the council, who came around one day while I was at work, dismantled it and took it away.

Life at Cedar Grove was a litany of attempts to save money or get owt for nowt. We lived for Friday and Saturday nights. Friday night was the lads' night out – strictly no wives or girl-friends. If I wasn't working with the band, I'd join my mates and we'd all go into town together, spend the evening in the pub, move on to a nightclub and usually end the night with a fight or a fuck or both.

Walking into a nightclub as a young man, the music blaring, the birds wearing skirts halfway up their arses, you were always going to attract trouble. It was just the hustle and bustle of youth. Some jealous bloke would inevitably come over. 'You staring at my missus?' he'd shout over the music. 'I'll punch you in the fucking mouth, mate.' And even if I survived the nightclub and went back to a lass's house, her boyfriend would often knock on the door and I'd have to scarper. It always hap-pened.

Saturday nights were different. This time wives and girl-friends were permitted, which could make things complicated if the lads had seen some action on Friday night. My best mate at the time was Dave Hewitt, with whom I'd come off the motorcycle given to me by Norman Trevethick. The first thing Dave and I would do when we met at the Clarendon was get our stories straight. 'Now don't forget, Dave, you held me down last night, and you give me that love bite, didn't you, Dave?' I'd say.

'Yeah, sure,' Dave would say. 'I'll say I give you the love bite to make Judy jealous and you tell my girlfriend I stayed at your house last night because I was too blathered to get home.'

Some evenings, I'd work on the door of a pub or nightclub – usually the Red Lion – to earn a few extra bob if the band wasn't playing. We'd all meet at half past seven in the

Clarendon lounge, have a couple of pints, then at ten o'clock I'd go and work on the door until two o'clock, the best place and time to pick up a lass at the end of the evening. The girls would have had a drink and as they were leaving I'd say, 'What you doing, pet? Do you want to go and have a coffee?'

A lot of my mates lived on their own in flats, so I'd borrow the key and take the lass there. I took a fat girl called Grace home one night. She was hugely overweight, but it was the end of the night and I wanted to get my leg over. At times like that, nothing would stop me. Grace had sunk a few drinks too many and couldn't get her legs up. Now I don't have the biggest penis in the world and I couldn't get it in. In those days, there was nothing in the way of foreplay – I hadn't even heard of a blow job – and we were struggling to get going. Then I hit on a brain-wave.

'Fart and give us a clue,' I suggested.

That was it. We collapsed onto the bed in fits of giggles. The moment was lost, but it paid dividends years later when I remembered it and used it on stage. It got the biggest laugh of the evening and for a while became a regular part of my act.

Given the way in which I was carrying on, it was unsurprising that Judy and I had arguments and fights. They were about women, drink and money. Mostly money, actually – 'you don't give me enough' or 'I don't get enough to give you enough' or 'you get five pound when you're on the door at the club, why don't I get any of it?' – but it was also about jealousy. I'd see Judy going out in a short skirt that barely covered her crotch and I'd see blokes staring at her. I couldn't help myself. 'You're fucking doing that on purpose,' I'd say. And then the argument would start.

'You never took your eyes off that girl last night,' Judy would snap back.

'What do you mean? I don't even know her . . .' But women

aren't daft. And Judy sussed me out straight away. I had a stray-ing eye and that caused a lot of grief.

And as with a lot of couples from Middlesbrough council estates, it often turned violent. When I look back at that time, I'm filled with regrets. I know I have it in me to be cool, calm and collected, but I wasn't like that then and neither was anyone I knew. And it was always just everyday things that triggered the rows. Us lads didn't know the difference between right and wrong. We didn't realise that we were big blokes and they were little women. I don't agree with slapping a woman but, having done it, I know why it happens. When violence is all you know, it's difficult not to resort to your fists when you've got nothing and you're living on top of each other and you're getting at each other all the time. Suddenly the only way to bring a stop to the bickering and the arguing is to pick something up and just throw it. Or to lash out. I've done it and I've had it done to me. I came from a background where that was the way we lived. And as a result, we never had an ornament in my parent's house that wasn't chipped or broken. It was getting to be the same where Judy and I lived.

The most trivial things would trigger arguments. I was watch-ing football on television one day when Judy got up and switched channels. 'What y'doing?' I said.

'Watching *Peyton Place*,' Judy said.

Or, as I called it, *Paint and Place*. I got up. 'I'm watching the football,' I said, changing channels back.

'No, I'm watching the soap,' she said.

I saw red. 'Fucking nobody's watching it,' I shouted. And I smashed the television, which was on rent from Burbecks in Station Road. The next day, I went round to Burbecks and said we'd been burgled. 'You won't believe this, but our house was broken into. They tried to steal the TV and dropped it climbing through the window,' I said. Burbecks didn't fall for that one. I still had to pay for it. Three shillings and sixpence a week for about three years.

One night, at the end of a gig with the Four Man Band, Dave Hewitt came up to me as I was packing up my drums. He'd been living with a girl, but they'd had an argument and the girl had thrown him out. He'd moved on to his mother's house, but his mother was fed up with him and had told him to pack his bags. 'Any chance of stopping at your house?' Dave said. So I put him up in the back bedroom.

Dave didn't become a permanent fixture. He stayed maybe two or three nights a week. The other nights he'd stay with a woman or his brother or another friend. We were drinking mates and I liked having him around. Judy was pregnant with our second child and she also enjoyed Dave's company when I was out gigging with the band, working the door at the Red Lion or out with my mates.

On 12 June 1969 Robert was born in his grandma's front room at 8 Cleveland Street in Redcar, opposite the post office. I was delighted to be a father again and proud to have two bonny sons.

One Sunday, a couple of months after Robert was born, Judy and I took the kids to visit Judy's mother. Richard, who was only a year old, picked up one of his toys and smashed it down onto his grandmother's coffee table, her pride and joy.

'You little sod,' I said, wagging my finger at Richard.

'Don't you call him a little sod in front of me,' Judy snapped.

'He's got to be disciplined,' I said. 'I know he's only a baby, but look at your face.' And I slapped Richard on the back of the leg. 'Naughty, naughty, naughty,' I said, thinking I was doing the right thing.

You would have thought I'd stabbed Richard. Judy and her mother went berserk, screaming and shouting at me. 'You're nowt but a bully,' Judy shouted. 'You're an arsehole.'

'Aye, and this carry-on is for *your* fucking benefit,' I said, pointing at Judy's mother, 'not for my benefit.' Slamming the door, I walked out. I got home at about half past four. At six o'clock, the Four Man Band was picking me up for a gig.

'Where's Judy?' Dec asked when he'd come inside the door.

'Eh . . . she's at her mother's, we've just had a barney. Nowt to worry. It'll be all right when I get back.'

But Judy wasn't there when I got home that night and it wasn't all right. I went upstairs. All her clothes were gone. She'd packed up everything and vanished. I'd always thought that kind of thing only happened in trashy novels. I never thought it would happen to me. And, like something out of a Barbara Cartland plot, there was a note on the table. 'It's obvious you don't love me,' Judy had written at the top of two pages that detailed all my failings and which ended with the words '. . . and I have found love with somebody else. Don't try and find us.'

I had no idea who my wife had run away with – and the parallels with my parents' break-up didn't dawn on me until many years later – but I was hurt and incensed. I'd defy anyone to receive a letter telling them that they're a cunt and not to lose their temper over it. No man likes to feel inferior and I reacted like any young bloke would. I vowed to kill Judy and to beat up the bloke she'd run away with. When I realised I couldn't do that, I did the next best thing. I wrecked the house.

I picked up the chairs and tables and threw them at the wall. I swept all the ornaments off the shelves. I kicked a hole in the kitchen door. And I picked up the television – another one from Burbecks – and threw it through the front window.

My temper had got the better of me once again. My wife had fucked off with another bloke and my reaction was to lash out first and ask questions later. I'd never been any other way. It was just my nature. And, as usual, I was the one who suffered. By the time I'd blown off all my steam, the house was a mess.

I went down the pub, sunk seven pints and went to the police station. Banging on the duty sergeant's counter, I demanded to know where my wife had gone. The sergeant just shrugged. 'This is a domestic argument,' he said. 'Nothing to do with us.'

'If I get my hands on my wife or that fucking shite she's run away with, then you will be getting involved,' I said before storming out and marching round to Judy's mother's house.

'Where is she?' I shouted between threats to put a brick through her mother's front window. 'I want her back!'

'She wants nowt to do with you,' her mother shouted. 'And good luck to her!'

I didn't hear word of Judy for more than six months. Dave had stopped staying over a couple of nights a week and I was living alone in our former family home when a letter arrived.

'Dear Roy, I know you have been wondering where we are,' it said. 'We have been living in a rented house in Bellingham. It's very overcrowded and Dad's ill . . .' There was a bit of news, but no mention of who her new fella might be. 'If you want to see the bairns, we are here,' it ended.

I borrowed a small van, drove up to Bellingham and sat in it at the end of Judy's street. In the distance I could see a little boy, playing with a ball beside the front gate. Could that be Richard? I thought. The last time I'd seen him, he was a toddler clutching on to his grandmother's coffee table. And sitting on a towel in the front garden of the house was a little baby. I wondered if it was Robert.

I waited in the van for half an hour, watching the two kids play in the summer heat. Then I saw Judith come out of the front door with a drink and give it to the older child. I started up the van and pulled up outside the house.

'Hiya,' Judith said, as if we'd just seen each other the day before.

'All right?' I said. We got talking, nice and gently. There were no accusations or recriminations, just a serious, adult conversation. We both realised the relationship was dead and that we had nothing in common. We'd been married less than two years, but we'd married too young and in that time discovered that we were two quite different people.

'I know you want to see your children,' Judy said. 'So could you find us somewhere to live in Redcar? We'll come back and live near you. We've got nothing here. Dave has left.'

'Oh, right,' I said. It was the first time I'd heard Dave's name mentioned. Suddenly it all made sense. 'I'll see what I can do.'

Driving home, I thought it all through. It was classic stuff. While I had been out drumming, Judy and Dave must have formed a relationship and fallen in love. No wonder I'd not seen him since the day Judy scarpered. Judy had been waiting for an excuse to walk out and I'd given it to her when I slapped Richard at her mother's house. Like my mam, Judy had just wanted a happy home relationship straight out of *The Waltons* – playing cards and watching television together, going to the club once a week for a game of bingo, the kind of things that most domesticated women want – but I was looking for something else.

Judy had accused me of being a ladies' man, but that was a load of bollocks. Why? Because my fucks only lasted three minutes and there had to be more to life than that. I loved playing the drums. I loved being up on stage. And when I told a joke and everybody laughed – well, there was nothing better. That to me was a marriage made in heaven and far more tempting than sex.

Only entertainers will ever understand the attraction of that nervous anticipation when you're standing in the wings or waiting in the dressing room, that clearing of the throat as the adrenalin tightens your voice just before you go on, the audience lapping you up and that feeling that you can do no wrong, that you've got complete control of a room of a thousand people. And then coming off and the buzz hitting you full on because now you can relax. It's a high that any entertainer will tell you is irreplaceable. With that to compete against, Judy didn't have a chance.

As I drove home, I also thought about the best way forward. Having seen the bairns again, I knew I had to be part of their lives. I decided to give Judy the house in Redcar that we'd shared and find myself somewhere else to live.

A few weeks later, I'd moved into a flat in Westbourne Grove and Judy and the boys were back home. On Saturdays or Sundays I'd take them down to the sea for a couple of hours. We'd kick a ball about on the beach and I'd buy them an ice cream or some chips. I only got a few hours a week with them, but owt's better than nowt.

Judy and I were lucky really. We had no money, we weren't really suited and, like most youngsters, we were too possessive of each other. But in spite of all the trials and tribulations of a doomed marriage, we still have good memories. We're still good friends – Judith does my washing every week and we chat all the time – but, best of all, we produced two fabulous sons.

If I had been more of a concrete bloke, we would still be together today, because I'm not one for ducking responsibilities. I can put up with most things, but I needed my space away from two screaming kids.

I've got a young wife now and I've discovered that the best thing to do is to give a woman a lot of space and freedom, something I was incapable of giving Judith. I would have been too jealous and possessive. And now that I've found happiness with Helen, I can see that love grows if you allow a woman to be herself.

But there's one thing I've also learned. It takes two to make things work and two to make things go wrong, but in the end it's always the bloke that takes the can. After all, my mother always blamed my father for everything.

CHAPTER EIGHT

HARD KNOCKS

LYING ON MY BACK, staring at the ceiling after the operation, I was just glad to be alive. I didn't want to underestimate it – but then, I also didn't want to *over*estimate it. Thoughts of exactly what had happened – had the surgeon removed a little nodule or had half my throat been taken away? – didn't matter. I knew I had survived and that I couldn't talk and that was all I needed to know.

Of course, I tried to talk. If they'd removed my leg, I would still have tried to run. This was no different. I wondered if I could say anything at all. What should I try to say? I settled on a gentle 'ah'. Nothing came out. Just a muffled hiss.

I looked around the hospital room. Beside my bed was a row of machines keeping tabs on my breathing and heartbeat. There were gas bottles and a steam machine that would soon become a familiar friend. Every few hours a nurse would come in and make me breathe steam to avoid any throat infections. It left my face looking like a ripe tomato, but it killed all the germs.

And sitting halfway along the side of my bed, silently waiting for me to wake up, was Helen. As usual, just the sight of her filled me with confidence. And once she started talking, telling me how much she loved me and missed me and how important I was to her and how I was the best thing that had ever happened to her, I was filled with a quiet determination to get better soon.

Mr White popped in a few hours after I'd woken up after the operation and told me that he'd removed a vocal chord and some scrapings from my throat.

'You need to take it slowly, Roy,' he said. 'Just think of it as one day at a time and we'll get you back to where you were before the operation. But first you'll need six weeks of radiotherapy.'

When Helen wasn't visiting and when the hospital staff weren't attending to me, I'd lie on my bed and worry. On top of all those usual everyday worries – like paying the bills on time and getting the car serviced and making sure the garden's being looked after and the kids are happy and wondering what's on the telly – there was now a new one: 'How long have I *really* got?'

It wasn't an entirely novel question for me. I think everybody wonders when they're going to die. And once you reach your late fifties or your sixties, you think about it all the more. Anyone who claims that question hasn't crossed their minds is lying. We're all the same. The young 'uns want to climb mountains and see a bit of life. The old 'uns want the comfort of a nice house and a nice garden. We all want enough money in the bank not to have to worry about things and to be able to go on holiday once in a while. And the one thing that unites us above all else is that we want to put off our final breath for as long as possible. That's why so many of the soldiers who went into battle in the Second World War were pissed or on pills. Faced with something they knew could mean certain death, they were petrified. They wondered if the bullet would strike them or their mate running beside them. They wanted to know which of them would be the lucky one. And so did I.

Four days after the operation, Mr White shone a torch down my throat. 'We're letting you go home,' he said. 'You know what the rules are. You've got to abide by them.'

I knew exactly what Mr White meant. And with little more than a rough growl where my voice had once been, there was a fat chance of me being an arsehole, going out and getting drunk, shouting and bawling all night. So I didn't bother trying to rasp an answer and just nodded instead.

As soon as I got home, I started to work on my voice. All day, every day, I whispered simple words like 'hello' so quietly that only I could hear them. It was a start.

Late one evening, a week after the operation, I whispered loud enough for Helen to be able to hear me for the first time. And what was my first word? Well, it wasn't 'fuck'.

'Is the late shop open?' I murmured. A whole sentence! And straight from the heart. I'd been off my usual diet of bacon, beans, cornflakes and bread ever since the operation. Instead it had been jelly and lukewarm soup. I was desperate for something crunchy.

'Packet of crisps?' I whispered to Helen.

When Helen returned, I opened the packet and popped a crisp in my mouth. It tasted wonderful as it melted on my tongue. The flavours were particularly intense after a week of bland, sloppy hospital meals. Then I slipped the sharp sliver of spud between my teeth, crunched it and pushed it cautiously to the back of my mouth. I swallowed. The instant it entered my throat, I was in agony. The tiny crumbs were like shards of glass. It was like rubbing my bell end on a cheese grater. I'd never felt such pain.

The rest of the packet went straight in the bin and I went

back to square one. This was going to take longer and be much more difficult than I'd anticipated.

●

A lot happened in the year or so between Judith running away with Richard and Robert and returning to Teesside with the two bairns. I passed my driving test and ended my days of driving stolen cars without a licence when I bought a MkII Jaguar. It was my pride and joy until I discovered that it had been welded together from two Jaguars involved in car crashes. More importantly, the Four Man Band broke up and I formed a duo with Mick Boothby, a long-standing mate who played bass. I knew from my time with the Four Man Band that bands playing cover versions struggled to make a reasonable living. Club audiences wanted a good laugh at the end of a working week more than they wanted to dance, so we decided from the outset that we would be a comedy-music act. All we needed was a good name. We spent a couple of weeks scratching our heads, then it dawned upon us. Mick looked just like Jason King, a popular television detective at the time, and all the characters I played on stage were hard nuts, so we called ourselves Jason & Everard.

Jason & Everard didn't last long, no more than nine months to a year, but I look back particularly fondly on those days. Mick wore velvet jackets and frilly shirts, like the dandy character of Jason King, and I wore a tartan or checked suit and a flat cap with the peak turned up so that the crowd would notice me behind the drums at the back of the stage. We developed an act based on a couple of well-known hits of the day interspersed with a few comic routines and parodies of advertisements. But with just Mick and me to carry the show – and I did almost all the comedy – I had to hone my audience skills fast. The first lesson I learned was that a decent comic always has to be two steps ahead of the audience. A quick-witted quip under pressure will not only get you out of trouble but will win over the audience for the rest of the evening.

We were in full flow at a club at Stockton-on-Tees when a woman who could have doubled for Mr Blobby started making her way through the audience towards the stage. I suspected she was a committee member with a message that someone in the audience needed to move their car or come to the telephone. It was exactly the kind of interruption I didn't need when I was running through my gags. The jokes were a bit close to the bone – 'I'm taking my Goblin Teasmaid back to the shop,' I said, 'because it's not doing what it promises on the label' – and needed to be rattled off in quick succession to keep the audience on my side.

With a face like a bulldog's arse and wearing a shabby white top with a trail of deeply embedded gravy stains, the committee woman arrived at the front of the stage and held out her hand for the microphone. I tried to ignore her, but I could see from the sour expression on her face that I'd be asking for trouble if I didn't give in.

'Ladies and gentlemen,' the woman said. 'This man is filthy and should not be on this stage.'

'Yeah, about as filthy as your fuckin' blouse,' I snapped back. She looked at me with contempt, but I didn't care. The audience was roaring and I was thrilled. With just one line, I'd turned a potentially fatal put-down into a devastating riposte at the woman's expense.

However, dealing with bolshie club committee members or pub landlords wasn't always as easy and successful as it was on that night. Another evening and we were playing Gresham Working Men's Club near Seaton Carew. We'd reached the part of our act where Mick would start playing 'Walk Right Back' by the Everly Brothers. After the first verse I would usually run off stage. Mick would then sing 'Walk Right Back' over and over again, getting increasingly angry and desperate until I reappeared on stage dressed as Terry Scott doing the Curly-Wurly advert.

But on this occasion, just as we started singing, a committee man stood up. 'Raffle tickets!' he shouted, completely ignoring us on stage. 'Meat prize!'

That was enough. I took the hump and walked straight off the stage, through the dressing room to the side entrance and out of the door. I got into our old post-office van and drove home.

The next day I bumped into Mick. 'Where the hell were you?' he said. I told him I'd had enough of the rudeness of club chairmen and had gone home.

'I sang "Walk Right Back" twenty-six times before I realised you weren't going to walk right back,' Mick said. 'It was funny afterwards, but at that time I called you all the fat bastards under the sun.'

Mick was the best-natured stage partner any musician or comic could have ever wanted. On the way to a gig at Middlesbrough Labour Club, we stopped off at Guitarzan, a shop in Slaggy Island, where Mick bought a brand new Shure microphone. Driving the van to the club, I watched as Mick, sitting beside me, took it out of its case and admired it.

'That's a lovely-looking mike you got there,' I said. 'Can I use it tonight? It'll make the gags sound better.'

Mick didn't hesitate. He immediately said yes. A couple of hours later, we walked on stage to face a rowdy crowd. I grabbed Mick's mike to start the show, but was immediately heckled.

'Get off!' someone shouted. 'Yer rubbish!'

Then a few of the audience booed. We hadn't even started.

'You're a bunch of fucking wankers,' I shouted in the direction of the hecklers. Then I threw Mick's brand new Shure microphone at them and stomped off stage. When we got to the dressing room, I could see Mick was upset.

'I paid eighty quid for a microphone that I will never speak into and which is now in little bits that I'll never find,' he said. Then he shrugged it off with a smile.

Mick and I were a good team, but I missed playing in a larger band, so I started to play a few gigs with a couple of other mates. The core of the band was my cousin Lee Vasey, who played guitar, with Davy Richardson on bass and me on the drums. We called ourselves The Nuts.

Other musicians would join us for a few gigs then drop out when they got a better offer or got fed up earning a pittance for an evening's work. Davy's brother, Barry, who was a Bob Dylan fan and a bit of a hard nut, played with us for a while. Towards the end of our time together, Mick Boothby joined us and with his good looks promptly became the ladies' man of the band. Mick brought along George Proudman, who always had something funny to say.

The Nuts were happy but poor – we had some good laughs, but we never made much money. And we were hopelessly inept at times. We were playing a small mining club one night, going down like a nun's knickers. Trying to get a laugh by singing 'King Of The Jungle', I was dressed as a gorilla, throwing bananas into the audience. One of the bananas knocked over a bloke's pint. He must have spent his last penny on that pint because he was straight up on to his feet and wading through the audience before I realised what had happened. The sight of this big miner approaching the stage was so frightening that it would have sent an egg back up a chicken's arse.

'Hang on there,' I shouted from the stage. 'The drink's on us.'

Those were some of the most stupid words I've ever uttered

on stage. The audience stood up as one and made for the bar. Every single one of them bought a drink at our expense and at the end of the evening we didn't get paid a penny.

Another night and we were playing the Ranch House Social Club at Hutton Rudby. I'd devised a sketch where I'd leave the stage, put on a vicar's costume, slip out of the stage door, leg it around the club and re-enter the concert room at the back, from where I'd make my way through the audience, taking a collection. Davy on stage would then pick an argument with me and the banter would flow from there. On this particular evening, I was stopped at the front door of the club by a doorman.

'You can't go in there, vicar,' he said. 'The Nuts are on. You won't like them.'

'I'm the drummer,' I said.

'But you won't like it, vicar. They are very blue.'

'You daft bugger. I'm the *drummer.*'

I couldn't do anything for laughing. The lads on stage realised what had happened and also cracked up. And our act fell apart. Again, we didn't get paid.

Like any band starting out, we owed everybody money. We learned to live on nothing and would steal whatever we could to get going. On many a Monday morning we'd take our instruments to Greenwood's Pawnshop beside the turning circle for the trolleybus in North Ormesby. On Friday, we'd go down to the social security office at 1 Grange Road (we'd say we were 'on the number one' if we were claiming dole) and give them a sob story.

'I haven't eaten for three days and I've been sleeping rough on the beach,' I'd say. 'You couldn't give me the price of a meat pie and a cup of tea?' If the number one didn't pay up, we'd borrow money from a mate to buy back our instruments.

In all this time, none of us thought of jacking it in. We'd

never known the luxury of a wallet full of wads so there was nothing to miss. It was a way of life for most of the people we knew, but it hardened our attitudes. 'So what if you've nowt,' I'd think. 'If you've nowt, you've nowt – but you can always look round for owt to steal.' So if we couldn't beg or borrow the money, we'd shoplift something and hock it at the local pub.

Like any decent band with aspirations, we wanted our own van. We found a cheap Thames van with sliding doors and the engine on the inside, between the driver and passenger seat. It was just after the heyday of flower power, so I painted big roses and tulips on the side. We thought we looked proper rock stars in it, like the Beatles or the Rolling Stones.

On the way to a gig one weekend we picked up two birds. Before they got in, we made a pact. 'Right, there's no swearing in the van,' George said. 'Nobody says fuck. No cunts, twats, bastards, tits, nipples or arse. We're not doing none of that. Right?'

It was all going well until, cruising on the Fishbourne Road just past Sedgefield, flames started coming out of the engine into the van. 'What are we gonna do?' George shouted as we pulled over on to the hard shoulder. All of our gear was in the back of the van and all of it was in hock or being paid for on the tick. My drums didn't even have cases on them.

Emergencies call for improvisation and quick thinking, so we all pulled out our dicks and pissed on the engine. Fifteen minutes earlier, we'd vowed not to swear in front of the birds, now we were all standing around the engine with our dicks in our hands. But it worked, so we climbed back in the van and drove on to the club in a fug of piss fumes. The girls weren't at all impressed.

On the way home from a gig a short while later, the van broke down. We parked it up on the A1 and called a mate to pick us up in his van and take our equipment back – after all, it had to be returned to the pawnshop by Monday morning. The van wasn't insured or taxed and all the tyres were bald. A few days later there was a knock at my door. A copper was standing outside.

'Mr Vasey?'

'Yeah?'

'Do you own a Thames van?'

'I don't, but my band does. There's four of us.'

'Ah . . . we thought it was a band's van – all the flowers. You're called The Nuts, aren't you?'

'Yes, sir, that's right.' I was trying to be as nice as ninepence.

The copper walked into my flat and shut the door behind him. 'I know it's not taxed, I know it's not insured,' he said. 'I'll give you fifteen quid for it'.

'Whaddya mean? Fifteen quid?' I looked at the copper. Cheeky bastard, I thought, that van's got one good tyre on it.

'Take it or leave it.'

'Make it twenty,' I said, cottoning on, 'and you can have it.' I never saw the van again and another bent copper crossed my path.

We bought another Thames van and it served us well until one day when we were driving along, telling stories and having a laugh on the way to a gig.

'Eh, look there. Somebody's lost a wheel,' I said as a wheel went rolling past. And as I said it, the van tilted to one side, swung around and toppled over. The wheel had been ours. The worst part was we were meant to be picking up twenty-five quid that night when we were already pink-lint.

When it came to The Nuts' act, I wrote most of the gags and the other lads orchestrated the songs. I'd be the first to admit that the jokes weren't that good, but they were funny to us simply because we were excited to be in show business. We made up for the lack of good material by being utterly tasteless, telling jokes about sex and shit, and using a talking bucket that had a big pair of tits painted on the side.

We weren't the only amateurish act. Most of the bands were made up of musicians who worked at ICI or Dorman, Long during the day, rushed home, had some tea and a bath, then turned up at a club at seven o'clock. They weren't bothered by how well they could play their instruments and many of them didn't even learn the words to their songs. We shared the bill one night with Alan Old, a fisherman from Redcar who played the guitar and sang solo. Alan was a right character with a very pragmatic approach to the business. When his van broke down, he'd drive his fishing tractor fifteen miles to a gig. When he forgot his bass drum, he'd use his suitcase instead. And Alan was well known for getting the words to songs wrong. Audiences had to endure '*Elaine is in my ears and in my heart*' sung to the tune of the Beatles' 'Penny Lane'. Other songs in Alan's repertoire included 'My Boy Giddyup' and 'I'm Leaning On A Jet Plane'.

Standing at the bar of a club one evening, watching Alan belt out 'Goodbye Ruby Wednesday' as a heckler chided him that he was a day late, I decided to put him right.

'It's "Goodbye Ruby Tuesday", Alan,' I said as he came off stage, but he didn't care.

'Most of the time, the fuckers don't even notice,' he replied. 'They're too busy talking and buying bingo books. And as long as I get my money at the end of the evening, it doesn't even matter. I'm not bothered – I've had a good day fishing.'

With an act that was often crude and rude, our reputation started to precede us and The Nuts stopped getting good work. The only clubs that would take us were so rough the piano legs had bandages and the arms on the chairs had tattoos.

At a nightclub in Billingham, a stag-night party sitting right in front of the stage got so rowdy and abusive that a fight broke out between us and them. We were heavily outnumbered and I was punched in the face, so I hit one of the stag-party lot over the head. He responded by putting his foot through the skin of my bass drum – a cardinal sin in any drummer's book.

The police were called. When they arrived, they found us locked in the dressing room and escorted us from the building. Our speakers, amplifiers, instruments and drums were wrecked, we didn't get paid and we were sent a large bill for damage to the club.

'I saw your act two weeks ago,' the policeman said. 'No wonder they attacked you.'

'Ha fucking ha,' I said.

I could see we couldn't go on like this. I'd been led to believe that show business was all sex, drugs and rock 'n' roll, but the best I ever got in The Nuts was a wank, a paracetamol and a Sandie Shaw record. We were losing more money than we were making and I'd not seen any decent action in months. Since Judy had left Redcar my sex life had been a bit hit and miss. I'd had a few knee-tremblers with some right monsters while working the door at the Red Lion, but nothing permanent.

Fortunately, the Red Lion was *the* place to go in Redcar. There was a pub and restaurant at the front and a disco at the back that attracted every good-looking bit of skirt in the area. It was packed with pussy. If you were up for it, you could not help but get a fuck.

I was working one night with a lad called Enoch who like most bouncers had a reputation as a bit of a bruiser. 'I'm up at court tomorrow,' he said as we waved a couple of birds into the disco. I should have been rooting for him, but when he said that only one thought passed through my mind: that girl standing next to you is a bit bonny. Audrey was very attractive. With long dark hair and olive skin, she could have passed as a Spaniard. A fortnight later, she walked into the Red Lion with some friends.

'Have you heard from Enoch?' I said.

'I went to see him in Durham jail. He got six months,' she said. It was the first I'd known that Enoch had been sent down.

Later that evening she was hanging around the door, so I thought I'd chance my luck.

'Can I take you home?'

'Yeah, if you like.'

'I'll get you a taxi.'

'It's all right, I'll get it myself. I'll pay for it.'

'Do you want a coffee?'

'Whereabouts?'

'I've a flat round the corner in Westbourne Grove, just near the Labour Club.'

'Aye, I'll come back, then.'

Bingo! Audrey was great. A fantastic shagger and a lovely woman. She'd bring me little presents and I'd always buy her a drink when she turned up at the Red Lion. It was nothing serious – for one thing, she had a four-year-old illegitimate daughter and after my experiences with Judy I wasn't ready to take on another child – but it was good fun while it lasted.

After about three months, Audrey stopped coming around to my flat or turning up at the Red Lion. I made a few enquiries. At the garage where Audrey had worked, they said she'd called in one day to say she was ill, then never appeared for work again. Her brother, who worked on a mobile shop, said he didn't know where she'd gone. Audrey's friends warned me off going around to the house where her father, a Sicilian seaman, lived. 'He's a fucking killer,' they said and gave the same explanation I heard from everyone I asked: 'Audrey? She's vanished into thin air.'

In the end, I assumed that Enoch had been let out early on parole and that Audrey had just upped her bags with him and left. I was a bit disappointed, but soon found solace in the arms of Lana, a woman I met at the pub.

Lana was gorgeous. Every bloke in Redcar was after her, but I'd been the lucky one who made his play just when she'd had enough of her boyfriend. I fell for Lana in a big way, having her name tattooed on my arm and buying her a second-hand engagement ring. Lana accepted my proposal – without her parents' consent because they hated the sight of me – and we made plans to get married. A few days after we'd got engaged, Lana dropped the bombshell.

'I'm pregnant,' she said.

'You what?'

'I'm pregnant. What are we gonna do?'

'We'll have to tell your mam . . .'

'No, I'm not doing that. I'm going to get it aborted.'

With Richard and Robert now living with Judy back in Redcar, I knew I didn't want any more children. I was happy to get married – it was what most people did in those days, no matter how fleeting the relationship – but children meant a more serious commitment than wedding bells and I didn't want that.

Although I was in love with Lana, I hadn't stopped playing around. At the end of an evening out with Lana, I'd kiss her goodnight on her parents' doorstep and catch a bus for the five-mile journey to Saltburn where, with a couple of mates, I'd rented a cold, damp flat. The bus ran along the coast road and was often empty late at night. I'd sit at the back with the entire top deck to myself. One night, the conductress came upstairs and sat down next to me. She was blonde, about thirty and her uniform clung tightly to her body in all the right places.

'Hiya,' she said. 'I know you. Don't you work at the Red Lion?'

'You want to fasten that button, I can see your tits,' I said. I told a few gags. By the time we'd left Redcar, the conductress had her hand down my trousers and was giving me a wank.

I never saw the conductress again and the wank had meant nothing to me more than a bit of fun, but such cheap thrills made me realise that, although I was happy to get married, I didn't want to be tied down to a woman and another child. So when Lana suggested an abortion I was very happy to go along with it. The only problem was that legal abortions were still difficult to arrange away from the big cities so Lana fell back on one of the old wives' methods of the day involving drinking a bottle of gin and sitting in a hot bath.

'You think that'll work?' I said.

'I dunno,' she said. 'But I really don't want this child.'

A few nights later I turned up to meet Lana in our usual place, the corner down the road from her parents' house, but she was not there. The next evening, I stood on the same corner at the same pre-arranged time but again Lana didn't appear. I walked up the road to her parents' house and knocked on the door. Her mother answered it.

'What do you want?'

'Is Lana in?'

'She's in hospital, no thanks to you.'

'It's got nothing to do with me.'

'Just go away or I'll call the police.' Lana's mother slammed the door in my face, so I rang her sister.

'Angela, it's Roy. What's happened about Lana?'

'She had a miscarriage. She was watching *Coronation Street* last night and she went up to the bathroom and started bleeding. Our mam and our dad are going to fucking kill you. They didn't know Lana was pregnant.'

I never saw Lana again. I suspect her mother poisoned her mind against me after that because she would have nowt to do with me. Six months later I was around at my mother's house. 'Have a look at this,' my mam said, thrusting a copy of the *Evening Gazette* across the kitchen table.

There was a picture of Lana on the front page beside a story saying that she had kicked a bus after getting drunk with some lad who was clearly her new boyfriend. It went on to say that she'd also hit the copper who'd locked her up. It didn't sound like Lana at all. When I knew her, she was one of those girls who was sugar and spice and all things nice. I was really shocked.

'And have you got a baby?' my mam said.

'What are you talking about?'

'Well, she's been round here, holding a baby, saying it's yours and asking if you want to see it.'

So Lana had kept the baby after all. 'That's all over now,' I said. 'Don't worry about it. I'm not seeing her any more.'

'Well, I think it's disgusting. You have responsibilities.'

'It's not me, Mother,' I said. 'Lana doesn't want to know.'

My mother didn't understand. She couldn't. Like most mothers, she was outraged at her son's morals and behaviour. And I didn't give it much thought. There was so much going on in my life then that I didn't have the time to think it over. I just lived day to day. I cared about only two things – playing the drums and telling jokes. Whatever else went on didn't matter. All the scams, escapades and misdemeanours never bothered me. It was like throwing a brick through a window and months later passing that window and seeing it had been repaired. I'd just be chuffed to have got away with it. Live for today, forget the past and fuck the future – that was my motto.

CHAPTER NINE

CHUBBY IS BORN

I HELD UP THE SIGN. 'Had throat operation,' it said. 'Please don't ask questions. Leave a message below.' And I asked Helen to tell my sons and anyone else who knew me: please don't ring me up. I'm sorry I can't talk to you.

For weeks I lived in a silent world, not talking, just pointing, grunting and scribbling messages on a notepad. And the strangest thing happened. Because I was silent, most people around me stopped talking as well. I'd gone dumb and they added deafness.

And when they did talk to me, it was always the same thing. 'Are you all right, Dad?' Or: 'How're you feeling, Roy? Are you okay, Chubby?' If I had a pound for every time I was asked that question . . . well, let's just say I appreciated the concern but was totally fed up with the limitations of my response – a smile, a shrug or a thumbs-up.

Even now I'll be in the shops and somebody will shout: 'Chubby! How's your throat?' I'll pretend not to speak. I'll point at my throat and silently mouth something and shrug apologetically. It makes them smile. And if the checkout girl's pretty and she asks 'How's your throat Chubby?' I'll leap on the opportunity.

'Why, do you wanna put your tongue down it?' I'll say. Or: 'Don't worry, I'm not shoplifting. I'm not hiding anything at the back behind my tongue.'

Back then, in the first weeks after the operation, I was desperate to be able to answer questions concerning my well-being with a quick quip. But I couldn't. First I needed radiotherapy.

The treatment started a week after the operation. Five days a week for six weeks I trooped into the hospital, laid myself down on a trolley and waited for the radiotherapist and the nurse to strap me into a brace that kept my head and chest absolutely rigid.

Just to relieve the boredom of it, I would always have a bit of a crack with the nurse. 'I've bought you some coffee creams, ladies, so treat me right today. Whose turn is it to get undressed?'

'Your turn, I'm afraid, Roy. It's always your turn.'

The nurse would help the radiotherapist push the trolley into a large machine that looked like a body scanner. The heat would come on and I'd try to keep as still as possible until the buzzer sounded. It was like getting a tan on a sunbed. It was that boring and that mundane.

'Are you all right, Mr Vasey?' the nurse would say afterwards.

'I'm fine, thanks.'

'Would you like to put your shoes back on?'

'Thank you.'

'See you tomorrow.'

'Yes – I'll bring some bread in tomorrow. Will you put it under the machine when I go under? I'd like some toast.'

'You know, we're going to miss you when you stop coming, Roy,' the nurse said. 'We'll miss the crack.'

For the first couple of weeks' treatment I felt no real change. I couldn't eat much anyway, so I stuck to my sloppy food and vitamin drinks. But in the third week I woke up to find that my neck was covered in purple and red blotches. It looked like I'd been beaten up or severely sunburned.

Having been blessed with baby-face skin, I've always scoffed at anyone who said it was impossible to lie about your age because the skin on your neck would give the game away like the rings on a tree trunk. I'd look at women my age – they had saggy necks from the age of fifty – and they'd look at me and say I had the skin of someone twenty years younger. But now I really looked my fifty-seven years. The skin on my neck was as tired, mottled and saggy as an old sack.

It wasn't just the side effects of the radiation that were getting me down. I wasn't sleeping well. At home after the radiotherapy, I'd lie down on my bed in the hope of sleeping. But as soon as I lay back the coughing started. It was one of those tickly coughs that never lets you rest. Irritating as hell and worse at night. I found it impossible to sleep, so I'd lie awake coughing and worrying.

In the morning, I'd try to get out of bed, but the lack of sleep and the radiation made me tired and lethargic. I didn't feel like doing anything, I had no energy and I couldn't swallow. The one thing I wanted was a chip sandwich, but the only things I could eat were ice cream and soup. Not having eaten properly for weeks, the weight fell off me. I went from nineteen stone seven pounds to seventeen stone two pounds. I was chuffed about the weight loss. I just wish cancer hadn't been on the end of it.

●

I had a friend called Ronnie Aspery, an alto saxophone player in Back Door, a jazz fusion group. Ronnie went on to record for Warner Brothers, tour the world and perform with Keith Richards, Ronnie Scott, Status Quo and Chris Rea. He wrote music for films such as *The Spy Who Loved Me*, *McVicar* and *Natural Born Killers* and for television shows such as *Baywatch*, *Friends*, *The Simpsons* and *Sesame Street*. But in the early 1970s, Back Door was a local band with a cult following and a residency at the Starlight Club in Redcar and Ronnie would play with Colin Hodgkinson on bass and a drummer called Tony Hicks.

Ronnie was a wonderful lad, a bit of an awkward sod but always funny. I was talking to Ronnie after watching him play one evening.

'What you doing with yourself in the daytime?' I said.

'I've opened a little shop in Lord Street, selling second-hand instruments. Ukuleles, banjos, guitars, flutes, trumpets, saxophones. You know, anything. I've got a tuba in there. Keyboards, drums.'

'Eh, that sounds great.'

'I want to extend the stock range. You know, it's only a small thing, but I want to get bigger.'

As it happened, I'd been talking to somebody who walked salerooms. I used to love auctions, all that buzzing around looking for a bargain and the auctioneer's spiel – 'Twennyfive-twennyfive-who'll-give-me-twennyfive . . . ah-thirtyfive-thirtyfive-give-me-thirty five . . . fortyfive-fortyfive-do-I-hear-fortyfive?'

According to the bloke I'd met at the salerooms, the mucky bookshop opposite the Red Lion in Westdyke Road was closing down. I made a few enquiries, found out the rent was ten pounds a week and told Ronnie about it.

'Did you say you liked to walk a saleroom?' he said.

'Yeah. Love it.'

'D'you think if I give you a float, you'd help us?'

I gave up all my other daytime jobs and Ronnie and I became partners in Alley Cats, his shop. I did the legwork, Ronnie paid the rent on the shop and we shared the profits on anything that I bought in for him. I'd buy watches, clocks, wooden ladders, buckets, any old junk for a pound here or ten shillings there.

After a month or so, Gerry Hartley, the manager of the Starlight Club, joined us as the third partner and we formed a tight team. I'd walk the salerooms, scouting for stuff for the shop. Then Gerry, the big boy with the cigar, would come in with a thick wad of cash and take over. He was that kind of person, the type that's good at driving a hard bargain and sealing a deal.

There were two flats above the shop, so I moved into one of them. It wasn't very pleasant – the shop was near a road junction and there was no double glazing in those days – but I did it up and decorated the stairwell. There was always the noise of traffic, but it didn't matter as the only time I went upstairs was to sleep.

The turnover in the shop could be phenomenal. Situated less than a mile from Redcar racecourse, the shop would attract the lads coming back from the races with no money in their pockets. They'd flog us a watch or a camera for a couple of quid so they could have one last drink before heading home. And the luckier lads, who'd won at the races, would pass by, spot the watch or camera and buy it. I'd give one bloke a fiver for his watch, put it in the window and ten minutes later somebody else would buy it for twenty quid. We'd make fifteen pounds' profit in no time.

And occasionally we'd pick up something really valuable from the salerooms – although we also had our fair share of missed opportunities. On one occasion, an old lady sold us a figurine. She only wanted a fiver for it, so I put it in the window. Two days later, a lad called Brian bought it for ten quid. Only an hour or so after he'd bought it, another lad came in.

'How much do you want for the figurine that was in the window?' he said.

'Sorry, mate, I've sold it.'

'That's a shame. I've been after a Queen Anne for ages.'

'A Queen Anne? What's that, then?' We knew nothing about antiques and such things.

'It's a rare piece of porcelain.'

'Oh, is it?' I said. I ran around the corner to Bradley's, a jeweller's shop. Peter Bradley was a bit of a dab hand at antiques. He looked up the figurine in his catalogues. It was worth about five hundred pounds. I had only one thing to say – 'Fucking hell!' – as I legged it out of the shop to track down Brian and force another ninety quid out of him.

About six months after we'd been in business, Ronnie's jazz career took off. Back Door recorded its first album, played a few sell-out nights at Ronnie Scott's Club in London and became a big thing. Ronnie departed for stardom, leaving Gerry and me to run Alley Cats. We split the profits down the middle and I started to make a decent living. I was still playing drums with The Nuts and with a bit of money coming in from the shop I could afford to move into a better flat, above a hairdresser's. When they did a perm downstairs, the stink of the chemicals would make my bread turn up at the ends, but the flat was larger and more comfortable and I really had a sense that things were looking up.

Gerry and I renovated the two flats above Alley Cats and rented one to Mick Boothby, the bass player from The Nuts, and the other to a woman called Beryl. Tall, with long dark hair,

Beryl looked a lot like Sandie Shaw and had a little boy called Gary. I fancied her from the moment I set eyes on her.

Beryl would come into the shop every now and then for a cup of tea and we'd have a laugh. 'Is he bent?' she'd ask about Gerry.

'I think he's either way, to be honest with you,' I'd joke.

Beryl told me she was working at Kings, a fish shop on the seafront. I'd pop in once in a while and she'd give me a free wrap of fish and chips or pie and chips. Gradually, we got to know each other. I told her that I was a drummer with a pop group and that I'd split with my wife. She said she was separated from a lad called Ginger. I'd heard of Ginger, who had a hell of a reputation, and of Beryl's brother, Billy Mundy, a Redcar lad I knew as a bit of a hard case. I invited Beryl along to a gig and bit by bit we got closer.

I was in the shop one day when a ginger-haired bloke came in. 'Is Beryl about?' he demanded.

'I think she's at the shops.'

'I'll fucking teach her.'

'What?'

'I'll fucking teach her.'

The penny dropped. I knew Beryl's husband had red hair. 'You'll be Beryl's husband, will you?'

'Yeah.'

'What's she done? We don't want any trouble here,' I said.

'This has got nowt to do with you.'

'I'm renting these premises and Beryl is renting the flat above it. I told you, I want no trouble here.'

Ginger went off on another rant, shouting that he would knock the living daylights out of Beryl. Just as he finished, Beryl walked by the front of the shop. Ginger ran out into the street, grabbed Beryl and tried to drag her into the shop. I couldn't stand by and watch him do that, so I ran out after Ginger and hit him so hard he fell over.

'You fucking bastard!' he shouted as he tried to kick me.

'You get your hands off her!' I shouted.

Beryl screamed. 'I don't want any trouble,' she yelled. Little Gary, her son, was beside her, crying hysterically, and everyone in the street had stopped and turned around to see what was going on.

Ginger lost his nerve, ran across the street and jumped in his van. As he drove off, I hurled a milk bottle at him. 'If you ever come back here . . .' I yelled as the bottle smashed the rear windscreen.

A couple of days after that Beryl and I started going out. I never saw Ginger again, although Beryl would take little Gary over to him on Sundays. Beryl and I became a solid item. We were as good as married, although that didn't stop me straying every now and then, but I was more committed to Beryl than I'd been to any previous woman.

Around this time – the early 1970s – my cousin Lee and Davy Richardson got fed up with The Nuts and packed it in, leaving just the trio of Mick, George and me. I'd recently taken to wearing a First World War flying helmet as part of my stage outfit, so we decided to play on that and name ourselves after Captain John William Alcock and Lieutenant Arthur Whitten Brown, the British aviators who made the first non-stop flight across the Atlantic Ocean. Part of the appeal of the name was our intention of tricking the audience into thinking they'd got a good deal because Alcock & Brown implied a duo. The three of us would walk on stage and announce ourselves as Micky Hall, George Cock and Roy Brown – and more often than not, it worked. The typical club audience member was not the brightest bulb in the room and we'd hear the collective sigh of recognition when they realised it was Hall, Cock and Brown instead of Alcock & Brown.

Club audiences were conservative and lazy. It was under-
standable that after a week's long, hard graft, they didn't want
anything too taxing on a Friday or Saturday night, but it meant
that our comedy had to be obvious and simple.

'Oh, for God's sake, tell us one we know,' they'd shout if we
told them a joke they hadn't heard before.

New material had to be introduced subtly and in small doses
to give it time to sink into their work-sapped and drink-addled
heads. Even a silly gag such as 'My father's a psychopath – he
rides his bike on the pavement' could be too much. It was just
one simple line, but they didn't want to have to think about it.
They wanted their jokes on silver plates with all the trimmings
and that meant explaining each line of it to them, explaining
why we were telling the joke, explaining who the people were in
the joke and explaining when and why the punchline came up.

And there was something odd about the mentality of club
audiences. The most easygoing and generous of people would
change into mean-spirited, stingy, awkward bastards the
moment they sat down in those stuffy, smoky rooms, bought
their raffle tickets and lined up their drinks beside their bingo
cards and fag packets. If an act walked on stage, put a rubber
tyre around its neck and set it on fire, burning itself to death in
front of the crowd, at the end of the night the audience would
complain that two weeks previously it had a bloke on who burnt
himself to death a lot quicker.

No matter how hard and long we worked, the audience was
always ungrateful. Often it was from resentment and I'd hear
the same old lines trotted out again and again when I met the
punters in the bar or the toilets.

'I have to work down the pit all day for the money you're on,'
they'd say.

'Well, there's the drums, there's the piano, there's a guitar,' I'd
say, pointing at our instruments. 'You go and fucking do it.'

Sometimes it would lead to trouble; sometimes I'd get away with it.

The northern club circuit was a miserable place to make a living, but fortunately I had George and Mick as accomplices. The two to three years I played with them in Alcock & Brown were some of the best I've ever had in show business. Very little of it was down to the clubs, their audiences or the club committees, the sanctimonious attitude of many of which could be summed up by the motto of the CIU (Club and Institute Union) clubs: *Recreation hand in hand with Education and Temperance*. Most of our good times arose out of our scrapes and experiences dealing with the clubs and the little despots that ran them.

Within every working-class neighbourhood, each community formed its own club. The steelworkers, the miners, the fishermen, the Labour Party members and the Conservatives – each group of men wanted to socialise only with their own type and so in any district you'd have half a dozen clubs. Big cities such as Sheffield would have three or four massive clubs just in the one street. And even in small neighbourhoods there would be several clubs dotted around. In Grangetown there was the Working Men's Club, the British Legion Club, the Old British Legion Club, St Mary's Club, Grangetown & District Social Club, Dorman's Athletic Club, The Transport Club and The Unity Club. Most of these clubs would have a concert room with enough space for 300 to 500 people. The largest clubs seated from 1,200 to 1,600 punters, while the smaller clubs would seat eighty to a hundred. The bigger clubs got the better acts, but there weren't enough artists to go around, so we'd play each club four or five times a year.

Until the early 1980s, just about every entertainer spent part of their career in clubland, many of them serving their apprenticeship and making their names on the northern club circuit.

Household names such as Marti Caine, Larry Grayson, Billy Connolly and Bernard Manning were born in the clubs of the Midlands, the North and Scotland. When they were on the bill, the queues would stretch right around the corner.

Even superstars such as the Beatles and Elton John paid their dues in the clubs and the clubs of the North-East were a fertile spawning ground for many big acts. I first saw Sting play at a club behind the Lion Inn, a pub on the highest point of the North Yorkshire Moors. Playing bass in a band called Last Exit, he was going by his real name of Gordon Sumner in those days, but he had a great voice and even then anyone could see he'd go far.

I first met David Coverdale when he was working in a men's clothes shop by day and singing in Redcar clubs and pubs in the evenings with a band called Rivers Invitation. I knew him quite well and bumped into him outside the Wimpy Bar one day. I asked him how he was.

'Eh, Roy. Not so bad, mate,' he said. 'You haven't got owt for a coffee, have ya?'

Dave hadn't eaten for a couple of days and was always scrounging food and drink off his friends. On this occasion, my sister Barbara was just passing by across the road, so I shouted to her to lend us a couple of bob and we went into the Wimpy for a drink and a bun.

The next time I saw Dave, he'd joined Deep Purple and had just got back from Sweden, where the band had sent their new lead singer to have his cock-eye straightened. Suddenly it wasn't 'Eh, Roy' any more but 'Man' and 'Hey, cool, mother, lay it down, man.' Now, Mick, George and I used to wear loon pants, cravats and flower chains and we'd all had our hair permed like Kevin Keegan – we looked like three lollipops – but this was different. We'd kept our Teesside accents, whereas Dave had bought into the hippie vibe lock, stock and barrel. He'd become one of them. One of the beautiful people

The Bay City Rollers also started out as a club act. The night that they were number one in the charts, they were on at a club in Redcar – and all because of the sheer bloody-mindedness that was the hallmark of most club committees. The Rollers had asked if they could be bought out of their contract because they were number one in the charts and because they had a big tour coming up. But the committee said no. They'd booked the Rollers and paid for the Rollers, so they were bloody well getting the Rollers.

Club committee members were the type of people who worked diligently all day, quiet as a mouse. Then, every evening, they'd go down to the club, pin a little badge to their lapel and turn into little Hitlers. It didn't take a degree in psychology to work out why they were so unpleasant. All day, at work, the little committee member would have been ordered about by his foreman. Then, at home, he'd have been bossed about by his wife. But when he walked in that club, he was on the committee and that little badge should have said 'God' because now it was *his* turn to boss people around. And so he took it out on anybody who crossed his radar, especially the acts.

'You *will* put that *there*. You *won't* put that *there*,' he'd snap. 'We want no blue stuff. We want no filth. We want three half-hour spots and make the first one twenty minutes and the last one forty minutes.' Those were the kind of demands and skewed logic we came to expect from club chairmen.

The bigger clubs had full-time committee members who drew a wage off the club and who through sheer greed ended clubland in the mid-1980s by refusing to scale back their wage demands when the audiences got smaller. Clubland went to the wall because it couldn't afford to support all the committee members' expenses.

The best clubs were those run as commercial concerns by an

entrepreneur – places like the Frontier Club in Batley, a little block of old-style Las Vegas in a West Yorkshire street of second-hand car dealerships and theme bars. The owners of these independent clubs could be just as ruthless as the chairmen of working men's clubs – there's a sign backstage at the Frontier that says: 'One-hour set plus the encore, please. Short show = short pay' – but they respected the acts as fellow professionals. The problem with working men's and social clubs was that they were run by amateurs who regarded professional entertainers as crooks who wanted to rip them off.

If there was one thing that united club chairmen, it was that they were awkward bastards to a man. In twenty years of playing the clubs, I never met a chairman who wanted to be helpful or cooperative. They just weren't nice people.

In those early days, it was up to the club chairman whether we got paid or not. If they didn't like our act or if we misbehaved in any way, the chairman would come into our dressing room and tell us we were getting 'paid off'. It meant we weren't getting a penny. Even if the audience had roared with approval and called for encores, the club chairman was the judge and jury. It was up to him to decide if we deserved our fee.

As Alcock & Brown we had an act that, while it wasn't good enough to sell out at the Palladium in London, was certainly a good clubland act. Most of it had evolved from the routines we'd developed with The Nuts, so there were a couple of parodies of adverts, a few silly songs and some gags based on props we brought on stage. We'd round off the evening with a couple of well-known hits to get the audience dancing.

Even the very best of clubland acts could have a bad night because few ever entertained people who had bought tickets specifically to see them. The punters had gone to the club for a pint, a fag, the bingo and the raffle. They could not have cared less who was on stage and they didn't realise it had taken us eight hours to get to the club and that we needed to earn our fee to put petrol in our van and to pay for our lodgings that night. Thinking we were earning a fortune, they'd moan at us for the couple of shillings it cost them to get into the club and wouldn't realise that we often didn't have a penny to scratch our arses with.

An agent had booked us on a tour of clubs in North Wales that was typical of our experiences in those days. On the first night, the club chairman said we were rubbish and we were paid off. The second night, they gave us half our money, which paid for fish and chips and some petrol. We didn't work the third night. The fourth night went well and we were paid in full. And so it continued. By the end of the week, we'd played eight shows, but had picked up our full fee only twice. Nevertheless, we were convinced that we'd earn our full fee of fifty quid on the last night, which would be enough to get us home, so we spent our last pennies on a few drinks. But when it came to the last show we didn't get paid, so George was forced to beg the petrol money off Alan Earle, his boss at the Guitarzan shop in Slaggy Island, where he did a bit of part-time work.

Having often not earned a penny all week and been insulted or belittled by a club chairman, I found it difficult not to lose my temper when we were pushed into a corner. Lashing out was always a mistake because as soon as any of us lost our cool, we were the bad bastards.

Playing a social club in the North-East one evening, we were nearing the end of our act. We were playing 'You Never Can Tell' by Chuck Berry and everybody was up dancing. Full of beer, they were having a great time, shouting 'More! More! More!' for an encore. It was eleven o'clock and we'd been on stage since eight, so we looked at the concert chairman. He held up his finger to signal one more tune. We crashed into 'Rock Around The

Clock' by Bill Haley and his Comets, the crowd whooped with joy, we played the last verse and chorus a second time and then finished with a big flourish.

'That's it, ladies and gentlemen,' I said as the house lights came on. 'Goodnight, ladies and gentlemen. You've been a great crowd. Please don't forget your coats and handbags . . .'

Up in the dressing room, we were taking off our shirts and jackets when the chairman came in. 'Right, get the gear off the stage. Come on, lads, hurry up. It's a lock-up club. We have to go home.'

'Can you just give us a chance to just to get our gear off?' I said.

'Don't be fucking answering me back. Just get your kit off stage.'

'Whoa, whoa. I've got a son older than you. Don't you talk to me like that.'

'Get the kit off or I'll get it off for you.'

'You touch any of them drums, them guitars, them amps, them speakers, and you're in a lot of trouble, mate.'

'Get the kit off *now*,' the chairman said. 'Or I'll get the police.'

'We'd better get the kit, Roy . . .' Mick said.

'No, just stay here,' I said. 'We've only been off stage for five minutes.'

Sure enough, two coppers turned up. 'Have you got a problem, mate?' one of them said.

'No, we haven't,' I said. 'We've just finished. We've gone over the time, people were late drinking in the club when they shouldn't be and that twat there—'

'There's no need for that language,' the copper interrupted.

'—just told us to get the kit off the stage and we haven't even had time to put our stuff in our bags yet. We *will* get the kit off the stage, no doubt about that.'

With five committee members looking on, their chests puffed out and their hands behind their backs, we dismantled our kit and carried it out, taking our time to do it carefully.

'You're being awkward. You *will* be arrested,' the chairman said. 'You're trespassing.'

I put down the drum I was carrying. 'Do you know, mate, not only will we never come back to this club again, but you'll need more than the police. You'll need the fucking army if you don't shut your mouth 'cos I'll smack you in it.'

We finished loading the van, got in, drove around the corner to the roundabout, went right around it and came back. We waited around the corner from the club until I saw the chairman go back inside. Grabbing a brick off the ground, I ran over to the chairman's car and hurled the brick through its windscreen. Served the cheeky bastard right.

Another time, we arrived late at a club at which there were three flights of stairs up to the concert room. As usual, I was the spokesman and I had to tell the chairman we'd had a flat tyre.

'Not another flat tyre,' he said.

'No, we only had the one.'

'I hear this from you bands all the time when you are late. Can't you get here on time?' He was standing with his left arm raised, totally for the benefit of the crowd. I could see the audience were looking at the chairman holding his watch out in front of himself, thinking: Good old Arthur, there he is, looking at his watch and giving the band a hard time.

'Do you see what time it is here?' the chairman said, pointing at his watch. 'You were on at eight o'clock.'

'Well, how are we doing?'

'What do you mean, how are we doing?'

'If we were on at eight o'clock, how are we doing?'

'Is that supposed to be funny?'

'Well, I thought it was funny.'

The chairman paced the stage while we were setting up our gear, tut-tutting and humming louder and louder. It was obvious to me that his wife had just bought him a new watch and that he wanted an opportunity to show it off. And throughout it all, I could see the audience watching the chairman's antics: Aye, Arthur will pay them off, you know. He'll pay them off. He won't have this, you know.

As I tightened the screws on my drum kit, I called over to the chairman. 'Will you do us a favour, mate? Will you stop walking up and down, looking at your watch? You are making us look cunts.'

'You should have been here at eight o'clock.'

It was too much. I took the stanchion that attached my cowbell to my drum kit and walked over to the chairman.

'Can I have a look at that watch?'

The chairman proudly held it out in front of me, revelling in making the point that it was nearly half past eight.

BAP! I hit the watch cleanly with a single stroke. I could have hit him on the knuckles. I could have hit him on the arm. But I didn't. I hit the watch smack in the middle. And it just disintegrated.

The chairman looked straight at me. 'My wife bought me that watch.'

'Well, she'll have to get you another fucker, won't she?'

'Will she?'

'Yes. And you'll have to ring the agent and get another band, because we are fucking off home.'

The lads looked at me. 'Get the gear off,' I said.

'But it's taken us half an hour to carry all the gear up the stairs . . .'

'*Get the gear off the stage*. We're fucking off. Or you are playing without a drummer.' Again, my temperament could only take so much.

But it wasn't always an awkward chairman that caused us problems. The audience could be just as troublesome and would think nowt of throwing a pint of beer over us if they thought we were no good. After one soaking too many, I had an idea. The next time we walked on stage, instead of my usual attire of a checked or tartan suit, I was dressed in a suit made of beer towels. 'Throw all the beer you like,' I said. 'I'm ready for it.'

We were playing a club in a village just outside Sunderland when a fight broke out between a stag party of about twenty lads and another dozen or so locals. I tried to calm it down from the stage but nobody took a blind bit of notice of me, so I walked off. I'd got back to the dressing room when I realised that my two prize Bose speakers, which were small but very powerful, were still on stage.

Standing at the side of the stage, I shouted: 'George, mind them speakers.'

George grabbed the speakers and inched through the crowd, fists and glasses flying all around him as he made his way to the dressing room.

'How are we going to get out?' I said.

'We'll get out the window,' Mick suggested.

George went first, sliding easily through the opening and dropping down into the car park outside. 'You're all right,' he shouted.

I went feet first and got my arse through the window, but then came to a sudden stop. 'My bollocks are caught in the catch, you bastard,' I shouted.

I couldn't see the floor outside, so George shouted: 'Just push yourself.'

I dropped onto a car, leaving a massive dent in the bonnet. George and Mick couldn't speak, they were laughing so much as we jumped in the van and sped off.

If it wasn't for the pranks and high jinks – and Mick and George's easygoing humour – I wouldn't have been able to put up with petty club chairmen and hostile audiences. We had a well-rehearsed revenge repertoire for the worst clubs. Most clubs had a bingo machine. Usually it was a simple glass box on four legs with a fan in the bottom and a set of table-tennis balls with numbers painted on them inside it. Someone on the club committee would start the bingo by switching on the fan. The balls would blow around the box until one got caught in a little chute. A small metal prong at the top of the chute stopped the ball from escaping, holding it in place until the bingo-caller removed it and announced the number. If we really had the hump with a club, we'd bend the wire prong. As soon as the fan was switched on, the balls would fly out of the chute and they wouldn't be able to play bingo until they'd collected them all.

A lot of the time we relied on basic spontaneity to relieve the tension of a bloody-minded audience or chairman. At Black Hill Social Club at Consett, our act was going down like a knackered lift. Nobody was laughing.

'There's nothing like a good act,' I said. 'And we're nothing like a good act.'

Instead of a laugh or some applause, I heard a click and then a whirring sound. I looked around. The electric stage curtains were closing on us. The bastard chairman was shutting them.

Thinking on my feet, I jumped in front of the curtains just as they came together and closed behind me.

'I think your chairman wants me off the stage here,' I said, 'but as far as I'm—'

Silence. The bastard had switched the microphone off.

'*It doesn't bother me,*' I yelled and started shouting the rest of our act. But there was no point. No one in the audience was laughing and I had to give in. I walked off stage.

At another small club where hardly any of the audience were listening to us, I asked Mick if he had any matches. He passed me a lighter and I walked out into the audience to where an old bloke was reading the newspaper, his feet up on a chair and his newspaper held up to obscure his view of the stage. I crept up to him, ducking beneath the bottom of his newspaper. I lit it. For a second or two, he didn't realise it was on fire. Then the flames caught and the paper went up in his fingers. Jumping to his feet, he shouted abuse. 'You big stupid fucking bastard!' His sudden exit from the club got the biggest laugh of the evening.

Often the laughs came when our act went wrong. The Alcock & Brown act relied on a lot of stage props and one of our best was a talking bucket. We'd put the bucket on a table with a curtain around its legs and get our roadie to hide beneath the table, operating the bucket.

It all went swimmingly until we took on a new roadie. His name was Derek, but we called him Spotty Muldoon because he was always covered in spots and because he wore a grey RAF greatcoat that was so big (and he was so thin) that he could turn around in it without the coat changing direction.

George explained the routine to Spotty Muldoon. At the end of each chorus of 'Can't Help Falling In Love With You' I'd turn to George and Mick to ask if they were all right. At that point, Spotty Muldoon would have to pull a string under the table to make the lid of the bucket lift up like a big mouth to say: 'Yeah, I'm all right.' It always got a big laugh.

'How will the audience hear me?' Spotty said.

'We'll give you a microphone below the table,' Mick said.

We reached the point in the act where I sang the song. 'You all right?' I said at the end of the first chorus.

The top of the lid rose up, then clanked down without saying anything.

I sang the last line of the chorus and asked the question again. 'Are you all right?'

Silence and no movement from the lid.

'I *said*: are you all right?'

'And *I* said: the fucking string's snapped,' Spotty bellowed over the PA. The whole club cracked up. Mick, George and I couldn't carry on for laughing. We tried to play the next verse, but our fingers wouldn't play the instruments.

At another venue, it was the support act that provided the laughs. We were on with two strippers and an act that I'd been asked to introduce. I met him in the slips at the side of the stage. He was shaking with nerves.

'What are you called?' I asked. Raving Rupert, he said.

'Ladies and gentlemen, please welcome Raving Rupert,' I announced over the PA.

The music started. Running on stage, Raving Rupert caught one of the girl dancers with his guitar, banged her on the head and knocked her over. He tripped over his guitar lead and caught his head on the microphone. Then, as he cleared his throat and tried to pull himself together, he leant forward to speak into the microphone and knocked his nose on it. Before he could say a word, his nose began to bleed, the audience started to laugh at him and he had to leave the stage. The biggest laugh came, however, as we walked on.

'Ladies and gentlemen,' I said. 'Raving Rupert, my arse. You mean Clumsy Fucking Rupert.' The place erupted.

One of Mick's many virtues was that he was a good mechanic. At first, we used a red Morris Minor van to cart our gear to gigs, stuffing all our equipment – guitars, amps, a drum kit and a PA system – in the back. Two of us would push the door shut while the other one locked it. Then Mick brought along an old Transit that he'd repaired. It was falling to bits, with a red toffee paper stuck over a light bulb in place of the glass on one of the brake lights. It didn't last long.

Our next band van was a Bedford. We packed it up one afternoon, ready for a gig in Darlington that evening. When it came to leaving at five o'clock, the van wouldn't start and I started panicking. We had to be at the club by seven o'clock.

'I know what's happened,' Mick said, opening the bonnet. Standing beside him, I peered into the engine. Everything looked OK until I noticed two big thick red books, larger and wider than phone directories, wedged either side of the engine.

'The engine mountings snapped,' Mick said. 'Them books are keeping the engine level, but it's slipped down a bit.'

'Where've you got them from?'

'The library,' Mick said. And then he started laughing. 'They're not due back for another week.'

'Well, we'd better get this gig done, then.'

Mick fiddled around for a bit. There were a couple of grunts and swear words, then he emerged from under the bonnet with a smile on his face.

'That should have done it,' he said as he fired up the engine. It made some stomach-churning noises on the way to Darlington, but we made it to the club on time.

As in the days of The Nuts and the Four Man Band, we rarely insured or taxed our vans. We just couldn't afford it. And when the money for petrol ran out, we'd wait until midnight, drive onto a caravan site, cut off the engine and glide towards a car, remove the fuel cap, siphon out some petrol, then scarper as fast as we could. At one campsite, Ronnie, our driver at the time, swallowed the petrol. 'Don't have a cigarette,' I said. 'Your arse will blow up and you'll get home before we do.' But running out of petrol was the least of our worries. We broke down so many times, Beryl thought I was having an affair with the AA man.

By late 1974, Mick and George started to tire of the stresses of erratic earnings and life on the road, and I was wanting to stretch my wings. I'd already started playing the occasional solo night when Mick and George told me they were packing in Alcock & Brown to form a duo that would give them more time to earn money from their day jobs. Meanwhile, I appeared on television for the first – and almost the last – time.

I had bought myself a little John Gray banjo-ukulele and would sit in my flat, practising George Formby songs. One day, an agent rang up while I was rehearsing.

'I've got a little acting job for you on a programme going out on Tyne Tees Television called *Sounds of Britain*,' he said. 'I can't get the whole band on it. They just want somebody, a big fella, so I thought of you.'

The agent explained what would happen. 'A monkey comes ashore at Hartlepool and you arrest the monkey.'

'What, a real monkey?'

'Oh yeah. It's from Scarborough Zoo. It's called Max.'

I drove to the beach at Hartlepool where the camera crew were waiting with Max, a massive chimpanzee. I was given a policeman's outfit to wear, ushered into a caravan for make-up and taken to meet the producer, called Heather.

'It's a history thing about who hung the monkey in Hartlepool,' Heather explained. 'What I'd like you to do is walk up and say " 'Ello, 'ello, 'ello" to the monkey. Max will just look at you. You then say: "Can I take down your particulars?" And that's it.'

We rehearsed a few times. Then they took the chain off the monkey's neck and he sat there on the beach. Holding a note-book and pencil, I went up to him.

' 'Ello, 'ello, 'ello,' I said. 'And what's your name?'

The monkey reached to grab one of the shiny silver buttons on my tunic, but accidentally grabbed my bollocks instead.

Thinking he'd got hold of a button and squeezing as hard as he could, he tried to rip off my testicles through my trousers. I was in agony. The camera crew were on the floor, howling with laughter.

Eventually, the crew prised the chimp's hand off my trousers and we nailed the scene in the next take. As I'd been such a good sport, Heather offered me a spot in the studio. A few days later, I was standing in the studio, pissed up, dressed in my Alcock & Brown flying helmet and a multicoloured patchwork suit I'd had made to replace the beer-mat suit because I thought it looked more professional. Playing the banjo-ukulele, I sang 'Jollity Farm', a mildly rude song by the Bonzo Dog Doo-Dah Band. At the end of the performance, a production assistant came up to me.

'Thanks very much, Roy,' she said. 'What should we call you on the credits?'

I thought for a short while. I didn't know what to say. Most people knew me as Roy Vasey, but my stage name in the trio was Mr Brown. I was just about to say 'Just call me Roy Brown' when I thought why not add my nickname around Redcar?

'I'm Roy "Chubby" Brown,' I said. And my stage persona was born.

CHAPTER TEN

MALTESE MAYHEM

SHE WORE A red scarf to cover a head made bald by radiation. Her skin was waxy and stiff like plastic. It was obvious that she was very ill.

'We used to come and see you all the time,' she said as we both sat waiting for our appointment. I smiled and thought I'd crack a joke, but at nine a.m. in a cancer ward the atmosphere's not conducive to comedy.

'Really?' I said. 'What's your name?'

'Pauline.'

'Hello, Pauline,' I said. 'How long have you been coming?'

'This is my third term,' she said. A term of treatment was typically six weeks. With maybe a couple of months between each term, that meant she had been coming to the hospital for the best part of a year.

'I read about you in the paper and saw you on the television being interviewed about your cancer,' Pauline said.

'That's right. But I'm not too bad now, thanks.'

We chatted some more, then Pauline was called for her

appointment. A couple of weeks later I was sitting in the waiting room when one of the regulars sat down next to me.

'Hiya,' I said. 'How are you?'

'I'm pretty good, thanks,' he said, 'but Pauline . . . you know, we lost Pauline at the weekend.'

'The lady with the red headscarf?'

'Yes. She went on Saturday.'

Life suddenly seemed very insignificant. I'd known lots of people who had died, but that morning I was struck by how life just doesn't mean anything really. Not a thing. It made me feel like we were put on this planet for a purpose and when we're finished with, we're slung out like a bin bag. Straight onto the rubbish heap.

Sitting in that waiting room five days a week, my mind would whirr like a computer. I couldn't help it. When you're frightened and anxious, terrible things go through your mind. Or at least, they went through mine.

Part of me was pleased to be sitting there, waiting for my daily blast of radiation, because I saw people who were worse off than me and it made me think that I had a better chance than them. I know that's a terrible thing to say, but I'd be surprised if I was the only one to have such selfish thoughts.

And although we all sat there sympathising with each other, saying 'Oh, you poor bugger, I am *so* sorry,' I knew that each and every one of us, at the back of our minds, was thinking the same thing – Thank fuck it ain't me. Thank God I am still here.

It's the dark side of what we call human nature. There's something in us that makes us sympathise and feel concern for someone and genuinely hope that they will pull through their illness, and then, when they die, we go home, sit down in our favourite armchair and think to ourselves thank fuck that wasn't me. When I felt sorry for Pauline – the eighteen weeks of radiotherapy burning and discolouring her skin, turning her bald, making her unable to eat, confining her to the toilet, making her cough all night – I wondered if it wasn't all a waste of time. And I wondered why, when the operations and the drugs and the doctor's attentions and the radiotherapy don't work, we all don't just give in?

So now, when someone says to me that they sympathise with people who have cancer, I want to ask them: have you had it? Because I thought I sympathised. I thought I knew what it was like. But I didn't until I had it myself. You can't sympathise or empathise with something you know nowt about.

And then there are the people who tell you cancer is not as bad as it used to be. They're the ones that say it was different thirty years ago, when cancer usually meant you had only weeks or months left to live. And because of that, cancer doesn't get the sympathy that it used to get. But what those people don't mention is that cancer is still the number-one killer, terminating 135,000 people's lives prematurely every year and bringing misery to many more families. And what they also don't say is that cancer discriminates. While I was getting my radiotherapy treatment, I discovered that people who come from deprived areas are at much greater risk of developing and dying from ten of the major cancers than people from better-off areas. When I heard that, it suddenly all made sense. It helped explain why so many people I'd grown up with in Grangetown had died young. And it also explained why, when I was a kid, people used to say that Middlesbrough, with its filthy air, dirty factories and run-down housing, had more hospitals with cancer wards than any other similarly sized city in Britain.

●

I didn't become a solo comic overnight. It was a slow, gradual process that began when I stepped out from behind the drums on the night of an early 1970s power cut at Haverton Hill Working Men's Club. While the other three members of The Nuts stood in the darkness, waiting patiently for the electricity to come back on, I attempted to keep the audience amused by shouting some jokes out into the darkness. From the moment that evening when the darkness returned the favour with a few titters – and then some guffaws and belly laughs – I wondered if I'd ever be able to keep the laughs coming for a whole set and with the lights on.

Over the next few years, when I was playing with The Nuts or Jason and Everard or Alcock & Brown, I'd slip in the occasional solo comedy spot when a club was looking for a solo comic. My first proper solo booking was at the cricket club in Redcar, a wooden hut beside a cricket green at the end of Coatham High Street. It wasn't the Palladium in London or the South Pier in Blackpool, but it was a start.

From then on, as well as practising my drumming or learning the banjo or rehearsing my piano playing, I started to work diligently on my gags. I set myself the task of writing around ten jokes a day, a practice to which I've stuck ever since then. As long as one of the ten jokes is good enough to keep in my act, I'd have 365 new gags a year and my act would never get stale.

I've always prided myself on writing all my own material, never relying on professional comedy writers to supply me with gags. Because I tour constantly and usually visit the same venues at about the same time each year, I add new jokes and drop old jokes all the time so that by the time I return to any venue a year after I last visited it, my act has changed completely and is entirely fresh to the audience.

Of course, like every comic, I borrowed heavily from other comedians' acts when I was starting out, but I was always happy to acknowledge it. I once came off stage at a small club where another comedian was playing after me.

'I wrote that gag,' he said referring to one of the jokes in my act.

'You wrote that gag? Are you sure now?' I said. 'When you wrote it, you hadn't just been watching Laurel and Hardy in *Way Out West*, had you? Because the bastard line's in that film.'

'No, I wrote that gag.'

All comics do it. Maybe they just need a pat on the back or maybe they don't want anyone to realise they get their jokes out of books or from someone else with a better brain than them.

When I started writing, most of my material would come from things about which the lads in the band would say, 'You should say that on stage, that's quite funny. You should use that.'

On one particular day we were all in the van, driving through Slaggy Island when a dog walked in front of the van.

'That fucking dog must have seen us, he must have seen the van coming, yet he still walked out in front of it,' said Mick, who was driving the van.

'It's probably an Irish Wolf Hound – walks backwards and wags its head,' I said. I used that joke in my act a few years later and when I appeared on *New Faces*. After that, I heard it again and again, particularly from other top professional Irish comedians.

Another gag that was mine was: 'Have you heard about the Irish Evel Knievel? He tried to jump twelve motorbikes in his bus. He'd have made it but somebody rang the bell.'

Again, I've heard dozens of comics claim it was their joke. I should have copyrighted it, but I've never copyrighted anything because I used other people's material when I was starting out – it would have been hypocritical. The longer I spent in the business, the more I developed my own style and my own ideas. And nothing gives me a bigger thrill than cracking a gag that I've written, not one that I've heard. It's what makes any comic want to get up in the morning.

Every day, I'll read all the newspapers looking for inspiration. My humour is built on the shared experiences of working-class people, so I'll look for the kind of stories that everyone will have been talking about – celebrity scandals, big news stories such as the tsunami in Asia or the terrorist bombings in London, titbits from *Coronation Street* and *EastEnders* or *Big Brother*, and whatever's going on in football. And if there's anything filthy or salacious, like the schoolteacher who mistakenly took a video of her bedroom antics into school and showed it to her pupils, then I'll seize upon it with glee because, more often than not, sex makes us all laugh.

I'll write a few words about a story from the newspapers on a page of my notebook, then below it I'll write the first thing that comes into my head. And I'll keep adding to the list, until I write something that somehow triggers a joke. It's a hit-and-miss process of word association, but it's always worked for me. So, in the case of the teacher with her home-made sex video, I wrote: Teacher . . . sex video . . . school . . . pupils . . . classroom . . . lessons . . . maths . . . history . . . dinosaurs . . . extinct. And then the gag came to me: 'Eee, did you hear about the teacher in Essex who took a home-porn video of her sucking off her husband into school? She thought the video was about the history of dinosaurs, so she put it in the video and played it to her class. And now the kids in that school think dinosaurs ruled the Earth *after* Miss Jones was fucked up the arse.'

As long as it makes me laugh, I'll jot it down in my notebook. I'll try it out on the audience that night and if it gets a good response and I still like it, I'll keep it in my act. Some jokes last a long time. Others make people laugh for only a few performances. Then they lose their currency. Others fall flat on their faces and get relegated to the notebook for ever. And on some days when I can't think of any new jokes, I'll look through my notebooks and spot something that might not have been particularly funny at the time but which, with a few changes to update it to a current event, becomes a winning gag.

When I look back at my notebooks from the early days, when I was playing my first solo gigs, the topics of my jokes are not that different from today. In those days, there were more jokes about clubs and club chairmen because I always played clubs and because clubland was a big fixture in the lives of my audiences, but otherwise the subject matter was the same: work, football and women. The only thing that has changed is that almost all the jokes were one-liners, whereas nowadays I tell more stories and sing more comedy songs.

'My girlfriend's a wardrobe – tall with drawers.' That was my opening line in those days. I'd then knock off eight to ten more gags in quick succession.

'She walked in tonight. The committee man said: "Are those your tits or are you smuggling coconuts?"'

'I told him that the doctors had put her on a stable diet – she needs her oats twice a day.

'I treat my women like dirt – I hide them under the bed.

'I had two girlfriends at the same time. Surrender Brenda and Give-In Kim. They named their bras after Middlesbrough Football Club – plenty of support but no cups.

'Brenda wouldn't hurt a fly, unless it was on the front of your trousers.

'When I met her, she said she was thirteen. "That's okay," I said. "I'm not superstitious."

'Kim had a tattoo on her chest: "In case of a sexual assault: This Way Up."

'I took them both fishing. My mate said: "Did you catch anything?" I said: "I'll let you know in two days' time."'

And so it would go on right through my set. A quick-fire onslaught of one-liners built around the basic things we all had in common. I'd grown up on a rough council estate and I knew that most of the club audiences were just like me. They'd all been snotty-nosed, raggedy-arsed kids who hadn't worn a uniform to school, who didn't take any notice of the teacher and who had left school without having learned anything, not even how to spell. So there was no point in trying to make them laugh with smart-alec jokes and sophisticated witticisms. Like me, they used humour as a way of getting away from the miserable realities of their lives. By turning everything into a joke, they made their lives more bearable. And because our lives were crude and harsh and unrelenting and unforgiving of any weaknesses, our humour was that way too.

Playing solo gigs was more satisfying – I got all the applause, I had full control of the act and I got all the money – but it also meant that I took all the abuse on my own. Pit-village clubs were the hardest venues of all, places like Blackhall Colliery, Easington and Houghton-le-Spring. Many of the miners had never experienced life outside their little village and they didn't have time for reading newspapers or watching television. I used to think half of them weren't even aware the *Titanic* had sunk, so there was no point in talking about things in the news. The outside world meant nothing to them. The miners were down the pit for eight hours a day and all they wanted in the evening was three or four pints of beer and a laugh before going home.

In the pit clubs, everyone had their own seat and woe betide anyone who came in and sat in Archie's chair. 'Archie's been sat there for the last sixteen year,' they'd say. 'He'll be in at ten to eight.'

And sure enough, at ten to eight the door would open, Archie would come in and you'd be told, 'You're sat in my seat, mate.'

The attitude of the pit clubs to outsiders could be seen in the way they treated visiting acts. At Peterlee Rugby Club, I had to get changed in the ladies' toilet. Until then, I'd always thought it was impossible for women to miss the toilet bowl, but in Peterlee there was piss all over the floor. Conditions were just as grim on stage. Faced with miners' attitudes, my jokes had to be as simple as possible, talking about things we all had in common, like women and drink and shitting and fucking. I had to go there cap in hand, arse-licking all the time just to get more work. If I succeeded in a pit village, they liked me for life. If they hated me, I'd never go back.

Standing at the urinal in the toilet in a pit-village club, midway through the evening, I was tapped on the shoulder by a miner. 'I didn't think much of your first half,' he said. 'In the second half, can you tell some jokes we know?'

That was typical.

I was playing Easington Colliery, a mining village between Hartlepool and Sunderland, where I'd been booked for a Sunday lunchtime in a club notorious for the ferocity of its members. Sunday lunchtimes in pit-village clubs always followed the same ritual. The doors would open at 11.30 a.m. to an all-male audience. A comic would come on first, then a stripper, then another comic, and finally another stripper. The comics, however, knew the audience were really there only for one thing: the girls.

By midday the miners had sunk two or three pints each and were well into their session. I could tell they were in no mood for comedy as I climbed onto the stage and began my act.

'Good afternoon, gentlemen. Welcome to Easington Working Men's Club . . .' I said as a miner walked through the audience towards the stage. I thought he was going to make an announcement, maybe ask one of the audience to move their car because it was blocking the door.

'Will you get off?' he said.

'What?'

'I want you off. Will you leave the stage?'

'I have come all the way from Redcar,' I said. I needed the money.

'I don't care where you have come from. I want you off the stage. You're crap.'

'I'm not coming off the stage. I've been told to do a one-hour slot and I am going to stand here for an hour by hook or by fucking crook.'

'No, you're not.'

I turned to the audience: 'Lads, the concert chairman wants me to come off stage. Silly bastard.'

Some of the miners laughed. Others started to hiss and boo. I didn't know if the brickbats were directed at me or at the concert chairman. 'I'm not coming off,' I said. 'So you can please your fucking selves.'

I continued telling jokes, running through my usual routine. Most of the audience watched and listened in silence. I could tell what they thinking – 'This lad has some bottle. Nothing fazes him' – but there were very few laughs.

Suddenly the side doors opened. I turned around. Silhouetted against the midday sun was the concert chairman standing in the doorway with two huge dogs tugging on leads either side of him. The dogs were growling like they'd had nowt to eat for a week. The chairman walked in with the dogs salivating and gagging to be let loose on me.

'Are you coming off the stage?' he said. 'If you're not, I'll set the dogs on you.'

'All right, all right, mate. I can take a hint,' I said as the audience started slow-clapping and the first of the strippers came on. Sometimes there was no point in fighting the mood of the crowd.

Working men's clubs outside the pit villages could be just as bad, particularly on Tyneside or on the Wear. At the Commercial Road Club in Sunderland, a fight broke out in the bar and spilled over into the lounge. By the time I was on stage, the fight had stopped, but the brawlers were in the concert room and giving me trouble. They'd had too much to drink and were heckling me. I was having a go back. Just the usual replies to trouble: 'You have got the brains of a fucking wasp, mate' and 'Don't kick him up the arse, you'll give him brain damage.'

I came off, thinking I'd had a fairly decent night and been lucky to survive. The chairman came into the dressing room. 'Eeh, you told that fucking load of bastards, didn't you?' he said.

'Aye, fucking did. They don't get far with me.'

Feeling pleased with myself, I carted my gear out of the club to find my van up on bricks. The wheels were gone and the hecklers had got the last laugh. I was furious, but I used it the next day in a gag that used to get a good response. 'I live on the Commercial Road Estate in Sunderland,' I said. Most of the audience knew the Commercial Road in Sunderland by its rotten reputation and usually there'd be a ripple of 'oohs' and 'aahs' around the crowd. 'The milkman come out of our house the other day,' I continued, 'and his donkey was on bricks.'

Towards the end of my stint with George and Mick in Alcock & Brown, I took on more and more work from a local lad called Brian Findlay. Brian was a well-known Teesside show-business agent who had booked The Nuts, Jason and Everard, and Alcock & Brown into hundreds of clubs in the late 1960s and early 1970s.

Even by his own admission, Brian was not a good business-man, but he was one of the lads. He was a rascal who liked a drink, a bet on the horses and a good card game. He once went on a trip with a bunch of theatrical agents from the North-East down to London, playing cards all the way to King's Cross. By the time the train arrived in London, Brian had to lend all of them their spending money because he'd won everything off them.

Brian liked to be around performers. He loved clubland, owned several clubs himself and would buy acts from or trade them with other agents. Most of the acts were dreadful (one was a magician who accidentally set fire to the dove he was hiding in his top hat) but there were so many clubs in those days that anyone could get a gig.

Towards the end of my time with George and Mick in Alcock & Brown, Brian started pushing me to go solo full-time, but he wasn't particularly ambitious for me. As far as he was concerned, we were just pals and his role in the friendship was to find me work. It was a good working relationship until I needed Brian to sort out some trouble. Brian didn't have a hurtful bone in his body and he was hopeless at confronting tough club chairmen.

I was about to play the Beechwood and Easterside Social Club in Middlesbrough, which had just built a new concert hall seating seven hundred people. It was Middlesbrough's largest club and I knew that people had been queuing in the street to see me. The club committee had packed the place to bursting point with punters paying two quid a ticket. The box office takings were £1,400 and I was getting just seventy pounds of that.

'Brian . . .' I said. 'Isn't it about time you tapped Beechwood for some more money?'

'You can't do that!' he said. 'If I ask them for some more money they'll say no. And they'll pull all my other acts out.'

So I found myself in the position of backbone to many of Brian's other acts. Brian would ring up a club and try to book a two-month residency for one of his less successful acts by using me as the carrot. 'You can't have Chubby if you don't take . . .' he'd say. It was blackmail, but all agents did it.

Alcock & Brown had just split up when Brian called me with

an offer of work in Malta. 'Roy, the money's not very good,' he said, 'but you get free accommodation, a free car, fifteen pounds spending money and four weeks to lie in the sun.'

I thought about it. I didn't have much on in Redcar and at least it would be a holiday of sorts. Although I'd docked in several foreign ports while I'd been in the merchant navy, I'd never been on holiday abroad, so I collected the tickets, flew to Valletta and made my own way to the Pescatora restaurant at St Paul's Bay, my home for the next month. At the restaurant, a lad in the kitchen gave me some keys to a villa and an old Ford Anglia car, which had neither driver's door nor windscreen wipers. The wipers didn't concern me – it was August, 114 degrees Fahrenheit in the shade and unlikely to rain – but the missing driver's door was a worry. Then I thought about the twenty-minute journey from the airport to the restaurant. The buildings I'd seen were in a terrible state, crumbling and pock-marked with bullet holes. They looked like they'd seen the end of the Second World War just a week earlier. And the famous green buses that cruised the Maltese streets had no windows, chunks missing from their tyres and passengers hanging on at the back. Dust rose from the roads when cars sped past – something I'd previously seen only in movies. So when I looked at that battered Ford Anglia, a car that would have been scrapped in Britain, I accepted that it was nothing unusual for Malta and that I would have to get used to it.

The lad from the restaurant took me to a house in Bugibba, a nearby resort. From the outside, the house looked like a Mexican hacienda. Inside it was dilapidated and dirty with a load of scruffy furniture stacked up in one room. I turned on a tap. The water came out orange. I opened the fridge and a green lizard crawled out. I looked carefully behind the fridge. There was no back to it. I was bewildered and slightly fright-ened, but I had no choice but to get on with it.

I drove back to the Pescatora to meet the band at four o'clock. They were called the Maltese Bums and were famous throughout the island. Basso, the bass player, looked like Demis Roussos and had lived in England with an English girl.

'Are you working for Benny Muscat?' he said.

'Benny Muscat? Who's he?'

'Listen, Roy, I don't give many people advice but just do as Benny fucking tells you.'

Benny was obviously the boss. He had luxury cars, a beautiful yacht and three or four large restaurants on the island. They were some of the smartest buildings in Malta and Benny, when I met him, was one of the smartest men. He wore dark glasses and a sharp suit. All the men who surrounded him were dressed similarly, but their suits were made from slightly cheaper fabrics and cut less generously.

So I just went along with it. Every evening, I did a forty-five-minute spot at the Pescatora, then jumped in my Ford Anglia and drove to Mosta to do another forty-five minutes of comedy at The Whisper, another of Benny's restaurants, opposite a church. One of the chefs would feed me at the end of my second spot, then I had the next day off until about eight p.m., when I had to report to the Pescatora.

After a few days, I got to know the bands at the two restaurants. They were both fantastic. Entirely self-taught, none of the musicians could read a note, but they were instinctive players and extremely good. I thought they were so accomplished because they had nowt else to do but practise. Then I got speaking to Paul, the drummer at The Whisper.

'When you finish here,' I said, 'what do you do then?'

'I play until twelve o'clock, then go home, get changed and go out with my father and brother fishing.'

Paul would fish from midnight until five or six o'clock in the morning. Then he'd go home and sleep until midday. In the afternoon, he worked in an office until six o'clock when he went home, got changed and ran to The Whisper in time for the band to start at eight o'clock. These three jobs netted him around fifty quid a week – about half what I would make on a good night at home.

I spent the first few days in Malta rehearsing with the band. I'd written a song called 'Fat and Tall' and I wanted the band to accompany me while I played the piano and sang. I was due to start playing at Benny's restaurants on my fourth day in Malta. We rehearsed in the morning and then I headed for the beach, buying a loaf of bread, a couple of tins of beans, some cakes and biscuits and some cans of drink on the way. It was ridiculously cheap.

The beach at St Paul's Bay was deserted and I lay in the sun for a couple of hours, thinking that this was the life. It didn't get much better than lying in the sun all day before performing a couple of gigs every evening with accommodation, food and spending money thrown in. I got back to the shabby house and wanted to take a shower, but the waterworks in Malta left so much to be desired that I gave it a miss.

Shortly after six o'clock I got ready for work. It was so hot, I'd been walking around the house in my underpants – and then I caught sight of myself in a mirror. I was red from head to toe. It was no wonder my skin had been stinging so badly. I'd burnt my face, neck, chest, back and the tops of my legs.

I didn't know how I was going to work looking like that, so I dabbed after-sun cream all over myself with a piece of cotton wool. I jumped in the car and raced to the Pescatora, where I ran on stage looking like a ripe strawberry with legs. At the end of my act, I took off my shirt. The skin on my back came away with it. I put on a clean shirt. It was immediately soaked with blood.

'I think you should go to hospital, Roy,' Basso said.

'I've got another fucking show to do and you've just told me that when Benny summons you, you fucking run.'

I raced to The Whisper and put on yet another shirt. The same thing happened – it was covered with bloodstains within minutes, so I walked on sideways, like a crab, so the audience wouldn't see the back of my shirt. I spent my entire act standing still, making sure that only the band could see the agony I was going through.

The next morning, Basso's sister picked me up and took me to Valletta hospital. I'd been there once before, when I was in the merchant navy and had contracted malaria. I was given a ticket and told to wait in a corridor. Hours later and sweating with the pain of my burns, I was called into a room where a bloke in a white coat was standing with a clipboard.

'Are you English?'

'Yes.'

'What can I do for you?'

'I'm badly burned.'

'Oh, you've been a silly lad, haven't you.'

Throughout the time the doctor treated me, a plumber was at work in the room, sawing a pipe a couple of feet away from the treatment table. There was dust everywhere, but they didn't seem to care.

I recovered from the burns over the next few days and had been in Malta for more than a week when I started to run out of the pocket money I'd brought with me. I needed the fifteen quid a week I'd been promised, so I went to the manageress of the Pescatora.

'I've been here ten days and I haven't been paid yet,' I said.

'You want to get *paid*?'

'Yes, I'm supposed to get fifteen pounds pocket money.'

'Oh, forget that,' she said. 'You just go in the kitchen and help yourself.'

'But I can't put food from the kitchen in the car.'

'You don't need petrol. You go to Benny's garage.' She gave me the address of a garage and that was the end of my quest for payment. I never saw a penny of the fee I'd been promised and I wouldn't ever have spoken to Benny had I not made a massive faux pas.

I used to do a routine in which I sat in a cot dressed as a baby, sucking a massive dummy and wearing a giant nappy. On my belly, which hung over my nappy, I wrote 'Empty' with a felt-tip pen. The act wasn't particularly sophisticated – I'd walk around the stage, making baby noises – but I knew I had it down to a fine art and that it hit a nerve because the audience would cry tears of laughter.

I unveiled my baby act on my first Saturday night at the Pescatora. On every other night, the crowd was predominantly British tourists, but Saturday was the big Maltese night out. There were a few laughs, but they soon gave way to a deadly silence.

'Benny wants to speak to you,' Basso hissed from behind his bass guitar as I headed off stage.

'Oh right, I'll ask him for my fifteen fucking quid.'

Benny was standing in the shadows backstage.

'Roy,' he said in a thick accent. 'I watch your act. Is very funny but I am asking you to take out the routine with the baby.'

'Why?'

'Is insult to Maltese people to show skin. I have lots of complaints about it.'

'Oh . . .'

'Very funny – I understand English ways. But *you* have to understand Maltese ways and we don't allow skin, especially in view of public . . .'

That was all he said to me, but he gave the band a right rollicking. They were told they should have told me, but it just hadn't dawned on any of them to say I could do the baby act any time but Saturday night.

A week after I arrived back in Redcar from Malta, Brian booked me into Blackhall Colliery Working Men's Club. I was standing at the bar when one of the stewards came up to me.

'Now then', he said.

'OK?' I replied.

'No, I am *not* OK. You spoilt my holiday.'

'I spoilt your *holiday*?'

'Yeah. I took my wife and kids to Malta for a holiday. On the second night we went out to this restaurant and you walked on stage. And you took the piss out of the North-East.'

'I am a comedian. That's what I do.'

'But you said there was that much muck and filth and dust and coal and slag and shit in Teesside, you could see a red light in the distance and it got clearer and clearer. And then you realised it was the end of your cigarette.'

'Yeah. It's a joke.'

'Not to me it isn't. Not to me – I protect the North-East.' And he droned on interminably about the North-East until I'd had enough and interrupted him.

'I spoilt your holiday?' I said. 'You went with Thomas Cook or some other travel company for a fortnight's holiday in Malta that cost you an arm and a leg and I spoilt it because I cracked jokes about the North-East?'

'Aye. That's right.'

'As far as I am concerned, you've the brains of a fucking thalidomide fucking wasp with piles and you want putting down.' It was an insult I used a lot in those days. Most of the time, it made whoever I directed it at laugh. But this time it didn't work. As I walked away, the steward hit me with a bicycle chain that he must have kept behind the bar.

I went mad. I jumped on him. I thumped him. I kicked him.

I punched him. I hit him as hard as I could. He tried to fight back, but we were pulled apart by a couple of bouncers. 'I will kill you,' I shouted. 'You fucking twat.'

I walked out and got in my van and left. I phoned Brian the next morning.

'Boy, is it great to be back home,' I said. 'Don't you *ever* book me into Blackhall Colliery again. I'm never going back there.'

'I wouldn't worry about it,' Brian said. 'I just had a call from Middlesbrough TUC Club. They want you.'

'But I've just done it, Brian,' I said, 'just before I went to Malta. I'll die on my arse, man. The same lads get in there all the time, the same football team, the same hairy-arsed scaffold-ers and welders. They'll know my act.'

'Well, they're asking for you back. The comic hasn't turned up and there's a couple of strippers and the Great Enrico. They want you to fill in for the comic and it's an extra fiver for you.'

We agreed to meet at the venue the next night. I got in my van and headed down to the TUC club on Longlands Road in Middlesbrough. I'd often joked about what TUC stood for – Ten Useless Cunts on the committee. When I arrived, Brian was waiting. The chairman told me the running order.

'We're putting the Great Enrico on first, then the strippers, then you're doing your spot, then the strippers again, then Enrico, then you on last.'

As I sat in my dressing room, trying to think of different gags and openers that the crowd wouldn't have heard the last time I played the TUC club, I didn't give the Great Enrico much thought. I'd not heard of him before and I assumed he'd be a tenor.

Shortly before the show was due to start, a huge Scottish bloke with tattoos and curly hair walked in.

'Where's that fucking agent?' he said in a thick Scottish accent.

'This is "that fucking agent",' I said, pointing at Brian. 'He's called Brian and he bought you. He's booked you off another agency.'

Enrico gave Brian a cursory nod, then busied himself getting his costume and props ready. While Enrico was rooting around in his bag, the club chairman came in looking for Enrico's sheet music to give to the band. 'Have you got your dots?' he said.

'I only need music to play me on and off,' Enrico said. '*I* am a *magic* act.'

The chairman walked out, leaving Brian and me looking at each other with raised eyebrows. It seemed a bit odd, a big lad like Enrico being a magic act, but I'd seen stranger things in clubland. Fortunately, Enrico soon relaxed and I found he wasn't quite so much the aggressive Scotsman that he'd first seemed. We cracked open a couple of cans of beer, I sat down on a tall basket that Enrico had brought into the dressing room and we chatted a bit until he was called on stage.

Tom on the organ and Bill on the drums played a fanfare as the concert chairman stepped up to the microphone. 'Good evening, gentlemen . . .' he said. Nobody paid a blind bit of notice. They continued drinking and talking as Enrico walked on stage.

'Good evening, gentlemen,' he said. 'My name is Enrico. It's nice to be here in the TUC Club in Middlesbrough. Has anyone got an apple?'

Silence.

'I said: has anyone got an apple?'

Again, silence. Enrico was staring so hard at a bloke in the audience that I twigged that he must have planted an apple with him earlier.

'Anyone got an *apple*?' Enrico asked, quite clearly directing his question solely at the one bloke in the audience.

'I've eaten it,' the bloke said.

There were a few awkward giggles and all the lads who'd been ignoring Enrico suddenly took an interest.

'You cunt, you've ate my fiver!' Enrico said. 'There was a fiver in that apple.'

That was it. The club erupted with laughter.

'Has anyone got a tomato?' Enrico said.

'You know fucking well we haven't,' another bloke shouted out. 'If we had, you'd have got it in the face five minutes ago!'

Enrico was getting all the laughs, but I wasn't sure if they were laughing at him or with him.

'I daren't ask if anybody's got my fucking orange,' he said.

'Aye, it's here,' someone shouted. And an orange flew through the air, hitting Enrico on the head. He was furious. I could see the steam rising inside him as he went through the rest of his act, trying to salvage his routine with some stupid one-liners when the audience was still laughing about the apple and the tomato. Towards the end, he dipped a torch in a wineglass containing some petrol and lit it. I'd seen strippers do a similar thing, running flaming torches over their bodies, pretending to burn themselves. But the Great Enrico was taking it a stage further. I could smell scorching. He was actually burning himself. Smoke was coming off his arm. This Scot was as hard as nails and he was out to prove it.

A balcony ran around the top of the TUC's concert hall. Standing on the balcony was a big gang of lads who looked like they were out for trouble. One of them shouted down to Enrico.

'Oi! Jock!' he yelled. I saw Enrico wince at being called Jock. 'Give us a light!'

Holding the wineglass of petrol in his hand, Enrico ambled over to the side of the stage near where the lad was standing on the balcony. He took a swig of the petrol and blew a long, roaring flame towards the balcony.

The head of the bloke on the balcony looked like it was on

fire. When the smoke cleared, he was standing absolutely still, his eyes the only white patches in his sooty black face. He looked like Al Jolson.

Enrico finished his act and walked off stage to a few claps, leaving me watching in the wings, wondering how I was going to top his act. It had been brilliant. If you could have bottled that routine, you would have made a fortune.

The strippers came on and I went back to the dressing room. Midway through me telling Enrico what a wonderful act he had, there was a bang on the door. I opened it to find the lad from the balcony standing there, smoke still rising off his hair.

'I want a word with that cunt,' he said.

'Oh, right,' I said. 'Well, he's just getting changed.'

'I want a word with him *now*.'

'Could you just hang on a minute, he's just putting his clothes on.'

Another five lads were standing behind the burnt lad. He must have talked them into giving Enrico a battering. I shut the door. 'You'd better get out now,' I said to Enrico. 'There's six big lads out there with that guy with the flame.'

'Aye, it doesn't matter.'

'No, if I was you I'd go through *that* door now,' I said, pointing at the rear exit. 'Go through that door and down them stairs, get in your car and I'll get Brian to send you your money.'

'I'm not frightened.'

'Look, these lads are fucking hard cases. They look like killers to me. So why don't you just . . .'

'No. It's all right.'

The lads waiting outside the dressing room started banging hard on the door.

'Hey!' I shouted, opening the door. 'Stop fucking banging on the door.'

'I want to see that cunt.'

'I know you do. Let him get fucking changed.'

Behind me I heard Enrico say quite clearly and slowly: 'Let them in.'

'Go on!' said the lad with the smoking hair. 'Let us in!'

'I know what *he* said,' I said. 'But look, *I* don't want any trouble. If you're going to cause trouble, the club will get the police and I'm in the middle of this.'

'We don't want any trouble with you, Chubby,' the lad said. 'I just want that twat.'

'It was just a bit of fun that went wrong. Enrico didn't mean to burn you – but you do look like Sammy Davis Junior.'

The lad's mates started giggling while the burnt lad twitched like Desperate Dan.

'Let them in,' Enrico said behind me.

So I opened the door fully. When I turned around, Enrico was standing bare-chested with a twenty-five-foot python wrapped around his neck, its head gripped in his hand.

'I want a word with you,' the burnt lad said.

'Aye? What you want?'

'Er . . .' the burnt lad said, his voice suddenly reedy and nervous. 'Is . . . is . . . that a real snake?' In an instant he'd gone from threatening to kill Enrico to outright surrender.

'Aye,' Enrico said.

'A real fucking snake?'

'Aye.'

'What's it doing here?' gulped the burnt lad.

'It's part of my act. Do you want to stroke it?'

'No, no, no, you're all right, mate. No, I'm all right, thanks.' Walking towards the door, the burnt lad stopped just before leaving the dressing room and pointed at his face. 'And by the way, *that*'s not fucking funny.'

As soon as the burnt lad had left the room, I asked Enrico: 'Where was that snake?'

'It was in the basket.'

'You cunt, I've been sat on that fucking basket for the last twenty minutes. You could have told me there was a fucking snake in it!'

'You're not frightened, are you?'

'No,' I said, 'but I'm going in the other dressing room.'

After a few more months playing the North-East clubs I was back in Malta. I wanted to show Beryl, who I was living with at the time, the Pescatora and the other restaurants in which I had worked. About a dozen of us went in a group, including Marty Miller, who'd lent me the money for my first drum kit, his wife Sue, a Middlesbrough taxi driver called George and his wife Margaret. Also with us was a theatrical agent called Norman Wales, who smoked a pipe and worked for Brian Findlay, and Norman's wife Louvane. Norman made us all laugh when he fell asleep on a deckchair one afternoon while the rest of us were swimming. He woke up after an hour to find that he'd fallen asleep with his hand on his chest, leaving a perfect white silhouette of his hand on his brown torso. His wife Lou was a lovely, clever woman who wore glasses and was a lot of fun.

Beryl and I spent many days with Norman and Lou, going to see the sights or swimming in the sea. Near the end of the fortnight's holiday we decided to take the ferry to Gozo, a neighbouring island where the locals made beautiful lace cloths and handkerchiefs that we thought we'd buy as presents for friends and family at home. But storm clouds were gathering by the time we got to the ferry port and the sailings were cancelled for that day.

While we were driving back to the hotel, the car that Beryl and I had hired broke down. Beryl got into a car with Marty and Sue and I squeezed in with Norman, Lou, George and Margaret.

Not far from the hotel, as we were coming down a mountainside near Rabat, the heavens opened. Over the next two hours, more than eighteen inches of rain fell on an island that usually got only twenty-four inches in a year. It rained so hard that we couldn't see our hands in front of our faces. The car had no windscreen wipers, so George pulled over to wait until the downpour subsided.

'I wish I was sat here in my swimming trunks,' I joked – but there wasn't time to laugh as the car was suddenly jolted upwards. The car moved sideways, then it rocked from side to side and started floating down the street.

A reservoir above Rabat had burst and millions of gallons of water were coming down the side of the mountain. Built on solid rock and with little vegetation, Malta had few fields or flood plains to soak up the water, which came roaring down the hillside. Sweeping up everything in its path, a wall of water lifted our car twenty feet on the swell. We all panicked. With water coming through the dashboard and the air vents, under the doors and around the windows, we had seconds to make a decision. Pressing my feet against the passenger door, I shouted to the others in the car as the car hit the side of a bank and flipped over.

'If we don't get out of the car, we're going to drown inside it!' I yelled as I pushed the door open and the water surged into the car. Grabbing Louvane by her anorak and Margaret by her arm, I pushed us all out of the door. We were floating in deep water gushing down the road in a gully between the mountainside and a high wall. The girls were screaming and other cars were swirling past us. A school bus and a van with some kids screeching inside it floated past, but there was nothing we could do. It was like something from a horror movie.

As the water swept down the road I kept hold of Margaret and Lou, my fingers digging into their arms. The water hit us again and again, like a wave crashing against rocks on a beach, as I pushed the girls towards some trees along the side of a boulevard.

'Get hold of a tree,' I yelled. '*Get hold of a tree!*'

I grabbed a palm tree at the side of the road and held on for my life. I looked round. George had grasped a tree and was climbing up a bank, pulling Margaret and Norman behind him. They were out of the water and were safe. Next to them Louvane was clinging to another tree, screaming as the water washed around her.

'My handbag!' she bawled. 'My purse! My passport!'

'Fuck your purse and your handbag!' I yelled. 'Keep hold of the tree!'

Lou let go of the tree, but I managed to grab her. 'Keep hold of me!' I screamed as I dragged the two of us towards another tree that had fallen over and lodged against the bank, its branches splayed all around it. 'Grab hold of the branches!' I yelled.

I looked at Lou. She had lost her glasses.

'Are you all right?' I shouted.

'I'm frightened, Roy. I can't see anything.'

'Just hold on to the tree! Hold on to the tree!'

I let go of the tree to push around it so that I could pull Lou up the bank. But when I got round to the far side of the tree, Lou was gone.

'Where's Lou?' Norman shouted from the bank.

I didn't know what to say. 'She's on the other side, Norman,' I lied. I couldn't tell him that I didn't know where she was. As I said it, I looked down the road and saw a massive wave hit the bank, sweeping everything in its path over the mountainside. I knew then that none of us would ever see Lou again.

I climbed up on to a wall. A cornfield waist-deep in water was on the other side, but at least the water there was still. I waded through it to a farmhouse where a farmer was stranded at an upstairs window, waving and shouting in Maltese. Turning back towards the bank, I saw Norman running along the top searching for Lou as a helicopter plucked Margaret and George off the bank. I got to the farmhouse and the farmer pulled me up to his first-floor window.

'English! English!' I said.

'Very, very bad storm,' the farmer said. 'You safe now.'

'My friend's car has gone.'

'Is OK. They take them Mosta. You go Mosta. We wait here and they take you Mosta.'

We sat on the windowsill of the farmhouse, waiting to be rescued, me half naked. The force of the water had washed off my shoes, socks, trousers and top. All I had on was my underpants. The farmer wrapped a potato sack around me, which immediately brought me out in spots, but at least I was warm and dry.

A large army truck pulled up and took us to the police station at Mosta, where I was left standing in a waiting room for hours. Then a policeman walked in with Norman.

'Where is she?' Norman said immediately.

'I don't know,' I said. 'I am sorry, Norman.'

Norman said nothing. He just stared blankly at me.

'I tell you where she'll be now,' I said. 'She'll be in a farmhouse or somebody will have taken her in and she'll be sat there wondering about you.' But as I said it, I was convinced that Lou was not with us any more.

'What if she has drowned, what if . . .' Norman started. And then he broke down in tears.

I wanted to say the right things, but it was difficult in front of a man as distraught as Norman. I put my arms around him. 'You are looking at the black side, Norman,' I said. 'Let's not think the worst until we know for sure what has happened to Lou.'

We gave the police all our details, then they dropped us back at the hotel. When I walked in, Beryl burst into tears. She had been told that we were probably all dead. (A premature report even made the local paper in Middlesbrough. 'Chubby Brown missing on holiday', the headline said.) Beryl and the others had made it back to the hotel without mishap. They'd spent the storm in the hotel's lounge, watching the water wash half the hotel's grounds and its swimming pool down the hill. There were uprooted trees and plants everywhere.

At least twenty people died that day. A Land Rover with four people in it had been swept off a viaduct. A woman had drowned in her wine cellar. But in those days most of Malta looked like it had just been through a disaster. The next day, much of the island looked as if nothing had happened. It was hard to tell the difference.

We all took taxis out to the bottom of the viaduct where Lou had disappeared. Word had got around the resorts that we were looking for an Englishwoman and more than two hundred English tourists turned up to help search for her. One of them came over to me.

'Hiya,' he said. 'Chubby, isn't it?' He was a small guy. With dark curly hair, a moustache and a suntan he looked a bit Greek.

'Yeah, that's right.'

'George Forster. Fairworld Promotions,' he said, offering his hand.

I knew who George was through reputation, but otherwise he was a stranger to me.

'Bit of a sad day,' he said.

'Did you know Lou and her husband?'

'Well, I knew Norman,' George said. 'What with buying and selling acts, I speak to Norman all the time on the phone, but I didn't know his wife. It's a very sad affair.'

We got on with searching for Lou. It was a beautiful day, the sky blue, the air warm and soft, but no birds were singing. It was eerily quiet. The police gave us long sticks to poke through the thick mud left on the road. And as we probed with our sticks, I didn't know what to say to Norman. I was sure that Lou was dead, but I didn't want to find a body.

Two days later, Lou still not found, we were due to fly home. Norman decided to stay on until he'd located Lou. The rest of us flew back in silence, all shocked by the tragic events.

Norman called the next day. Lou had been found two and a half miles out to sea. Two fishermen had netted her body in the bay. The police said she'd been pulled under the surface of the water, gone under a bridge and into the drains. She was unrecognisable. Norman had identified Lou by her wedding ring.

Norman flew back and was met at the airport by his two sons. I went round to the house. As I walked up the path to the door, I heard one of the boys howling. 'My mother! My mother!' he screamed. Lou had died on exactly the same date as her mother, and they'd both been thirty-nine when they went.

'They want seven hundred pounds for us to bring my mam's body back,' one of the sons said to me. I knew Norman didn't have it. He was a junior insurance agent who lived hand to mouth and who put in extra hours with Brian Findlay to earn enough money to put tobacco in his pipe. Other than that, he didn't have a penny to scratch his arse.

I made a call to Brian. 'Why don't you put on a special Chubby Brown show at one of the biggest clubs and we'll give all the money to Norman?' I said. 'That should be enough to bring Lou's body back and pay for a funeral.'

I called the show Chubby's Fresh Brown Eggs – I don't know why – and pulled together the best North-East musicians I knew. Paul Smith on drums, Tubby Ian on bass and Paul Flush on piano. I also roped in Les Desouza and Art McArthur, two great singers for a show that ran from eight o'clock until midnight with an hour's comedy from me. We sold out and, with the tickets at two pounds each, we raised enough money for Norman to bring Lou's body back.

When Lou was buried and everything had settled down, I sat at my piano and wrote a little ragtime two-step called 'Louvane'. I thought a ragtime suited Lou because she was always jokey and giddy and full of fun. It was mainly instrumental. At shows I'd introduce it as a song dedicated to a girl who lost her life on holiday in Malta and at the end of every sixteen bars I'd just say 'Louvane.' Norman was dead chuffed with it and the audiences loved it, so I put it on my first album, *Fat Bastard*.

I paid for a plaque to be put on the wall near where we'd last seen Lou. Ten years later, I went back to Malta on holiday. Norman died five years after he lost Lou – he'd started drinking heavily after her death and had a heart attack. I went to have a look at Lou's plaque. It was corroded and filthy. The lettering was impossible to make out. The next day, leaving the rest of the holiday party sitting by the pool, I went to an ironmonger's in Valletta. I bought some steel wool, a wire brush and some black paint. I cleaned the plaque up, repainted the lettering and planted a flowering bush in front of it. It was the least that Lou deserved.

CHAPTER ELEVEN

SOLO STEPS

THE FIRST CALL after I arrived home from hospital came from Bernard Manning. Many people in the northern comedy world believe there's a great rivalry between Bernard and me. But there's not and there never has been. I've always admired Bernard and he opened a lot of doors for people like me. We've been friends for years and I recently did the entertainment at Bernard's seventy-fifth birthday party.

Plenty of other comedians had written to me after news got out that I had cancer. Ken Dodd, who has always been my hero, wrote to wish me good luck after I sent him my most recent video. 'It's so good to hear that you are doing well with your treatment,' Ken wrote. 'I'll try not to do too much of your material on my next show!'

Bob Monkhouse, as well as phoning as soon as he heard of my diagnosis, wrote several times, on one occasion just after returning home to find more than a thousand letters from readers of two Sunday tabloids that had him at death's door. 'We hope with all our hearts that you are recovering strongly from your op,' Bob wrote. 'Let's fight on, you and I! We've both faced some tough battles on the stage and this is another one we can win. Keep polishing your helmet.'

More letters came from other comedians and club owners with whom I'd worked over the years. And then the phone calls started. Joe Pasquale, Duncan Norvelle, Dave Lee, Micky Miller and many others called. The message was always the same: we're thinking of you at this time. I'd gone through life thinking that few people knew who I was; now all these celebrities were phoning and writing to me.

I appreciated them all but Bernard was different. He has been like a comedy godfather to me, so when he called it was something special.

'Eeeeh, is this Chubby?' Bernard said.

I did my best to croak, 'Yeah.'

'It's Bernard.'

'Hello, Bernard.'

'I'm sat here worried about you, son. I have been told some hurtful things.'

'Yeah,' I rasped.

'Well, I don't know what to say. Keep your pecker up, won't you?'

'Yeah. How are you, Bernard?'

'I'm on eighteen tablets a day for me kidneys, for me angina, for me arthritis and me gout.'

'I bet you rattle when you trip up,' I rasped.

'If I trip up, no fucker's strong enough to pick me up, are they?' he said. Then he told me a gag about Michael Jackson. 'What's Arthur Scargill got in common with Michael Jackson?' he said. 'Hasn't seen a helmet for fifteen years.'

Bernard laughed. 'You can have that,' he said, like it was one of his own. 'If you want anything, give me a ring. *Please* give me a ring. And please keep in touch with me.'

'Right.' I wanted to tell Bernard how much I appreciated his concern, but my voice wasn't up to it.

'Thank you very much,' I said. It was all I could manage.

●

I'd been playing solo gigs for about two years, getting my name about as a solo comic while still playing with George and Mick in Alcock & Brown, when Brian got me a job at Jollys, a pre-mier-division club at Stoke-on-Trent. 'There's strippers on the top of the bill,' he said. 'Then you.'

Jollys was a venue with a big reputation. Along with Batley Variety Club and the Double Diamond at Caerphilly, it domi-nated the club circuit. I knew what would be expected of me. There'd be 1,800 men on pie-and-pea suppers washed down with jugs of ale before the strippers, of which there'd be about half a dozen, came on. My job would be to do a twenty-minute warm-up before the strippers and to step in during the show with a few gags if there were any delays. For a novice stand-up it was a daunting proposition, but I took on the gig and set off in my van from Middlesbrough with my cousin Dec, arriving at Jollys four hours later.

As we pulled up, Dec read out a poster outside the venue. 'Bernard Manning, 12 Exotic Dancers plus support,' it said.

'Eh, Bernard's on here soon,' I said as we walked inside. 'I wonder when.'

In the dressing room, the manager introduced himself. 'Bernard's on at nine,' he said.

'Hang on?' I said. 'Bernard what?'

'Bernard's on at nine o'clock,' the manager said. 'You do twenty minutes, then we'll put some strippers on. Bernard goes on for an hour, some more strippers, then you do another twenty minutes.'

'I'm on here with *Bernard Manning*?' I said. If I had been upside down, the shit would have come out of me collar. I was petrified. Bernard's reputation went before him and I was on the same bill.

Bernard was the king of the club circuit. The top comic. He was the boy. I'd never thought in my wildest dreams that I would ever work with Bernard Manning, but here I was, on the same bill, even if it was as 'plus support'.

At eight o'clock, the four-piece house band struck up a tune and the compère stepped up to the microphone. 'Good evening, ladies and gentlemen. Welcome to Jollys. We've *some* show for you tonight,' he announced. 'First of all, a young man, a comic who's just starting out but who we think is going to be a big name in the future. He'll keep you laughing for twenty minutes or so, then we'll bring on some of the girls. At the top of the bill, Bernard Manning will arrive at the building at nine o'clock, then . . .'

I walked onto the stage. Jollys was the biggest venue I'd played until then. It was a classic old-style nightclub, with rows of tables banked up from the stage, each with a little lamp on it. The lads were sitting four, six or eight to a table and the bars ran right around the back walls in a horseshoe from the stage. The waitresses wore bunny ears, like in the Playboy Club in London, taking orders for trayfuls of drinks. I did my set – it went down well, but I knew my place and I was very much bottom of the bill behind Bernard and the strippers – and left the stage, hoping to meet Bernard.

Bernard's ways were renowned in clubland and one of his many habits was always to start his set at nine o'clock and never to arrive before five to nine. He didn't like to sit in his dressing room, taking his time getting dressed and preparing for the show. Bernard would sit outside the venue in his white Rolls-Royce until the very last minute. He was well known for it.

At five to nine, Bernard arrived in full view of the audience in his usual costume – a white shirt and a black suit – and slipped on a bow tie. There were no inhibitions or starry antics with Bernard. If the venue was small, he wouldn't even bother with the dicky bow.

I grabbed Bernard's driver as he walked past. 'Excuse me, is there any chance of an autograph and a photograph with Bernard?' I asked.

'Course you can. Just do it before he goes on.'

I met Bernard in the wings of the stage. 'What do you do?' he said in a deep, gravely voice that could strip paint.

'I'm the warm-up comic,' I said.

'Do you want some gags, do you?' Bernard said with a smile. 'What d'you do, then?'

I ran through my repertoire. Bernard needed to check we weren't doing the same jokes. I told him I did a few adverts off the telly and a few parodies.

'Oh, right, that sounds fine,' he said and walked straight on stage.

I watched Bernard's act with open-mouthed wonder. He walked off the stage into the crowd, picked up someone's pint and drank it. Then he borrowed a cigarette off somebody else. He hadn't told a gag, but he already had the audience in his hand.

'Eh, these are nice,' he said, taking a drag on the cigarette he'd cadged. 'How much are they these days?' He patted the pockets of his jacket. 'I've got some fags,' he said and pulled out an old packet of Woodbines. 'I've had these since 1939.'

It was a simple act, based on having a go at the audience, but it was clever and very funny. Since then, I've known Bernard's routine off by heart and like all the 1,800 blokes in Jollys that night I loved his act. He was a great genuine man and a fabulous storyteller.

After an hour, Bernard came off. He would usually leave immediately after changing his shirt, but on that night he came into my dressing room after I had finished the second of my two twenty-minute sets. 'Where the fuck have you come from, son?' he said. 'Even I don't use that word.' He meant 'cunt'.

I had a shower and went out into the backstage corridor. Bernard's driver was waiting inside the stage door.

'Do you think Bernard liked what he saw?' I said.

'If Bernard gives you a backhanded compliment, he likes you,' the driver said.

A little later, Bernard came walking down the corridor.

'What do you think, Bernard?' I said. 'Did you like the act?'

'You want to pack it in,' he said. 'You're rubbish.' We shook hands. 'All the best to you, son,' he said.

'Thanks, thanks, Bernard, take care of yourself,' I said as he walked out of the club and climbed into his white Roller. That's a star, I thought, a real star. I was more excited about having worked with Bernard than I had been about playing in front of an audience of 1,800 and them all laughing at me. As far as I was concerned, Bernard was the King of Comedy and I was thrilled to have met him.

Bernard opened a lot of doors for controversial acts like mine and in those days I never thought I would ever reach Bernard's level. I don't think anyone ever thinks they're going to get to the top of their game. Kelly Holmes says she never thought she would be an Olympic champion when she was starting out. She thought she was a good runner and vowed to do the best she could. Edmund Hillary didn't begin his mountaineering career thinking he was going to be the first man to reach the summit of Everest. He just kept climbing higher until the day came when he thought he'd have a go at the biggest prize.

And when I was starting out, I saw myself as one of the thousands of club comics. A warm-up act for the big boys. I thought that was all I would ever be. I never thought my name would be on a ticket. I never thought people would pay eighteen quid to see me. I was just a warm-up comic who got a low wage. And for many years that was what I did. I worked with a lot of stars at different venues throughout the country, but I was still on two hundred quid for a week of six shows, always a bit skint, whereas they would be on daft money.

I worked on the same bill as Bernard a few months later at the Mayfair Ballrooms in Newcastle, where I was better known than in Stoke. Halfway through Bernard's act, someone shouted out: 'Where's Chubby?'

Bernard knew he was in my home territory and immediately snapped back. 'You can shout all you like, as long as they don't get the wage packets mixed up.'

Over the years, Bernard and I kept in touch. I did a few gigs for his charities and we occasionally shared the same bill. He is a gentleman with few pretensions, just a bloke who tells jokes.

A few years ago, when Danny La Rue was on a farewell tour and several comics held a dinner for him, Bernard came into my dressing room. 'How are you, Bernard?' I said.

'If it wasn't for me angina and me arthritis and me knees and me back, me deafness and that, I'd be fine,' he said. That evening, I went home and wrote a poem about Bernard called 'I Should Be All Right for the Shape I'm In'.

I'm fine, honestly, I'm quite all right, there's nothing wrong with me.
There was a time, in 1961, I had just a touch of dysentery,
And at the moment I can't catch my breath. It's just a little wheeze,
And, yes, I've backache and angina and arthritis in the knees.
I've got a few teeth that's rotten. I can't hear, you'll have to shout,
I'm overweight 'cos I drink a bit. And someone said it's gout.
No, I don't sleep at night with fallen arches and it affects both fucking
  feet,

The cramp gets worse when it's cold. That smell? It's called Deep
   Heat.
Dizzy spells, I'm used to them – my head is in a spin,
Without paracetamol and Nurofen, and of course my saviour which
   is aspirin.
Eyesight? God, what's that sign? Now I have to be told,
But don't worry, it happens to all of us. It's a case of getting old.
Aches and pains and cystitis. I'd have rust if I was made of tin,
But I'm doing well for seventy-five. For the shape I'm fucking in.

There was no better way of learning the ropes of clubland than sharing the bill with big names such as Bernard Manning. From them, I learned how to control audiences and how to deal with club committees. Of all the hazards of the game, not getting paid was one of the worst. Each club was different, but they were all united by one simple policy – don't spend money. If they could avoid paying you, they would. The chairman would tell you that you were being 'paid off', although the phrase was a misnomer. The 'paid' part of it didn't apply. You were 'off' and that was that.

It happened to every act that came up through the clubs. I heard that even the Beatles and the Rolling Stones had bad nights when they would be paid off. The unfortunate thing is that it was the bad nights that audiences remembered, not the good ones. Within five minutes of picking up the microphone, I knew whether I was going to do well or not that night. And if I wasn't getting the laughs, the clock would start ticking until someone walked up to me and said: 'You're off!' The only unanswered question was whether the committee official had a heart. If he did, he'd let me do half my act and give me maybe half of my fee. If he was a bastard, like the committee member at the Tanfield Lea Club in County Durham, he'd let you run through your entire act, then stitch you up like a kipper. I'd played a full one-hour set when I came off and the concert chairman summed up my act in three words: 'You were shite.'

'Was I shite after ten minutes?' I said.

'Yeah.'

'Well, why didn't you tell me to come off after ten minutes? I could have got in my car and gone home.'

'I can't take you off after ten minutes,' he said. 'The bingo doesn't start until nine o'clock.'

'So you let me suffer for an hour, sweating like fuck, worrying myself sick and then walking off to the sound of me own fucking feet because the bingo doesn't start until nine?'

'Yeah. What's your fee then?'

'You know what the fee is. It's fifty quid. That's what I'm on. Fifty quid.'

'We don't pay that type of money here.'

'The agent told me to pick up fifty pounds.'

'I work down the pits all week for that, you know,' he said. I'd heard that same line so many times before. 'We are going to give you five for your petrol because you have come a long way.'

It had taken me an hour and a half to travel from Redcar. There were no motorways or dual carriageways in that part of the country in those days. 'Five pounds?' I said. 'No, I'm not taking that. You keep the fiver for putty.'

'Putty?'

'Yes, *putty*. Because I'm putting all these fucking windows in.'

'You what? I'll get the police.'

'You get who you like. Get the Coldstream Guards, the Green Howards. If you don't give me my money, I'll smash every fucking window in this club.'

The chairman walked off and I thought I was going to get my money until he returned from the bar with two big bruisers – six foot, four inch Geordie equivalents of the Kray Twins.

'So yur gunna put wor windas in?' one of them said in a thick Geordie accent. 'Ahm gunna put *yer* windas in!'

'Hang on . . . hang on,' I said. 'I don't speak your language. I'm from Middlesbrough. I don't talk Geordie. Is there a translator in the house?'

'Don't get fuckin' funny wi' weh. I'll punch yer fuckin' face in. Ye knaa what ah mean, leik?' And they picked up my gear – very nice of them – carried it out of the club, dropped it in the street and dumped me beside it. I never got a penny. Not even the fiver.

As an act, you were powerless. There was no redress. If you had a complaint, you could go up in front of the local consultative committee, but the committees were staffed by members of all the clubs in a town or village. They made the rules, they sat in judgement on the rules and they made sure the rules always favoured the clubs, not the acts. They ruled with iron fists. If you did anything wrong, you'd be banned from the clubs for a minimum of six weeks. It was a racket.

But it wasn't just the clubs that would refuse to pay if they didn't like what they heard. I was booked to play a wedding at Wallsend British Legion Club. I always had the worst trouble on Tyneside. 'Good evening, ladies and gentlemen,' I said. 'Welcome to this glorified fucking cowshed. My name is Chubby "Whoops" Brown – the vicar dropped me at the christening.'

Immediately I realised that the groom's family on the right side of the room loved my act, but judging by the silence on the left of the room the bride's relations hated me and there was nothing I could do about it. I cracked a few more gags.

'I've seen the bride. No wonder they're all queuing up to kiss the groom,' I said. 'Has the fat sod had a shower? And what about the best man, eh? He's thicker than the cake and he left the ring on the curtains.'

A woman in a big white hat stood up. 'Get off! Yer rubbish!' she shouted.

'Who's the twat in a hat?' I said.

'The bride's mum,' yelled someone on the groom's side of the room as everyone around him cracked up laughing. With the right side of the room in stitches and those on the left booing, it wasn't surprising that a fight broke out between them. The wedding party came to an abrupt halt and again I wasn't paid. And they say until death us do part – it was my death and they parted.

The pit villages were the hardest venues to play, but at least they usually had decent facilities. The rugby clubs were diabolical. Some of the smaller clubs wouldn't even have a changing room. At best, there'd be a toilet with piss on the floor. At worst, they'd ask you to get changed in a corridor or in your car.

At Whitehaven Rugby Club, a hut on the side of a field, there was no microphone, no lights and no stage. When I told the chairman that I needed a stage and somewhere to put my speakers, he found an old beer crate. There was no point in complaining. I'd travelled for three hours to get to Whitehaven on the Cumbrian coast and I needed the fifty quid. I stood stock-still on the beer crate for a full hour and twenty minutes, playing my instruments and shouting joke after joke after joke as loud as I could.

Workington Rugby Club was even worse. 'Where's the stage?' I asked when I arrived.

'We don't have a stage,' said the concert chairman. 'The comics just stand in the corner.'

'I'm not a fucking dunce.'

'Well, they just stand there and do it.'

'Where's the PA system?'

'We don't have a PA. Everybody can hear – we all go quiet to listen.'

My 'stage' was right beside the entrance. Every time someone came in the room, the door would swing round, blocking me from the audience. And when they could see me, my face was in darkness – the only lighting came from a fifteen-watt light bulb suspended from a wire that stretched across the room.

'Good evening, ladies and gentleman. My name is Roy Chubby Brown,' I started as the door opened.

'Hiya,' said a latecomer.

'Hiya,' replied half his mates in the room.

'Well, there we are,' I said. 'Latecomers, I know what to get you for Christmas. A watch . . . Well, anyway, I come from Middlesbrough, a quaint little town . . .'

And the door opened again. It was like Woolworths on a Saturday afternoon. The punters were walking in and out as if I wasn't there. 'I wish I was as strong as these hinges on the door,' I said as a round of greetings rippled around the room.

'Hiya.'

'Hiya, June.'

'Hiya.'

'Hiya, Brenda.'

'Don't mind me,' I said. 'I'm just delivering the milk.' I took a step forward. 'I'll do this act, ladies and gentlemen, when everybody's arrived.' Meanwhile I turned to the committee man. 'How dare you book a fucking comedian? How dare you book *anybody*?'

'I thought you had a good reputation.'

'Yeah, I have, but I thought you had a stage and a fucking PA system. You are clueless,' I said, thinking he could stick his club where a monkey sticks its nuts.

As well as rubbish venues and tight-arsed committee men, clubland comics had to deal with the mixed blessing of the heckler. No comedian likes to be heckled. It stops the flow, interrupts your concentration and often breaks the timing and rhythm of your jokes. But equally, a quick response – comics call them ad libs, although they're mostly thought out in advance – can get the biggest laugh of the evening.

As much as hecklers are the bane of a comic's life, there's also something very exciting about batting back their insults with a quick ad lib. It makes the sweat drip on the back of my neck as I wait for the heckler to respond. The trick is to be confident in your material, self-assured in your responses and, most importantly, much funnier than the heckler.

A good supply of ad libs is a vital part of a comedian's armour. I worked for years on mine until I had more than five hundred one-liners with which to put down any heckler, so that the art of countering a heckler was simply choosing the right one.

For hecklers who simply shouted out inanities, I had a stack of replies, including: 'When you go to the cinema, do you shout at the screen?'; 'If I wanted to talk to a turd, I'd go for a shit'; 'If you were that important, the seats would be facing you'; 'Shout all you like. I'm a pro. Like your mother'; 'What're you shouting at? Has your probation officer gone for a piss?'; 'Whatever medication you're on, come on, share it out'; 'If I wanted to be shouted at, I'd have brought the wife'; 'Was the ground cold when you crawled out of it this morning?'; 'You sit right there until the blind knife-thrower comes on'; 'Gotta admire your Dad, building a shithouse like you with just one tool'; 'Was Wakefield jail overcrowded?'; and 'I bet your father threw bricks at the stork.'

Women heckled much less than men, who seemed to think that taking on the comic would make them look hard, but I kept a couple of ad libs especially for drunken hen parties, which could be worse than any male hecklers. 'When you're working, I don't jump up and down on the bed,' I'd say. Or: 'With a tongue like that, I bet you can lick your husband's arse through the letter box.' Or: 'I'll do the funnies. You go home and get your beauty sleep – stay in bed a month.'

Any comic resents people turning up late, simply because it distracts the audience and upsets your timing. 'Thanks for coming late,' I'd say. 'The babysitter called. She said it was only a head wound.' Or: 'What happened? Was the over-eighties night cancelled?'

And if someone got up in the middle of the act, I'd deal with the disruption by drawing attention to them and hurling a volley of abuse at them. It discouraged other punters from doing the same. 'You scruffy cunt. Is that your tractor parked outside?' I'd say. Or: 'Don't worry, that suit will come back into fashion.' Or I'd say: 'That was your mam on the phone. You can go home now. She's cleaned your cage out.'

If the heckler wouldn't shut up, or if they were particularly offensive, I'd match their rudeness. 'I'd call you a cocksucker, but I know you're trying to give it up,' I'd shout. Or: 'You're a good impressionist. From nowhere you became an arsehole.' Or: 'You're so thick you probably think a female peacock is a pea-cunt.' Or: 'If your dick was as big as your gob, you'd be with a bird.' Or: 'See what happens when brothers and sisters fuck each other.'

I soon got a reputation among other comics for my put-downs. 'Don't go for the bar when Chubby's on,' they'd say, 'because he'll get you.' I was like a sparrow-hawk looking for a mouse.

It was also important to have a quick reply ready if something unexpected happened. Any unforeseen disruption could stop an act in its tracks. If someone dropped a glass, I'd say, 'Don't bother washing that' and continue with my joke. If someone tripped up as they walked past, I'd say: 'No dancing while I'm on.' If someone knocked all the drinks over, I'd say: 'Eh, look at that. One Babycham and he'll fight any fucker.'

The only problem with having a go at hecklers was that they could try to make up for it after the show. I was playing

Farringdon Social Club in Sunderland and doing pretty well, but a gang of lads at the front kept interjecting, shouting, 'Fuck off, you big fat Geordie bastard'.

'You want to buy a road map, mate,' I said. 'I don't mistake you Mackems for Geordies and I am not one either. I'm from Yorkshire and proud of it.'

They kept on heckling, so I applied my usual tactic for dealing with a rowdy group of lads – pick on one of them and ridicule him in front of his mates. It usually worked.

'What're ya gonna do for a face when that elephant wants his arsehole back?' I said and continued with my act.

The concert chairman came up to me when I came off. 'May be a bit of trouble here, Roy,' he said.

'Why?'

'That lad you picked on is the hardest lad on the estate. He's from a very rough family and he's been telling everybody that he's going to rip your head off.'

I'd seen worse than that lad in other clubs, so I got on with getting changed and carrying my props to my van. I walked out the side door to find the Mackem hard nut waiting for me.

'Ah want a word wi yee,' he said.

'Could you hang on, I am just getting my speakers out.'

'Ah want yee – heor,' he said, pointing at a space beyond my van and the club. I looked at him. He was a big lad with a face that looked like somebody had been chopping sticks on it. He had a flattened nose and scars all around his eyes. It was obvious he was a fighter.

'Fuckin won't tell ye agyen, leik,' he said. 'Ah want *yee – heor.*'

'Could you just wait a second?' I said. 'This stuff is expensive. Can I just put it in the car?'

Bouncing from foot to foot and psyching himself up, he watched me while I loaded my van. I knew he was going to have me as soon as he got his chance. I needed to click my brain into a higher gear. How was I going to get out of this one? Should I pretend to pass out? Two lads were standing in the shadows a few feet behind him. Once he knocked me down, I suspected they'd kick the shit out of me. I'd seen it done before.

The Mackem moved closer, poking me in the back as I put my speakers in my van.

'Could you hang on? I'm just putting these speakers in,' I said.

'I'm fucking taaking te ye, fuckin loudmouth. Tell me *noo* me face is leik a fuckin elephant's arse.'

'Could you just let me put my speakers down, please?'

'Howay then,' he said, squaring up to punch me. 'Put yer speakers doon, leik.'

'Whoa, whoa, whoa. Hang on here,' I said. 'What's all this about?'

'Nobody tells me me face is leik an elephant's—'

'It was just a bit of fun, mate. I'm a comedian, for God's sake. You've seen the way I'm dressed – like an arsehole. What do you want to be fighting with me for? You might knock me teeth out but then I'll have to take you to court and sue you.'

'You'll hev ne fuckin heed, leik, when I've finished wi ye.'

'This is a bit silly, isn't it? I've got nothing against you, mate, but all you want to do is rip my head off. It's a bit stupid, especially coming from a bloke like you.'

'What dyer mean, a bloke leik me, leik?'

'Well, you're not going to tell me that you aren't shagging yourself to death.'

'What the fuckin hell as tha got dee wi it, leik?'

'Well, look at you. You are a good-looking bloke. You must be shagging yourself to death and here you are going around, beating people up, and getting a reputation for yourself,' I said. 'If I looked like you, do you know where I would be now? I'd be down the nightclubs pulling a bit of pussy.

You must get . . . I bet you get more pussy than you can handle.'

'Ah get a bit, leik.'

I knew I had him. 'Be honest with me, now. How many times have you been told you look like Elvis Presley?'

'Well . . .'

'When I saw you sat there, at the front, at that table in front of the stage, I thought: fucking hell, that lad looks like Elvis. That's why I thought I could have a bit of banter with you. Because you've nothing to hide. You're a good-looking bloke and you can handle yourself.'

'Aye . . . is that what you think?'

'I'll tell you what – it's amazing. I've never seen owt like it. A dead ringer for Elvis.'

On my bairn's life, I'd convinced him he looked like Elvis. As he puffed out his chest and turned his collar up, I thought, you thick twerp, I've brainwashed you.

'Are these yer speakers, leik?' he said.

'Yeah.'

He picked them up and put them in the back of my van. Then he shook my hand.

'Well, Ah thowht ye were fuckin geet, mate,' he said. 'If ye come roond heor Farringdon way, if yee hae any trouble, just fuckin ring me an I'll sort it oot.' He gave me his phone number. 'I'm Nosher. Everybody knows me. An I'll sort them oot.'

'Right.'

Nosher walked towards his mates and I got in the van. I turned the key and thanked God that it started. I put it in first gear and slowly moved off, winding down the window as the van picked up speed.

'Elvis?' I shouted out of the window. 'You look more like fucking Quasimodo's arse, you big ugly cunt!'

About a month later, Brian rang me. 'Farringdon Social Club want you back,' he said.

I told Brian the story. 'I wish I'd been there,' he said when he'd stopped laughing. 'And I don't think you'd better ever go back there again.'

I relied on a lot of props in my early solo days, mainly because we'd used props such as the talking bucket in Alcock & Brown and because in those days I found it easier to come up with visual gags than the patter. At one time I had more than a hundred props, including a wooden gate, a toilet seat, a balloon, a giant guitar, a telephone and a dog called Spunk that I'd sit on my knee for a routine.

There would always be a gag attached. I had a railing with 'Gents' toilet' painted on it. 'Could you please excuse me?' I'd say, then I'd walk behind the railing as if I was going down some stairs, press a button on a tape recorder and set off a sound effect of running water. The audience loved it. 'Oh God, I needed that!' I'd say and the place would be falling about. People laugh at the silliest things.

I had a telephone that would ring on the press of a button. 'Hello? Yes? Your Majesty?' I'd say. 'Yes. How are you? How's Phil? . . . Really . . . I passed your house the other day. Fucking hell, it's like a palace.'

All my bits of kit were props in more ways than one. Not only stage props, they also propped up my act because I hadn't developed enough gags to last an hour on my own.

I'd got fed up playing with Mick and George in Alcock & Brown because I thought they lacked ambition. Wanting only to earn beer money, they seemed quite prepared to sing the same songs, night after night, with no rehearsal or attempt to improve our act. They knew it meant we'd never earn decent money, but that didn't seem to matter to them. They just wanted a bit of fun a couple of nights a week, whereas I wanted to make a career of show business.

I'd vowed not to work with anyone else after splitting with Mick and George, but then I met Terry Harris, an impressionist who'd also been the lead singer with Sugar and Spice, a local group. Like me, Terry wanted to earn better money, so we decided to combine our acts in the hope that we'd get more and better work that way.

Still working under the banner of Alcock & Brown, our act was immediately more successful than it had been with George and Mick, with whom the act had been a very straightforward half-hour of comedy followed by half an hour of music. With Terry, it was ninety per cent comedy and we weaved the various bits together in a much better way. Terry did his impressions, I told a few jokes, we did the slapstick routines that I'd been working on as a solo act and I developed a few new spiels, including engaging with the audience as I'd seen Bernard Manning do. I'd look through women's handbags or take the mickey out of a bloke at the front. 'What's the matter with your face?' I'd say. 'Did you paint your teeth lemon on purpose?' If I spotted someone not laughing, I'd pull them out of their chair and get them up on stage. 'Make *me* laugh, you miserable bastard,' I'd shout at them. They usually giggled helplessly with embarrassment, the audience lapped it up and I loved relying solely on my quick wits. Occasionally there would be an awkward bastard who'd threaten to punch me if I picked on him, but that was inevitable when we were working six nights a week, and more often than not I could use it to my advantage. 'Ooh, have you come on?' I'd say if the misery guts was a bloke. He'd have to be a right miserable sod not to laugh at that.

Terry and I worked well together on stage, but off stage it was a different story. I felt resentful as I thought I was always the one who had to be the creative, innovative member of the partnership, the one who came up with new gags, whereas Terry was happy to stick to the tried and tested impressions of the day such as Harold Wilson, Prince Charles, Ted Heath, Norman Wisdom and Michael Crawford as Frank Spencer.

However, the greatest source of friction between me and Terry '14 Combs' Harris was his vanity. We once had the opportunity of doing a spot on a daytime television talk show in Edinburgh, but we nearly missed it because Terry spent so much time staring at himself in the hotel mirror, just in case there was an attractive woman he could pull at the studio. Also, sometimes I would buy food and drink for Terry all day and then watch open-mouthed when he did not even pay for his fish and chips at the end of the evening.

Terry and I worked so hard that we had little time for fun – and compared with Mick and George, Terry wasn't up for fun anyway – but there was one incident I'll never forget. We were playing a series of gigs in South Wales and went to the swimming pool to kill time one afternoon in Cardiff. We were sitting in the steam room when someone I recognised walked in and sat down beside me.

'You're Frankie Vaughan?' I said. I was right. 'We do a club act,' I added, explaining where we'd been playing. 'Oh, by the way, happy birthday.'

'Has someone told you it's my birthday?' Frankie said.

'I know because it's my birthday too. We were both born on the third of February.'

'That's some coincidence,' Frankie said. 'I think it calls for a celebration.'

We left the steam room, sat at a table beside the swimming pool and shared a bottle of champagne. Frankie was a lovely man, a wonderful person. I've met many people in show business who have let their success go to their heads. But Frankie was not one of them. A fabulous singer and very good-looking, he looked like a British Robert Mitchum. His wife Sheila must have had her hands full over the years because I think at one time every woman in Britain wanted to bed Frankie Vaughan. He was utterly charming.

Twenty-five years later, we met again. 'How you doing, Chubby?' Frankie said. I'd now made a name for myself and Frankie had recognised me.

'Do you remember a duo in Cardiff and a bottle of champagne?' I said. I told Frankie the story of our last meeting.

'Eeh, I remember that,' he said. 'Was that you – the bloke with the same birthday as me?' And this time I bought the champagne.

Terry and I didn't last long. I felt I was doing everything – driving us to the gig, setting up the gear, buying all the props and keeping Terry watered and fed – because Terry worked as a car salesman during the day and spent whatever spare time he had with his latest squeeze. The most recent was a girl called Brenda, a bottle blonde with black roots and a flat in Peterlee which Terry had swiftly made his little love nest, forever going on about how great Brenda was in bed.

I would rehearse all day while Terry relied on what he had. It was like a bad marriage in which one partner does everything and the other takes the piss. Terry was getting on my nerves and I was looking for a chance to bring an end to Alcock & Brown when Terry told me he had to go to Canada to visit his sick mam. We'd been together for eight months and I was glad to see the back of him.

'I'll work on my own until you get back,' I said to Terry, thinking that I'd avoid ever re-forming Alcock & Brown with him.

'Oh aye, yeah,' Terry said. 'I've been talking to Brenda and she feels that, in the end, I'm better off working on my own. So I that's what I am going to do.'

'Are you, Terry?'

'She thinks I'm carrying the act.'

She thinks I'm carrying the act. I'll never forget those words. *Carrying the act!* On stage, I was running about like a blue-arsed fly. I played the drums, piano, banjo and ukulele. I wrote all the comedy sketches, and I rewrote the lyrics to all the advert parodies. All Terry did was half a dozen impressions in the first half of the show. Also, off stage I did *everything.* And Terry had the cheek to say he was carrying the act! I've never got over it. The cheeky bastard.

'How much notice are you giving us?' I said. 'Because I will need to get somebody else.' I wanted to stay in a duo because I had enough material for an hour-long double act, but only enough solo material for a twenty-minute support slot.

'I'm leaving on Sunday.'

'*This* Sunday, ya mawky get?' It was now Thursday.

'Yeah.'

'Thanks for letting me know.'

Terry left for Canada – or so I thought. For the next month I worked night and day until I had enough new material to add to my older gags, songs and slapstick. I practised the banjo and ukulele incessantly, playing along to Sandy Nelson tracks until my hands were bleeding, and I wrote hundreds of gags, then honed them down to the best fifty.

I got all my comedy books out and scanned through them for inspiration. I knew I already had a good half-hour act, but most clubs wanted two half-hours and some wanted three half-hour spots. I couldn't afford the time to work up a full ninety minutes of material, so I relied on some rather hackneyed Paddy and Mick jokes – the comedian's bread and butter of the early 1970s – and practised stringing them out to make them last longer. A joke about Dublin mission control sending Paddy and Mick up towards the moon in a milk bottle would be stretched out almost to the point at which it snapped and was no longer funny, just to fill time. 'You know where Dublin is?' I'd say. 'It's in Ireland. Did you know they had a space launch pad there? Well, they tied Paddy and Mick to this rocket . . .' and I'd keep it going like that.

I played a few local warm-up gigs in Redcar to bed in the new material. When I came off stage after the fourth gig, I was confident that I could hold a show on my own so I rang Brian's office on the Friday. 'Am I out at the weekend?' I said. I was booked for Sunday night. Two spots at the Excelsior Club, a working men's club in Newcastle.

Walking into the Excelsior on Sunday evening, I was confronted by a big notice: Top Class Entertainer – Terry Harris.

Terry Harris?

He was waiting in the dressing room. 'Hey, how are you?' he said.

'I thought you were going to Canada?'

'I've been. I came straight back.'

'Oh, did you?'

'I'm on at eight o'clock,' he said. 'Then you're on at half past.'

Standing at the bar, I watched Terry do all my material. He was doing routines that formed the heart of my act, much of which predated his time in Alcock & Brown and the remainder of which was material I'd written. I went to the dressing room.

'What do you think of me first spot, then?' Terry said.

'You've a fucking cheek. It's all my stuff, Terry. I can't go on now.'

'Well, you know, I helped put that together,' Terry said.

'No, you didn't, Terry. And you know it.'

'Oh . . . I would have thought you would have put something else together by now.'

'I have, but it's only been four weeks. All that stuff that you did there, it's the first half of my act. You *know* it's my stuff.'

I found the concert secretary of the club. 'That lad who was just on, he used to be working with me,' I said.

'We were told that.'

'He's just done all my stuff,' I said, with a shrug.

I felt like giving Terry a ploat, but I got in my car and drove off. I never spoke to Terry again. Twenty years later, I saw him at a football match. He had lost all his hair at the front and ballooned in size. He was bigger than me. I looked at him, he looked at me and said hello. I didn't reply.

Terry tried to make it on his own, but got back together with Sugar and Spice. For all his overweening vanity, it seemed he didn't believe in himself enough to walk on stage by himself and take a battering. Standing behind a microphone, on stage is the loneliest place on earth if the audience doesn't like you. If you're dying and not getting a laugh, well, there's nowhere worse. Sitting in solitary in a prison cell has nothing on it.

CHAPTER TWELVE

LEARNING THE ROPES

AT LEAST I was losing weight. What with the liquid diet, the radiotherapy, the alcohol ban and the long walks I took to while away the hours of doing nothing, the pounds were falling off me and physically I felt better than I had in years.

My mental state was another story. The physical symptoms of the radiotherapy – the red-raw swollen throat and the loss of hair – were a breeze compared with the psychological side effects. I felt depressed and listless, I was getting headaches, I couldn't do my job and I was totally pissed off. There were days when I woke up and had to be at the hospital at nine o'clock and I didn't want to get out of bed. I'd pull myself together, get dressed and wash, climb into my car and set off. Then, sitting in traffic on the way to the clinic, I'd think: 'Ah, fuck it. What's the point of going through the pain and discomfort of radiotherapy? I'm going to die anyway.'

The only thing that stopped me from turning my car around, heading home and giving up was the thought of Mr White. That doctor just saved your life, I'd tell myself, so get out of bed, you lazy fat twat. Get yourself in your car, you stupid bastard. Fucking get down there to the hospital, grit your teeth, you lily-livered coward, and get on with it.

In the end, I kept going for Mr White's benefit. He saved my life and that was all there was to it. There was no romance to recovery, no fairy dust or pot at the end of the rainbow to keep me going. He saved my life, so I was indebted to him. If he'd phoned up just as the kids were opening their presents on Christmas Day and asked me to see him immediately at the hospital, I would have done it. If I'd been about to go on stage at the London Palladium to receive a gold medal for services to comedy and Mr White had called me into his surgery, then I would have turned my back on the Palladium and done it. At that time, family and work were secondary to his demands. That man saved my life. And for that I was eternally grateful and would never let him down. That's just how it was.

●

Terry Harris did me the biggest favour of my working life. If it hadn't been for his sudden resignation, it might have taken me a lot longer to summon up the courage to go out on my own full time. I might have drifted into another group or duo. But Terry left me with no choice but to chance my luck as a solo stand-up.

In the mid-1970s there were so many venues that any act could find plenty of work. No one was booked weeks in advance simply because they didn't need it. Agents would phone up several times a week, offering a choice of gigs. And some towns had so many clubs that you could play two gigs at neighbouring clubs on a Sunday dinner time, then another three gigs that evening at three more clubs a few hundred yards down the street.

I played my first gig as a full-time fully fledged solo stand-up at Newport Working Men's Club in Middlesbrough, a lovely little venue with a small stage and a red velvet curtain. I was familiar with being the front man, walking on stage to face an audience. But now it was different. Until that evening, I'd always walked on with a band or partner behind me. And if I'd been doing a solo spot, the pressure hadn't been on me because I was only the support to the headline act. If things were going badly, I could turn around to the lads in the band and crack a joke – 'I'm fucking struggling tonight, aren't I?' I'd say to the bass player and it would usually get a laugh – but now there was no one to lean on, no safety net. I walked on that night and there was just me, the microphone and the microphone stand. It was a competition with the crowd that I wanted to win. I had tried and tested material which I knew the audience would laugh at and I knew I could always rely on slapstick – walking up to the microphone, pretending to trip up, looking around and saying 'Who put that matchstick there?' – but now my big problem was my nerves. I'd never had trouble going on stage before, but now that I was the solo headline act my bowels took over and I found myself running for the bog, always needing a shite before I went on.

It took me many years and more than two thousand performances to get a grip on my nerves. Only then did I feel that I'd earned the right to be up there on stage. After years of sold-out performances in front of packed houses, I realised it wasn't my fault if on one night the audience didn't laugh at gags that had worked dozens of times before. As long as I stuck to the same formula every night, then I'd know what to expect. But if I veered away from my usual set, it was very difficult to predict the audience's response.

I'd been out on my own for about a month when a leg came off my most treasured stage prop, the papier mâché black and white dog called Spunk. I would stand beside Spunk, shout 'Fetch!' and give it a kick up the arse to send it scuttling across the stage towards the dressing-room door. On this night, I gave it a particularly hard kick. Flying up in the air, the dog did two somersaults high above me and landed on its feet on the other side of the stage. Thinking the aerial acrobatics were intentional, the club erupted with applause. I could have tried the same move a thousand more times, but I wouldn't have been able to repeat it and I even forgot my next line, I was that gobsmacked.

When I came off stage, I discovered one of the dog's legs was cracked. Beryl, the girl I was living with at the time, had a brother-in-law called Terry who was a bit of a dab hand at DIY, so I asked him to repair it. Two days later, Terry rang me to say he'd fixed the dog and offered to drop it off at the club I was playing that night.

I got to the club. It was packed and I was on with a couple of singers and a group. As I was waiting to go on, the concert chairman walked into the dressing room. 'The girl singer plays piano, so I am putting you on first to warm up the audience,' he said. 'By the way, a bloke has dropped your dog off. It's near the microphone stand on the stage.'

I could see the dog near the microphone stand, which was where I usually placed it, so I got changed into my patchwork suit, flying hat and goggles.

After the concert chairman announced me to the club, I walked on stage and launched into a song about being a dog.

'It's awful being a dog, walking up and down the street,' I sang. 'All you ever see is other people's feet . . .'

At the end of the first verse, I shouted 'Fetch!' and kicked the dog up the arse. It didn't budge an inch, but the audience laughed, probably because the dog was ignoring my orders. My foot, however, was in agony. I wanted to double up with the pain of it, but I had to continue the act as if nothing had happened while inwardly screaming with agony. After half an hour, I limped off stage and phoned Terry from the backstage pay-phone.

'What the fucking hell have you done to my dog?' I said.

Terry, who had a double-belt-and-braces approach to DIY, had built a frame of metal tubing inside the dog and put iron bars in each leg. The dog was stronger and steadier than it had ever been, but it also weighed so much that I could hardly lift it.

'You fucking twat,' I said. 'You've broken my toe.' I was limping for about three months. I still kept the dog in my act for years, but the days of kicking it were long over.

On other occasions, an unexpected turn of events or a spontaneous ad lib could have a less successful outcome and I would need real bottle to rescue the gig. The worst thing any comedian can do is say something really stupid, like making a joke about Hillsborough on a Liverpool stage. I was accused of that, but it wasn't me. It was another comedian – I'm not that stupid. And during the Falklands War I was accused of saying 'I am going down like the *Sheffield.*' Again, I didn't say it but, because I am known to be crude and controversial, newspapers often point the finger at me when a story goes round about a comedian saying something offensive.

But I did make a joke about Diana, Princess of Wales, the day after she died. I knew I had to be careful, but with Diana dominating every news bulletin, I thought there was no way I could ignore her tragic death, so I made a harmless crack about Princess Diana holding on to Prince Charles's ears, then I said: 'Let's hope it's not windy on the day of the funeral, it might blow Charlie away.'

I thought I was on safe ground – after all, the joke was about Charles, not Diana. A few faint titters and a handful of half-hearted boos broke the silence, but most of the audience just stared at me open-mouthed. Clearly I had overstepped the mark.

'Ah, come on,' I said, desperate to rescue the very uncomfortable situation. 'What difference has Diana made to your life? She was only going to marry the playboy son of an Egyptian shopkeeper. And she's had more cock than there's handrail on the *Queen Mary*.'

Up on stage, the hairs on the back of my neck stood up and I was in a cold sweat. I don't know what made me say something that tasteless so soon after Diana died, but I had an instinctive sense that something really crude was more likely to break the tension than a few mealy-mouthed comments. Moments later I knew I'd said the right thing when I heard a ripple of recognition – the audience seemed to be conceding that I had a point – and then a round of warm applause rolled around the theatre as the audience relaxed. It was only a joke, after all.

Another night, I was at the British Legion Club at Larkhall in Scotland, about forty miles from Glasgow, the night Scottish fans invaded the pitch at Wembley and stole the goalposts after Scotland beat England 1–0 in 1978. 'I'm not a comedian,' I said as I walked on stage. 'I've just come to get the fucking goalposts back.' About twenty glasses flew through the air at once, not one of them hitting me. I ran off stage and locked myself behind the dressing-room door.

Of all the audiences, those in religious clubs were the hardest to second-guess. A joke about religion would work in one Catholic club, but not in another. It was a lottery. I played one Catholic club where the colour television had been stolen from the lounge. Pointing at the crucifix above the stage, I said: 'Oh, I see you caught the cunt that stole your telly.' I was booed and hissed off stage. I was booked to play Christmas Day dinner at another Catholic club. Nobody was laughing, so looking up at the crucifix, I said: 'Why aren't you laughing? It's your birthday.' Everyone in the club gasped, but then they laughed and the rest of my act went down like a dream.

Another time, I was playing the Stella Maris Social Club at Washington in County Durham. Not being religious, I didn't know Stella Maris was another name for the Virgin Mary. It was a beautiful club with the plushest red curtains I'd ever seen, but as soon as I walked on stage the audience hated me. By the time I got to the end of my opening line – 'Why's this a religious club? You've certainly not got three wise men on the committee' – most of the seven hundred punters were booing or calling for me to get off the stage.

A large crucifix dominated one of the walls. 'Are you talking to me or him?' I said, pointing at the cross and trying desperately to be funny in the face of total hostility. ' 'Cos we're both stuck here, hanging about.'

A bloke out of the audience came flying up to the stage. 'Off!' he shouted. 'You ought to be ashamed of yourself.'

But I soldiered on. 'If I had met Mary before Joseph, she wouldn't have been a virgin,' I said. I could hear myself wheezing and breathing. The room was that quiet, I could hear a mouse passing by on tiptoes. After fifteen minutes I'd had enough and walked off. The same bloke who'd shouted at me on stage came into the dressing room, his hands pressed together in front of his chest as if he was praying.

'May the Lord forgive you,' he said.

'What for?'

'May the Lord just forgive you and cleanse your mouth with soap.'

'Oh right, thank you very much.' I knew it took all sorts, but this was ridiculous. What on earth was a Catholic club doing booking a comedian with a reputation for dirty jokes?

Soon after I started on my own, Brian sent me on a week-long tour of Doncaster and Rotherham. There were loads of huge clubs down there – the Clay Lane, the Grangetown, the Belmont, the Yarborough, and largest of all, the Wheatley Hill Working Men's Club – all full of hairy-arsed miners and rough steelworkers. Before I set off, I rang up the concert chairman of one of the clubs to ask if there were any theatrical digs in the area.

'There's one at Rotherham that they all stay at,' he said. 'It's called Pandora's Box and it's at 1 Vesey Street.' I booked a room for three pounds fifty a night and two pounds for break-fast, which amounted to around thirty quid out of my two hundred pound fee for the week.

At the club that evening I arrived first, did my act and had a fair night. South Yorkshire venues were hard clubs full of lads who would get their bollocks tattooed without flinching and I wasn't nearly as slick as I made myself out to be, so I considered it a fair night in those days if I got half a dozen laughs.

I put my bags in my little red van, asked a copper where Vesey Street was and drove round to the boarding house, my first-ever pro digs. Having paid my deposit and dumped my bags in my room, I walked into the lounge, a big room with a string of sofas and chairs around the walls, a television blaring in one corner and about a dozen lads and lasses all getting well stuck into the drink. In the middle of all of them was a bloke about forty years old with silver hair.

'All right, son?' he said.

'Yeah, thanks.'

'What you doing, then?'

'Oh, I'm an entertainer,' I said.

'*Really?* What does that mean?'

'Well, I do the clubs, you know.'

'You mean you actually stand on stage?'

'Yeah, yeah, but it's just a job.'

'What do you do, then?' the silver-haired bloke said. 'Can you give us some idea?'

'Well . . .' I said. I didn't want to brag or anything.

'I'll tell you what,' he said. 'Let's pretend this is a stage . . .' He put a cushion down on the floor. By now, everyone in the room had stopped talking and was watching me.

'Well, what happens is I stand here by the microphone,' I said.

'What, like this?' the silver-haired bloke handed me a broom. 'And you walk on, do you?'

'The microphone's here and I say, "Good evening, ladies and gentlemen. My name's Roy Chubby Brown", and then I tell my jokes.'

'Really? What, so people laugh at that?'

'Yeah.'

'I bet some funny things happen to you in the clubs,' he said.

'Yeah, they do.'

'Well, tell us about them, then.'

So I told them some of my clubland experiences, including what had happened to me a few nights before at Seaton Delaval Social Club when, dressed in a flat cap and miming with a wooden shovel to a Bernard Cribbins song, 'There I was, a-digging this 'ole, 'ole in the ground, so big and sort of round . . .' the concert chairman walked up.

'Oi, mate,' he said. 'When you've finished digging that hole, fuck off!'

And I told them about another recent experience at a social club in Yorkshire next to a big wood yard. Halfway through my act, a siren went off and everybody in the club ran to the windows. Outside, the wood yard was going up in flames. Inside, I was talking to the audience's backs. 'Eh, have I ever wished I were Joan of Arc,' I shouted at them. 'At least you would be facing the right fucking way.'

Halfway through telling my stories, I looked at the silver-haired fella again and thought to myself 'I know that bloke.' As I looked around at the other people in the lounge, I noticed that few of them were laughing out loud at my stories. There'd been a few titters, all right, but when I looked closely I realised that several of them were biting their lips.

'That's really funny,' the silver-haired bloke said when I'd finished relating the last of my tales. 'You know, I'm Johnny Hammond.'

I looked at him and the penny dropped. That was where I'd seen him before. Johnny Hammond was a local legend. He was one of the biggest comics in the North-East and had opened for Andy Williams, Val Doonican and dozens of other big stars. He'd recently won the first *New Faces All Winners Show.*

Pointing at each of the dozen faces around the room, Johnny introduced them. 'That's Bobby Thompson, that's Linseed and Aniseed, those two are Frank and Jessie . . .' They were all big clubland names. '. . . That's Larry Mason . . .' He was one of best impressionists around. Now I knew why they'd all been biting their lips.

'I can also fight,' I said.

'Oh.'

'I'll knock your fucking . . .' And then I smiled and the rest of them burst out laughing.

'Come and have a drink,' Johnny said. 'It was just a bit of a laugh.'

As I sat down, Larry Mason stood up. 'Goodnight, lads,' he said. 'Nice meeting you, son. I'll see you at breakfast in the morning.'

'Aye,' I said as Johnny poured the first drink and we got chatting. He was a lovely man and since he came from Hartlepool, just up the coast from Middlesbrough, we had a lot in common.

Five minutes later, Larry walked in, stark naked with a bowler hat on his head. With his cock and bollocks hanging out, he stood by the bar, ordered a drink and said, 'Can't anyone get any fucking sleep in this house?'

I realised then that they were all nutters like me and that show business didn't have to be a battleground. It wasn't quite the cliché of one big happy family – there was too much professional rivalry for that – but we all respected and liked each other and became great mates over the years.

But back then I was the novice, wet behind the ears and eager for advice, which they all happily gave. After years of struggling to get to grips with the strange practices of some of the clubs, at last I was being told the golden rules of the game. Get your money when you walk in a club; always be friendly; learn by watching others; learn when to speak and when not to speak; always make a concert chairman feel like he's God; say your pleases and thank-yous and don't talk down to him because he's the one with the money in his pocket; always be polite to the backing band and always have your dots ready (in those days, I didn't even have any sheet music); if you're going to use a club's drums, give them a fiver; make sure you park your car near the stage door for a quick getaway if there's trouble; make sure you go to the toilet before you go on, even if you have to piss in the sink; make sure the door's locked when you piss in the sink; if you're in a bad mood, don't take it out on the audience – remember you're an entertainer, so be professional; if the microphone goes off, use it in your act and pretend it goes off every night; if there's a fight in the concert room, just say 'Ladies and gentlemen, I'll be back on in . . .' and go to the dressing room, then get out fast.

There were hundreds of little tips that they passed on to me and I realised then that I could read all the books I wanted and watch every movie I could find, but the real thing about show business was watching those who between them had more experience than I would ever gain on my own. I learned something from every comedian I watched, but Johnny Hammond taught me the most.

What I really liked about Johnny was that his material was common. He talked about the coalman and the milkman's horse and things like that. And that was a revelation. There's a market here for being common, I thought, for being the man off the building site. And what do men on building sites do all the time? They eff and blind. 'John, pass that fucking brick,' they say. The swear words fly about like they're about to be outlawed and pleasantries are never heard. I'd worked on enough building sites to know that the swearing was a release valve from what was often a miserable, back-breaking job. And I guessed that if I took the man off the building site and put him on stage, then the swearing would become a release valve for an audience looking for some relief from the misery and mundanity of their lives.

I watched Johnny Hammond like a hawk and learned a lot. The way Johnny told jokes within stories was a lesson to me. Up until then, I'd always been a one-line gag merchant, but Johnny showed me how to link jokes into themed stories. And, in time, I came to realise that Johnny was a straight man telling funny jokes, like Bruce Forsyth or Bob Monkhouse.

Bob was widely regarded as the cleverest comedian on the circuit. Everyone called him the Governor. He was the finest comic this country had for years and his material was second to none. But he wasn't a funny man. His material was funny, but because he told it in a straight way, audiences admired the quality of his jokes, but they didn't really laugh.

Tommy Cooper was the other extreme – a funny man telling straight jokes. Audiences laughed as soon as Tommy walked on stage. He didn't need to say anything. He was just a funny

person. If you listened to his jokes, they were usually rubbish –
often intentionally so – but it didn't matter. Tommy's act was all
about his personality and his personality was hilariously funny.

For me, Ken Dodd was the best comedian of all. He had
both strengths. The consummate all-rounder. When I saw
Doddy on stage I laughed at him and I laughed at his material.
And that, to me, was the benchmark. I wanted to combine the
visual slapstick of Tommy Cooper, the clever storytelling of
Dave Allen and the one-liners of Bob Monkhouse, but bring it
together for the common man, the hairy-arsed builder or factory worker who lives in a council house with little money and
not much to do except shag, drink and swear.

But I also knew that if I based my act around the behaviour
of the rougher end of society, then I wouldn't have much of a
future on television and would probably remain a club act. I'd
already had a few small tastes of the world of telly and I was
getting a sense that television and I were not easy bedfellows.

Shortly before the George and Mick incarnation of Alcock &
Brown came to an end, I got a chance to audition for *Opportunity
Knocks*, the top talent show of its day. I travelled down to London
and I found myself in the same room as Little and Large and
several other acts I knew from clubland. I performed a five-
minute routine in front of two stony-faced television executives
in an empty room. With no audience reaction, I had no idea
how well I was going down. On stage, you feed off the atmosphere, you feed off the laughs. The audience gives you love and
affection. But there was nothing in that room. I might as well
have been practising in front of a mirror. It was one of the
longest five minutes of my life.

Afterwards, one of the *Opportunity Knocks* executives came up
to me. 'You were good, mate, but you let yourself down there by
saying arse,' he said. 'You spoilt yourself.'

In those days, I saw myself as a member of a group or duo,

so I didn't really care that I'd not passed the audition as a solo comic. But a few years later, when I was asked to compete in the 1976 series of *New Faces*, I was determined to prove my worth as a solo comic.

The night before *New Faces*, I appeared before an all-male audience of 1,700 in a club in the Midlands. I was waiting in the dressing room when a skinny black-haired stripper came in.

'I'm sorry I'm late,' she said.

'Don't apologise to me, pet,' I said. 'I'm on with you.'

'Oh yeah, you're Chubby Brown aren't you? I think we've worked together before.'

'Aye, we probably have,' I said.

The club manager walked in as we were talking, but the stripper took no notice of him.

'Do you mind,' she said to me, completely ignoring the manager. 'I'm busting for a slash.' And without waiting for an answer, she cocked her arse in the sink in front of two men in the dressing room. As far as she was concerned, we were invisible.

Five minutes later, she went on stage. With 1,700 blokes shouting at her and bawling 'Show us your tits! Show us your arse!' she whipped off all her clothes, rubbed cream and baby oil all over her body, then set to work on herself with a vibrator. After twenty minutes, she came back into the dressing room.

'I *knew* I worked with you before,' she said as she sat down. 'I was racking my brains while I was on stage and then it came to me.'

'Oh yeah?' I said. 'Where?'

'Wallsend Labour Club. I was the singer Carrie-Anne.'

I remembered her. She'd been a great singer. 'What did you pack it in for?' I said.

'Couldn't do it any more. I lost my bottle.'

The next morning I auditioned for New Faces at a club in

Halifax. Standing in front of a panel at half past nine, I knew that this time I had to be spotless. Not a mention of the arses, tits and fannies that had peppered my act at the stag party the previous night.

The many nights drinking in pro digs had put several pounds on my waistline. Tipping the scales at twenty-two stone in those days, I thought I couldn't avoid mentioning my weight, so I wrote a song especially for the audition called 'It's Awful Being Fat'.

'It's awful being fat,' I sang. 'I'm trying to diet to lose a bit of fat. People say I suit it, well, it's just the way I'm sat.

'I breathe in all I can and I try to look my best, but the fat still sticks through the holes in my vest.'

I played the piano and told a few jokes. 'You know, we were that poor where I grew up, I once opened the oven and next door was dipping their bread in the gravy,' I said. 'Christmas Eve, we'd all sit around the fire. If it got really cold, we'd light it . . . and then we'd get the Bible out. You know, a big thick book like that burns for three hours.'

'Fabulous, fabulous, lovely,' a very camp stage manager said at the end of it. 'We'll be in touch.' A few days later, I got a letter detailing a date for when I should record my appearance in front of the *New Faces* panel.

Before the recording, they asked me to take out the joke about the Bible, but other than that I stuck to the same act as at the audition. It all went very well, except for a painful moment in the song, when the lid of the piano slammed down on my fingers.

At the end of my five-minute routine, I told the joke I'd just written about the Irish Evel Knievel who tried to jump twelve motorbikes with his bus and would have made it but someone rang the bell. Then I stood stock-still on the stage, the spotlight trained on me, and waited for the panel's verdict.

Tony Blackburn was first. 'I think he's very funny, this lad, I'd like to see him over an hour,' he said. I thought it was the best compliment I could have hoped for, but I only wished he'd been one of the 1,700 punters at the club I'd played the night before. Then he would have seen what I was like over an hour.

All the panel, which also included Mickie Most and Dave Dee, gave me good scores, but at the end of the show I was pipped to the post by a country band called Poacher that went on to win at the Country Music Awards and become a big name.

I'd hoped that *New Faces* would have lifted me out of the club circuit, with its sadistic concert chairmen and uninterested audiences. I was disappointed as I drove back to Teesside, but it was still a lot easier than standing at the bus stop at seven a.m. in the pouring rain, getting to ICI and carrying bricks up and down ladders, mixing darbo and cement for laggers, carrying and fetching and arguing and being on time and having to clock off and go home and fall asleep in the chair – all the things that a normal Teesside everyday bloke would do. Show business promised a little bit of excitement, as long as I had the bottle to do it.

A few days later, I was in my little red van, driving back from a music shop in Slaggy Island, when I passed my auld fella standing outside Baxter's, the bakery on Bolckow Road in Grangetown from which as a kid I'd bought that sack of broken biscuits with a stolen pound note.

I stopped on the other side of the road. 'Dad!'

'Hiya, son!'

'How are you doing?' Dad was wearing a long grey mackintosh and a flat cap, a fag wedged in the corner of his mouth. Typical Andy Capp.

'I'm fine, fine.' Dad had been retired two years. 'What you doing?'

'I'm working tonight. I'm at the Stockton Engineers' Club.'

'Oh right. How's Beryl? Is she all right?'

No wonder I couldn't get fixed up
(John Herring)

Man, do I look like a kamikaze pilot
(Roland Kemp)

Burlington Bertie from Bow

The cot and spoon routine.
The Hunchfront of Notre-Dame

How's that?

This was my first successful album – I sold five copies at three quid a time
(Jeff Costello)

Fuck off, daft arse

It's not the first time I've been on a tram

Me as my mother. Oh God!

I make a lovely tart

Les Dawson. I loved him

Sir Norman. The master – enough said

It's not unusual to be loved by anyone.
Thanks, Tom

My mentor and adopted dad

Didn't dare tell Shane I'm a Corrie fan

Jim Davidson with his fifth wife – me

The best. I had to point him at the camera

A real gentleman and tireless campaigner for charity

The modern-day Jesus of Nazareth

He's just asked me for Posh's number

Try not to chuckle, lads

Carol Vorderman – would I . . .

My two lads, Robert Colin Vasey and Richard Armstrong Vasey with Dad, Royston Vasey. Funny how we all have the same name

A pound's worth of broken biscuits, please

(Robert Uhlig)

My sister came to watch me receive the Club Comic of the Year award at Lakeside Country Club

My beautiful, loving wife Helen, who I call Sweetyheart

Never ask a vicar to take your
wedding photo

Married in Vegas –
because it's cheaper

My adorable family: Reece, Sweetyheart and Amy

(Dave Evans)

'Yeah, she's fine.'

'Betty's just sent me down to get some bits,' he said, holding up a bag of scones and tea cakes.

'Right, well, I'll probably speak to you tomorrow or the day after.'

That night I was on stage at the Engineers' Club when I noticed a policeman standing at the back of the hall. He walked over when I came off stage.

'It's your dad, Roy. He's had a heart attack,' the copper said.

I rang home. Betty said Dad was in hospital but stable, and that I should wait until the morning before visiting him, so I immediately drove back to the Ponderosa, the filthy dump of a doss-house that all the neighbouring Redcar residents hated and where I had a flat. Early the next morning Beryl came round from her house. She was crying.

'What's wrong?' I said.

Beryl couldn't speak, she was crying that much. I put my arms around her and comforted her. When she'd calmed down, she spoke. 'I've just had a message,' she said. 'Your dad's died.'

I started crying myself. 'It was only yesterday morning I was talking to him,' I said.

Washed and dressed, I drove round to Dad's house. Parked in the street outside, a black funeral director's van with blacked-out windows contained my auld fella lying in a box. Inside the house, Betty and my sister Barbara were waiting, crying. I hugged them both. 'Why?' I said. 'It doesn't seem right. What has he ever done to hurt anybody?'

Betty told me what had happened. As usual, Dad had gone to the club at half past seven. At half past eight he was back home, complaining of not feeling well. He went upstairs and lay down on the bed. At about nine o'clock, Betty heard a long, low groan and a wheeze come from the bedroom – they call it the death rattle, don't they? – so she ran upstairs. When she went in, Dad was unconscious. Betty rushed my auld fella to hospital and he died that night. It was 3 September 1976. Dad was sixty-eight. He'd worked all his life, never taking a day off from the steelworks, then he'd retired and two years later he was dead. It struck me that was no kind of decent life.

All Dad's workmates and all the lads from his club came to the funeral. There's not much to say about it except that it was incredibly sad. I looked at his casket and struggled to make sense of it. I couldn't believe I wasn't going to see him any more. Even now, thirty years later, I can see him as clear as if it was yesterday, standing on that corner outside Baxter's bakery with his flat cap and bag of scones. And I can still see him when I was a boy, pegging it along the street on his bike after work, making his way home to where I'd cleaned and hoovered and cooked us egg and chips for tea. It seems only yesterday that I was waiting outside his club, hopeful of a tanner to buy a bag of chips or a bottle of pop, waiting for Dad to come and pat me on the head and send me on my way.

Sometimes you don't realise just how much somebody means to you until you haven't got them any more. We'd been together from when I was born. Dad was the one person who'd always been there. He'd been father and mother to me, and for a time I'd been son and wife to him. He'd been the one who took me to the football matches. He was the one who held my hand and who sat in the garden with us. When he had a bit of spare cash, Dad was the one who took me to the seaside or on a trip with the club or to Blackpool on holiday.

I don't really know how I functioned in the months after Dad died. Everywhere I went, there were memories of him and of all the times we shared together. In the end, I had to force myself to stop thinking about it because I was getting nothing else done.

When Dad was cremated a few days later at Acklam crematorium, Barbara and I were asked if we wanted a plot with a stone in the garden of remembrance. Neither of us had any spare cash. With a string of bills owing, a van to run, maintenance to pay for Judy and the two boys, I was still pink lint even though I worked every hour God sent. It breaks my heart that I didn't have the money then, but I didn't and there's no point in looking back.

Dad left everything to his new wife and her children. Barbara and I didn't get a penny, so Betty asked us if we wanted to choose one of his belongings. I took a pocket watch that had been presented to my auld fella by his club. I kept in a drawer for years, until my house was burgled one night and the watch was pinched. I was certain that I knew who did it – he was a right rogue and he'd left his socks on the kitchen doorstep – but I couldn't prove it, so I never got it back. It was all I had left to remember my auld fella by and again my heart was broken.

Even after Dad died, my mam was forever criticising him and she was probably right, but I could never fault my auld fella. Whatever had gone on between my parents, he was still my dad. Most of my friends and just about everyone I work with are forever going on about their parents and they never seem to have a good word to say about their mothers or fathers. I never felt like that. I've never yet met a man who says 'I can't wait for the weekend. My dad's coming over. I don't half love him.' They don't know how lucky they are.

CHAPTER THIRTEEN

THREE'S A CROWD

I WAS FULL of good intentions but once I got to the cancer clinic and lay down on the radiotherapy machine, fear and depression would often get the better of my resolve to recover. When that happened, there was one nurse who made all the difference. Nurse Noleen would sit beside the radiotherapy machine, clutch my hand gently between her own hands and speak to me. When she did that, I felt like a million dollars. 'Now, are you all right?' Noleen would say. 'Is your weight all right? Has it been checked this morning? Are you sleeping well?' She had some kind of supernatural ability to make me feel calm. Listening to Nurse Noleen was like taking some great big tranquilliser pill.

'Is your hair all right? It's not falling out, is it?' Noleen said one day.

'My hair's all right but my pubes are gone,' I replied. I'd always used humour to avoid confronting uncomfortable things in my life and having cancer was no exception. If I could make someone laugh about it, I used to think, then it wouldn't matter.

Escape your troubles with a laugh – it was like something sold under the counter at chemists.

But it was difficult to make jokes about friends such as Ronnie, the lad who'd been our van driver when I was in the Four Man Band and who swallowed petrol when we siphoned it from cars parked at campsites. After he stopped driving for us, Ronnie got a job as a hospital porter. Feeling ill one day, he showed a lump on his stomach to one of the doctors. By the time they'd done a biopsy and discovered that the lump was cancerous, it had spread to his brain. Ronnie tried everything, even travelling to Ireland to drink special water and to Lourdes on pilgrimage, but none of it helped.

So when I felt depressed and hopeless, I'd think of Ronnie and think that there was always somebody worse off than me. As long as I kept thinking that, I stopped worrying about recovering. I stopped worrying about the unimportant things, such as if my cock was hanging out, or how much money I had. Cancer taught me that materialistic things didn't mean anything. All I wanted was to live a little longer so that my wife could put her arms around me and make me feel good.

●

Maybe it was a reaction to my auld fella's death, but not long after he died I started doing the dirty on Beryl. I had a comedian friend called Billy Kelly, who later drank himself to death. Billy was the compère at the Fiesta Club at Stockton-on-Tees and we'd often meet for a drink and a natter. When Billy's wife Shirley died of breast cancer, Billy needed some time off to get himself together, so he asked me to compère the shows for him.

The Fiesta was a classy venue, a typical 1970s nightclub with all the tables arranged so that everybody could see the stage. The men were dressed in dicky bows or ties, the women were dolled up and always looked a million dollars. Cocktail waitresses took orders – there was no queuing at the bar. All the top acts stopped at the Fiesta: Shirley Bassey, Freddie Starr, Tom Jones, the Four Tops, the Hollies, the Big Three, the Shirelles. Anyone who came to England at that time would work the Fiesta.

I had a great time at the Fiesta. The night Russ Abbot handed his notice in to the Black Abbots, I was there. You could have cut the atmosphere with a knife. I was there the night the Paper Dolls split up and there was a big cat-fight in the dressing room. And one night, one of the biggest television sitcom stars of the 1960s and 1970s appeared there. I was thrilled to see such a big star walking the corridors backstage – and even more thrilled when I walked in on him getting his leg over with his on-screen wife on the settee in his dressing room.

I'd been compère at the Fiesta for a few months when there was a knock at the back door. I opened it to find a large woman in a scruffy coat standing outside, a heavily laden plastic bag in each hand. 'Where'z da drezzing roomz?' she said in a deep, hoarse voice.

'What?'

'I zaid: Where'z da drezzing roomz?' she growled again. It was uncanny – she sounded just like Tommy Cooper's stage voice. I'd never heard such a strange voice from any woman. I pointed the woman down the corridor to the dressing rooms and turned to a mate loitering behind me.

'I know what you're thinking,' he said. 'Tommy Cooper?'

'Yeah.'

'You won't believe it. She's his wife.' And sure enough, a few minutes later Tommy appeared and headed down the corridor in the direction of his gravel-voiced wife.

Whenever Tommy Cooper played the Fiesta, he asked me to help him with one of his routines by passing him an aluminium ladder through the stage curtains. Standing in the slips in his trademark fez, Tommy instructed me what to do. When he waved his arms and said 'Ah-zazzz', I was to push the ladder out from the curtains by six inches. Then he'd say 'Ah-zazzz' again and the audience would see another six inches of the ladder emerge from the curtain. Every night, this amateurish magic trick had the audience in hysterics. But one night I replaced Tommy's eight-foot ladder with a much longer fourteen-foot one and kept on pushing it out long after Tommy stopped saying 'Ah-zazz'. The audience fell about, but Tommy didn't see the funny side of it at all. When he came off, I thought he was going to kill me. He went berserk.

'You ever fuck my act up again . . .' he said.

I hadn't fucked up his act, but he certainly lost his rag.

Standing at the bar of the Fiesta one night, I noticed a regular customer who hadn't previously crossed my radar. She was a great looker with nice eyes, lovely teeth and long dark hair, but the first thing that went through my mind was, 'By God, they're big tits.'

I'd been seeing Beryl for seven or eight years by then. We'd never lived together, mainly because I needed my own space, but otherwise we were as good as married, so I kept my distance from the top-heavy lass. We exchanged a few words while she was ordering a drink and that was it. The next night, we talked a bit more and I found I had a lot in common with Pat. She played the guitar and had written a few songs; I was teaching myself the piano. We swapped chords and words and began to realise that we were interested in each other.

It was gone two o'clock in the morning, we'd been circling

each other for a few weeks and we were both heading home when Pat asked me if I wanted a coffee.

'Yeah,' I said as we crossed the road. 'That'd be nice, if it's all right with you. Where do you live?'

'Here,' she said. It was less than a hundred feet away. As soon as we got in the door – my God, she was faster than a whippet. Forget the coffee, it was straight down to the nitty-gritty. I knew she wanted it and she knew I did. And boy, she had the loveliest, biggest pair of tits I'd ever seen.

We became lovers and had been going at it hammer and tongs for a couple of months when I gave her an indication of how I felt. Problem was, it came out all wrong.

'I don't like you hanging round the bar,' I said. 'All the blokes slathering all over you.'

'No, they don't.'

'Well, how do you think I met you?'

'What about you, stood on stage? All the women looking at you, thinking you're gorgeous?' It was just kids' stuff. Immature jealousy, but it caused a big argument and we split up. Then we got back together. Then we split up again. We were on and off like Christmas-tree lights.

Pat was great fun, one of the funniest women I've ever met. She always had a quick answer for anything and would have made a great comedienne if she'd had the bottle to get on stage. But you couldn't trust Pat as far as you could throw her. Everyone told me the same thing: 'You want to watch Pat. She likes a bit of dick.'

'You don't have to tell me,' I said the first few times I heard it. 'She likes dick and I'm happy.'

But it soon became apparent how much she liked blokes, particularly ones in bands. We were watching a band one evening when I noticed Pat staring at the guitarist. 'He's gorgeous, isn't he?' I said.

'I know him,' she said.

'Do you?' I found out that she'd slept with him before we met. And I discovered that as far as Pat was concerned, anyone who was in a band or group was a target. Talk about a dog of war. All the time I was with Pat, I was never sure if she was seeing someone else on the side. But then, I couldn't complain – I was still with Beryl.

My career at that time was no less complicated than my private life. After the disappointments of *Opportunity Knocks* and *New Faces*, I'd realised that I had to make a decision. I was faced with a simple choice. Did I want to be one of thousands of clean comedians trying to establish themselves and getting paid twenty-five or thirty-five pounds for a gig or did I want to be a blue comedian, with the potential to earn a lot more money but from a much smaller market? I knew there were only three or four blue comedians in the country that got regular work and that they were paid a hundred quid a gig.

On the face of it, the decision was easy. I was skint and there was little sign of my prospects improving. But I also knew that if I failed as a blue comedian, it would be much more difficult to find regular work as a clean comedian. The thing that swung it for me was realising that I had a talent for being filthy – or rather, the Chubby Brown character I'd created could get away with being crude and rude because my stage persona was a hapless fool, a lecherous Billy Bunter who boasted about his virility but was quite obviously a dead loss with women. I'd already discovered that I could get away with a lot more dressed in my multicoloured patchwork suit and flying helmet than dressed normally, so turning blue was simply a matter of throwing a few more well-timed 'fucks' into my routine. But once I started that, there was no turning back. A lot of people stopped noticing the material. All that mattered to them was the fact that

I'd said 'fuck'. And once I started doing that, many doors were slammed in my face.

Like many comics of that era, I had two acts. A clean act for most clubs and a blue act for stag nights and men-only after-dinner gigs. In those days, many clubs in the North-East didn't admit women. And all clubs were men-only on Sunday dinner times. It was a very male world.

Max Miller used to have what he called his white book and his blue book – clean jokes and dirty jokes – and I had just the same, except it was all in my head. Since the age of about twelve, I'd sworn like a trooper in the street, but I stopped as soon as I walked in the house out of respect for my auld fella and because he would have given me a thick ear if he'd heard me swear. Likewise, I'd swear all the time I was getting my stuff out of the van – 'Where's my fucking microphone?' 'What fucking time am I fucking on?' – but as soon as I walked up to the microphone I stopped swearing because if I did I wouldn't get paid.

I told a lot of clean jokes, even performing in old people's homes. 'A man went into the baker's,' I'd say, 'and said: "I see your sign outside. If I order any sandwich and you haven't got what I want, I can have something else for free." The woman behind the counter said: "That's right." He said: "I'll have an elephant sandwich, then." And the woman said: "That's okay, could you come back in three hours." And he went: "Ha ha ha ha! I knew you wouldn't have it." She said: "No, sir, you've mis-understood. It will take three hours to butter the bun".' It was simple humour and the old dears loved it.

Or I could play Saturday nights in clubs, where it would be jokes about the mother-in-law, the car, debts, about dancing and young girls and navy-blue knickers. A bit of naughtiness, but nothing too rude because it was a mixed crowd and the club didn't want to get a reputation for being rough.

The next day, Sunday dinner time, I could be back at the same club and there would be eight hundred scaffolders with broken noses and scars and no respect for a comic who came on and talked about navy-blue knickers while they sat there with their pints and plates of cheese and biscuits, waiting for the strippers to appear. They'd throw you through the window. I had to walk on and I had to be aggressive. I had to tell gags about dildos and fucking and prostitutes and – in those days because it was what scaffolders and builders expected – about black people and Asians. That was what they wanted to hear because they'd spent their entire lives on building sites and docks or in steelworks and mines. They liked to play the part of the hard man and there was no way they were going to mince their words, so comics couldn't either. They liked jokes such as: 'My mate's really hard. None of his tattoos are spelt right' or 'He's had his nose broken in three places. The back kitchen, the front room and the bath-room.' Subtle wit and social awareness would get you beaten up in those clubs.

Word started getting around clubland that I was ruder, cruder and more combative than many other comics. I was in great demand in the rough-arsed clubs, but my reputation also got round to the more respectable venues. 'Oh, we don't want him, you can't get up to go the toilet. He takes the piss,' I heard the committee members tell each other. 'Every other word is eff this or eff that. Have you heard some of the things he comes out with? He's brilliant on a stag night, but we have lady members and we don't want all that muck.'

And then, of course, concert chairmen spoke to each other, clubs discussed acts and suddenly my phone didn't ring as much. I'd have standing ovations at stag nights and on Sunday dinner times, but a raft of sour faces at small mixed clubs, not because my act was no good but because my reputation had preceded me and they'd decided they didn't like my sort.

Of course, some clubs and some bookings exploited the fact that I could be a bit too blue for some audiences. Cleveland Police Force, which was giving out bravery awards to people for feats such as diving into rivers and saving dogs, had invited up some top copper brass from Scotland Yard. Charged with organising the entertainment after the awards ceremony, one of the desk sergeants booked a band and me to appear at the Ladle Hotel in Middlesbrough, although I suspect he'd employed the time-worn way of having a go at a boss who didn't swear, namely booking a blue comedian.

I arrived at the Ladle to find all the men dressed in red dinner jackets and bow ties. All the women were in long dresses, white gloves above their elbows and box hats with veils. The sergeant took me aside. 'Roy,' he said, 'I don't want you to be too blue.'

'Well, what did you book me for?'

'You can be a bit saucy but don't go too far . . .'

'I've travelled here tonight, I'm only on seventy-five quid for a big do and now you're telling me I can't do what I want to do?'

'Well, just play it by ear . . .'

I walked on stage in a room dripping with candelabra. I cracked a joke and nobody laughed. So I cracked a joke about the police force. Again, nobody laughed. Then I cracked another joke. Silence. I looked down at a table in front of the stage, where two stuck-up women were gazing at me aghast.

'What the fucking 'ell's the matter with you two, Minge and Bracket?' I said.

There were gasps and ooohs at the front of the room, but at the back of the room all the regular coppers fell about. It was obvious they'd set me up.

'Obviously I'm pissing against the wind, ladies and gentlemen,' I said. 'And there's only me getting wet.' I walked off stage and went to the dressing room.

I was all over the place. Some nights the audience loved me; other nights they hated me. There was no halfway house. My blue act went down a storm, but the success of my clean act depended on the prejudices of the audience. It was a constant battle, but I was learning that show business was like that. And I was ahead of my time. Nowadays the word 'fuck' doesn't mean a thing. It's on telly every night. Graham Norton talks about twats all the time. No one would have got away with that when I started.

I felt in need of a holiday, so I offered to take big-breasted Pat to Majorca. We'd been together nearly two years. I also took my sons Richard and Robert, who were about nine and ten years old, but I didn't tell Judith, their mum, about Pat. The boys made friends with her, but I told them to say nowt. Pat was just a friend of Daddy as far as they were concerned. She took them swimming and bought them ice creams. They thought she was great.

But when the plane landed back at Middlesbrough and was taxiing to the terminal, the thought went through my head that Beryl or Judith might be waiting for me to arrive. Panicked by the prospect of being caught with Pat, I warned her that 'just in case Judy's here, I won't be holding your hand going down the stairs.'

Clambering down the stairs with the kids, pulling one and pushing the other as I lugged our hand luggage to the terminal, I left Pat struggling to lift her bag down from the luggage rack and leave the plane on her own. Inside the terminal, I whipped our cases off the conveyor belt and rushed through Customs to the arrivals lounge, where Beryl was waiting. The kids loved Beryl, but I didn't give them any time to say hello as I rushed them out of the airport, terrified that Pat would catch up with us.

I rang Pat the next day. She wouldn't speak to me. A week later I rang her again. 'You just fucking used me,' she said.

'I didn't.'

'You *did*. You couldn't wait to get off that plane. You could have taken me to the fish shop or had a drink before you went home, but no, all you wanted to do was get away. You must have somebody else.'

'I haven't. Honest. You're talking rubbish.'

But Pat was right. When you are seeing bits of pussy on the side, you're ducking and diving all the time, and you always get caught in the end. No one is that clever.

A few months later, Pat got a job at a Butlin's camp. I went to visit her, but she refused to let me on the site. We'd always meet off the site – at a garage, maybe. We'd go for a bite to eat and then have a fuck in the back of the car. I found out that a bald white-jacketed piano player in the Butlin's band was giving her one, but I didn't really care that much. I wasn't in love, just in lust, and much as I liked Pat, I knew she had a problem: she was too fond of dick. That problem, however, got a whole lot more complicated in 1979, by which time Pat had moved back to Redcar and we'd been seeing each other for about three years.

'I'm pregnant,' Pat said. 'And it's yours.'

For all Pat's reassurances that the child was mine, I didn't trust her. A couple of previous squeezes, who I'd casually knocked off on the side while seeing Beryl, had claimed they were pregnant with my child. One was a bird who worked on the tills at the local Tesco branch. She was engaged to another lad, so I had little reason to believe that the child was definitely mine. Pat, however, took deviousness to another level. I'd had too many experiences of turning up at nightclubs for a drink and finding Pat on the dance floor with another bloke on a night when she'd told me she was staying home to wash her hair. I was forever hearing tales from other blokes of Pat's shenanigans. She'd tell me she was staying home, then I'd go round to visit her and discover she wasn't in. A couple of days later, a mate would say he'd seen Pat in a club with another bloke. It happened so often that it got beyond a joke. And even after she told me she was pregnant and claimed there'd been no one else in her life for a while, there were stories that Pat was seeing a policeman and a footballer in Hartlepool. I felt I had no choice but to ask her for a blood test.

'If you don't want this baby to be yours,' Pat replied to my demands for proof, 'it's not yours. I'm not bothered. I'll just tell the social that I don't know who the father is.'

Some days I did want it to be mine, other days I didn't, but most of the time I simply didn't want the responsibility of fatherhood. I'd neglected Richard and Robert for the job, so it seemed wrong to take on another child when I couldn't give the boys the attention they deserved.

As if my sex life wasn't already fraught enough, while Pat was pregnant and I was living with Beryl I met another woman. From the moment we met, Maureen was very clear about what she wanted. All Maureen wanted was a good old-fashioned fuck, plain and simple. She lived in Stockton-on-Tees and I would drop by after a gig for a leg-over before going back to Beryl or Pat. There were days when I'd sleep with all three of them in one night. I'd arrive at Maureen's house. We'd share a glass of wine on the couch, I'd shag her and then I'd say 'See ya.' On the way home to Beryl, I'd remember that I'd promised Pat I'd drop around, so I would go through the whole spiel again with Pat before heading home to where Beryl was waiting in bed for me. It went on like that for about six weeks, by which time I felt like the walking wounded.

Maureen was very discreet – she was separated from her husband and waiting for a divorce – but what I didn't know was that a comedian friend of mine who was knocking off Pat lived opposite Maureen and that his son had spoken to Pat.

'What was your car doing outside Maureen's house?' said Pat one night.

'What are you talking about?' I said, turning red as a beetroot.

'It was outside there on Tuesday and on Saturday.'

'Oh . . . where's that? Near the Malleable Club?'

'Yeah.'

'I broke down, didn't I?'

'You broke down for three nights?'

I just couldn't lie and I admitted it all to Pat. 'She's just a friend,' I said. Pat and I got over it and I stopped seeing Maureen. Then one day, several months later, I bumped into Maureen at a car-boot sale.

'Why don't you come round to mine?' she said. So I did, but this time I left my car around the corner.

A few weeks later, I was playing a club in Sunderland. I came off stage at nine-thirty, got in my car and drove around to Pat's flat. We'd arranged to meet at ten o'clock. 'Shall I bring some fish and chips round?' I said.

'No, just drop in,' she said. 'I'll be waiting.'

I walked in. There on the sofa in the front room of Pat's flat, sitting in a line like those see-no-evil-hear-no-evil-speak-no-evil monkeys, were Beryl, Pat and Maureen.

'Whoops!' I said. 'I think I've dropped a bollock.'

'I think you better sit down,' said Beryl.

'I can't stop . . .'

'You sit yourself down now. We need to talk to you about what's going on here,' Beryl said. 'You've got some explaining to do.'

'I've no explaining to do. Work it out yourselves.' They looked at me. 'Well, I've been caught . . .'

I walked out of the house. I had no answers for them, so I thought I might as well let them get on with it. I went back to my flat, shut the door and didn't answer it for several days.

About a week later, Beryl came round. 'So what have you got to say for yourself?' she said.

'Well . . . you know . . . a couple of drinks, you know . . .'

'How long has it been going on?'

'I don't know. I can't remember.'

'Pat's pregnant.'

'Yeah.'

'Is it yours?'

'She said it is.'

'Are you sure?'

'Well, I've asked her for a blood test and she told me to get lost.'

'What you going to do?'

'Nothing.' I looked at Beryl. Out of all three of them, she was the one I loved, even if I had a funny way of showing it. 'I am sorry,' I said. 'I do love you and . . .'

'Well, it's up to you. Do you want to carry on or not?'

'Do *you* want to carry on?'

'I don't know,' she said.

We drifted apart after that. All of us. When Pat's baby was born, I made an effort to visit the two of them in hospital. Michelle was a bonny girl, but I didn't feel anything for her because I wasn't sure she was mine. As for Pat, I bought her clothes, I decorated her house, I bought her a washing machine and a television, and I gave her fifty quid a week. Then Pat moved away. We kept in touch by phone, but I rarely saw her or Michelle again.

Beryl and I realised that, after ten years together, our

romance had run its course. She made no effort to rekindle dying flames and neither did I.

And Maureen? I never heard another word from her after that day in Pat's front room when the three of them caught me with my pants around my ankles.

CHAPTER FOURTEEN

GORGEOUS GEORGE

WHEN THE RADIOTHERAPY was finished, they examined my throat. The verdict was good and my mood improved dramatically, but I still couldn't speak. Again the question resurfaced of what I would do if I didn't regain my voice. Having spent more than thirty-five years on stage, speaking for two hours a night, it felt as if I'd lost a limb. I'd spent half a lifetime being funny every day of my life and I couldn't get used to not being funny. I needed to speak and to have something for which to write.

So I wrote to Cancerbackup, an organisation that helps people with cancer and provides information. They sent pamphlets and books advising me to drink carrot juice and eat broccoli. Above all, they said, try to do the things you've always done.

But instead of doing what I'd always done – get up on stage – I had to lay off my crew. I'd paid them for the first eight weeks of my illness, but I couldn't continue to pay that kind of money when there was nothing coming in. They all found jobs elsewhere.

After seeing Pauline in the red headscarf die after three courses of radiotherapy, I decided to devote my time to raising money for cancer charities. With my son Richard, I helped raise money for a cancer hospice at James Cook Hospital in Middlesbrough. Richard climbed Kilimanjaro with his mates, almost collapsing six hundred metres from the summit and raising £12,500. I was thrilled at the achievement, even if I felt that the government should have provided it for the working men and women of Middlesbrough who'd toiled all their lives and paid their tax and national insurance only to find that when they got ill there was no one to look after them.

●

The late 1970s were not easy times. After splitting up with three women – Beryl, Pat and Maureen – all at once, my love life was in tatters. And although I was gaining a good reputation in the clubs, it was as a crude comic who took no prisoners, which limited the number of venues that would book me. I certainly had a sense that these were the dark days and that, if I persevered, things could only get better.

Anyone going through difficult times needs good friends and fortunately I'd found one of the best in my driver at the time, Peter Richardson. We first met one night when I noticed a river of piss running down the pavement past my van. I looked up and there was Peter stood in the shop doorway.

'Sorry, mate,' he said.

'It's all right,' I said. 'You couldn't do me a favour? The van won't start. Do you live anywhere near Redcar? Can you give me a lift?'

That was a mistake. Peter drove home along the moors roads in a steam bucket of a car. To this day I don't know how we made it – I was petrified – but a friendship was forged that night that led to Peter working for me on and off for more than fifteen years. In that time, Pete was everything to me – chauffeur, personal assistant, protector and confidant. He loved a bargain and a practical joke, which led to some great laughs on the road, but the best thing about Pete was that he was all heart and fiercely loyal.

Pete understood the difficult love-hate relationship that I had with my audience and the kind of trouble to which it could lead. It's a well-known fact that I've had my fair share of trouble – the tabloids delight in reporting it – and often the public think I had it coming to me. People assume that because I swear and I'm crude on stage, I'm the same off stage. They presume I provoke the trouble and then get my come-uppance. But that was rarely the case, although my on-stage persona did mean I had more admirers in prison than outside. Several times, women came up to me and said: 'My husband thinks you are absolutely wonderful. *Fantastic*. He *lives* for you. All he does is sit and watch your videos. If he knew I was talking to you now, he would be stood there with a hard-on, but unfortunately he's inside for the next five years.' The people who came to my shows weren't frightened to walk around with a T-shirt printed with 'Fuck you' or 'Bollocks to Chubby Brown'. They were rough people from rough houses on rough estates and they knew I was just like them, except I struck lucky and found a way out. I loved my audience dearly, but it did mean I got more trouble than most comics – and that was where having a friend like Peter came in handy.

We were stopping at the De Vere, the best hotel in Blackpool. Waiting at the reception desk for my key, Peter standing beside me holding my bags, I was nearly knocked off my feet when this huge lad crept up behind us and jumped on my back.

'Chubby Brown!' he shouted. 'You fucking big fat cunt.'

'Yeah, hello,' I said. 'Just keep your language down, please. There's girls behind the reception.' I thought he was just another over-friendly, pissed-up fan.

'You big fat fucking bastard . . .'

'Listen, we've established what I am,' I said. 'Could you just keep your language down, please?'

'What are you going to do about it?' he said. 'You big bastard.'

He walked towards me as if he was going to throw his arm round my shoulders, but I was worried that he had more violent intentions than giving me a friendly hug. I put my hand out to push him away. 'Look, I'm not in the mood,' I said. 'Leave us alone.'

As I turned around to pick up one of my bags, the lad swung his fist around and punched me smack in the mouth. He must have been wearing a ring with a spike because his punch went straight through my lip and into my gum. Blood squirted everywhere. I was shocked. I hadn't expected it. It was like being knocked down by a car.

'Fucking hell,' Peter said. 'Look at your gob!'

I touched my swollen lip and looked down. Blood was running down the front of my T-shirt. 'You fucking bastard!' I shouted and ran after the lad, who ran out of the door and got away. But his mates, about a dozen fellas who were drinking in the bar, stood up as one.

'Come on, then!' they shouted. 'Come and get it, you fat cunt!'

Fists flew everywhere and Pete took most of the punches. He was bitten around the head and hands, kicked and punched, all just to protect me. The hotel security turned up, saw how vicious these lads were and ran off, so I picked up a table in the foyer and smashed it against the lads to get them off Peter. Then I grabbed a vase and broke it over one of the attackers' heads. Kicking the lad as he dropped to the floor, I shouted to Peter to get out of it quick. We ran to the lift, jumped inside it and managed to get the door shut while the dozen lads tried to pull us out.

Arriving at the top floor, we found a phone in a corridor and rang down to reception. 'It's Chubby,' I said breathlessly. 'I'm bleeding pretty badly and so is my mate. I'm going to have to get out of this hotel and get him to hospital.'

'We've sent for an ambulance,' the receptionist said 'The police are here now.'

The coppers had rounded up the attackers by the time we got down to reception. 'Do you know which one did it?' said one of the bluebottles.

'No, but if I see him again,' I said, 'I'll know him.'

The copper explained that our assailants were showmen from a travelling fair associated with some of the amusement arcade owners in Blackpool. One of them had a birthday, so they'd booked up the De Vere and commandeered the place with little respect for anyone or anything else in the vicinity. They'd driven cars across flower beds and the police had found stolen credit cards on the showmen they'd arrested.

Pete and I went to hospital. A doctor put a stitch in my face and four stitches in Peter's head. Then we went back to the hotel, collected our gear and went home. I cancelled the show, something I do very rarely. I was that upset about it.

A couple of years later, Peter and I stopped at another hotel in another seaside town. There were two lads at the bar, both with earrings and both a bit Jack the lad. 'Hiya, Chubby,' they said.

'Hi. All right?'

'We're coming down to see you tonight. It was great last year.'

'Oh, smashing.'

'Do you want a drink?'

'Aye.' We got talking.

'You know, you're not the bloke I thought you were,' one of them said.

'How d'you mean?'

'That night at the De Vere that you had a fight, I was there. I thought you were an animal. I've never seen anybody go mad like that.'

'You were there?'

'Yeah, I'm a showman.'

'So were you involved in the fight?'

'No. I kept out of it.'

'So who were they?'

'You don't want to know . . .'

'Yes, I do.'

'No, I'd forget it if I was you. If there is six of you, there'll be eight of them. If there is ten of you, there'll be twelve of them. And they are all fist fighters. They'll come from miles around to have a go at you, so why don't you just forget it, it's all over and done with now.'

'You actually know the lad with the ring?'

'Yeah. He's an absolute cunt. And so is his family.'

'Where are they from?'

'Here. They own all the amusements on the seafront.'

Sometimes it's best not knowing. That lad in the De Vere marked me for life. And for nothing but a stupid bit of horse-play. When I get a tan, the scar he gave me on my lip stays white. I'm still as mad as blazes, but I had to realise it was time to put it behind me, else I'd carry the anger for ever.

Although incidents such as the fight weren't commonplace with Pete, there were dozens of other occasions when he came to my rescue, particularly as Pete looked very similar to me and could often pretend that he *was* me when I had a bit of trouble. And whenever something funny happened, Pete was also usually there.

We were staying in a pro digs in Wales that we called
Pansey's Down because we couldn't pronounce its proper
Welsh name. Staggering in, laden with bags, we dinged the
bell at the reception desk. This fella appeared, six foot four
and thin as a rake.

'*What?*' he said.

'Chubby Brown, Peter Richardson . . .'

'*Yeeees?* What do you want?'

'We booked in.'

'*Did you now?* When did you book?'

'Our office will have booked it.'

'Are you sure?'

Peter and I looked at each other. This fella didn't have the
moustache, but in every other way he was just like Basil Fawlty,
so much so that it was like he was doing an impression.

'Right. Right,' he said. 'I see . . . Yes . . . Have you much luggage?'

'Yes, lots.'

'Well, you'll have to carry it yourselves. No porter.' We didn't
know whether to laugh or not. 'Right! That's your key. OK?
Your key.'

'What number's my room?' I said.

'Are you blind?'

'No.'

'Well, can't you see it's number fourteen?'

We went to our rooms, then met in the lounge, where the
Basil Fawlty fella was serving behind the bar. He did everything
in that hotel – reception, room service, waiter in the dining
room and barman.

'What's everybody having?' I said.

'What's the beer?' said Peter.

'*Could* you make your mind up?' the Basil Fawlty fella said. 'I
haven't got all day.'

'Would anyone like some crisps?' I asked Peter and some of the other performers we knew in the lounge.

'*Crisps?*' the Basil Fawlty fella said. 'You want *crisps?* We've got two flavours. Take it or leave it. It's up to you.'

As he passed me the crisps, I noticed he had a plaster on his finger.

'What happened there?' I said.

'*What?*'

'What happened to your finger?'

'Why don't you ask *him?*'

'Who?'

'*Him.* In the cage.'

As if his manner wasn't enough to convince you he was John Cleese, a sad-looking parrot sat in a cage at the end of the bar.

'The parrot bit your finger?'

'Yes. And he lived to regret it.'

'Oh, right.'

'He was squawking. Squawking all the time. *Squawking.* Couldn't talk to the customers. Couldn't hear myself think. So I opened that window there. And I opened the cage and I shook the cage and I said go! *Fuck off!* I don't want you any more. Get lost!'

'Christ, what happened?'

'He flew out the window. I thought that was the last I'd see of him and the bastard flew back in that one.' He pointed at the other window, further along the wall. 'I didn't have the heart to throw him out again so I put him back in the cage. He fucking bit me!'

We were crying with laughter.

'Look!' he said. 'Fucking bit me! I'll get him back.'

At another hotel in Skipton, Pete and I stayed up late in the bar with Kay Rouselle, a jazz singer who worked with a six-piece band. Kay was lovely, one of the lads who liked a drink, a cigarette and a shag. She could fart like the rest of us. And she could handle the blokes. She always used to say she could fuck all night.

Whenever we worked at the same venue, Kay would introduce me on stage; she really knew how to deal with hecklers. If any of the lads shouted 'Get your tits out!' Kay always had a reply. 'You wouldn't know what to do with them,' she'd snap. Or: 'Go home, your mother's waiting there for you. It's time for your breast feed.'

Peter and I were sat in the lounge at the Skipton hotel having a drink with Kay when we noticed a bloke at the end of the bar who kept staring at her. He turned out to be the manager and bought us all a drink. 'Not a bad bloke,' Kay said after the manager had bought us a second drink. 'Quite handsome.'

The manager only had eyes for Kay, but then, she was the only bit of skirt there. 'Are you married to any of these lads?' he said.

'Oh no, my husband is on the *QE2*,' Kay said. 'He's a trumpet player.'

I thought no more of it and went to bed around half past one. Next morning, we were all sitting at breakfast when Kay walked into the dining room. Sashaying through the room, a fur coat over her shoulder, she winked at a group of us sitting at a big table.

'Morning, lads,' she said, smiling.

'Morning, Kay,' we said.

'There won't be a bill this morning,' she said with a dirty smirk on her face. She'd obviously spent the night with the manager. 'No charge after last night.' And she was right – there was nowt to pay.

Peter was invaluable in those days. He shared the laughs and he helped fend off the trouble but, more significantly, he was there when things got really miserable. And miserable would have been a compliment to some of the clubs I played in those dark days. The worst of all was a club at Queensferry in North Wales. The graffiti on the dressing-room walls was a master-piece. Like an obscene version of the Sistine Chapel, every square inch was covered with cocks, fannies and filthy com-ments. As for the sink, it was full of piss. And there was dog shit on the floor. I've never forgotten the smell. It stank worse than anywhere I've ever been. I only wish I'd had a camera at the time because it would have made an ideal photograph to show how I started. The toilets were cleaner than the dressing room.

The worst night I ever had in that period was so bad it ended up on the front page of a newspaper. I'd been booked to play a stag night at the Dial House, one of the largest clubs in Sheffield, with Dennis Beard, a magician, and four strippers. If someone had told me that Tommy Cooper had pinched his entire act from Dennis, I wouldn't have been at all surprised. Born at the turn of the twentieth century, Dennis had a wrinkly little face, always wore a fez and specialised in magic tricks that went comically wrong.

Word had got around that Chubby Brown was on and by the early 1980s I had a bit of a reputation, so the tickets sold out in four hours. But about a hundred tickets had been sold to people from Rotherham, most of whom turned up in football strips to rile all the Sheffielders. Daggers were drawn before the show started. By the time the first stripper came on at about nine o'clock, most of the crowd were on their fourth or fifth pint. It didn't take long for a fight to break out. I stepped out of my dressing room and peered out from behind the stage cur-tains to see chairs, tables and glasses flying through the air as about forty Rotherham supporters took on about eighty Sheffield fans.

It was like a western, when a fight breaks out in the saloon and everything gets smashed – the furniture, the bottles of drink, the glasses and the mirrors on the walls. I could see that the action might put my eye out and I could hear police dogs barking, so I decided not to venture out from behind the stage. After about an hour, the police carted the fighters off in police vans and the girls got dressed. Emerging at last from the dressing room, I found a bloke with blood on his white shirt standing in a room that looked like a sawdust factory.

'Committee man?' I said.

He nodded. 'Steward.'

'Eh, what was all that about?'

'They sold the tickets to the wrong people, man.'

'That's *some* damage you got here.'

'I'm not bothered,' said the steward, opening up the palm of his hand. He was holding four solid gold chains, about half a dozen rings and a thick wad of money. 'I've just picked that up off the floor. It'll pay for some of it.'

In spite of having absolutely nothing to do with it, I was blamed for the fight. *Geordie Comic Incites Riot* said the headline in the Sheffield evening paper the next day. I don't know what the biggest insult was – calling me a Geordie when I'm a Yorkshireman or blaming me for sommat that had nowt to do with me.

On 3 April 1982, Brian Findlay phoned me. It was a Saturday night and Brian wanted to know if I was going to pick him up the next day on the way to playing a club he'd booked me into in Thornaby. I agreed to pick him up from a little caravan he kept at Hutton Sessay, about twenty miles from York. The next morning, I got a phone call from Brian's wife, Rita. Brian had been making a bacon sandwich at about ten o'clock that morning when he'd had a massive heart attack. He was only forty-eight.

After Brian's funeral, Rita tried to take over his talent agency, but she didn't have a business brain and all the acts suffered. There was no work coming in and when she did get work for her clients the money was terrible because Rita was too nice to demand a decent fee for her acts.

I needed to find a new agent and remembered meeting George Forster shortly after Louvane's death in Malta. I put on a blue suit and made an appointment to see him at his office at Chester-le-Street. Everyone I spoke to in show business advised me to keep away from George who, as the son of a Geordie docker, had a reputation as an unpleasantly hard man.

'He's ruthless,' they said. 'He's a sixty/forty man.'

George, they said, kept a tight grip on his acts' earnings and would sack them at a moment's notice. And apparently he was underhand and had no friends. 'George Foster?' one act said to me. 'Work for him? I wouldn't work for him if he was the only agent on this planet. I'd pack the business in.'

'Why?' I said.

'He's an out and out cunt.'

But I believed in making my own judgement, so one day in November 1982 I knocked on George's door. Stuck on the first step of the show-business ladder, I wanted to climb higher and I thought George might be able to help me.

Dark and handsome, but not that tall, George looked a bit like Paul McCartney. I told him I was looking for new management. 'Do you fancy taking over?' I said.

'OK,' said George. 'As from when?'

It was that straightforward. George came across as all right to me and I believe in taking as I find. I could see that George was all 'me, me, me' and I'd have to be all 'George, George, George' but I liked him and refused to have owt said against him. 'He's all right with me,' I'd say to anyone who asked.

About a month later, he sent me to Wallsend British Legion Club and told me to pick up £125 for the gig. I'd never earned that much before. I was a seventy-quid-a-night comic at best.

'I can't ask for £125,' I said. 'I'm not worth it.'

'Look, Roy, they've asked for you, they want you and they'll pay the money,' George said. 'You just go and do the job.' It was a very different approach to Brian's.

I had a good night on stage. George rang the next morning. 'I've just had the club on,' he said. 'I hear you had a fantastic night.'

'It was great George, yeah.'

'Did you get your money?'

'No, I didn't.'

'Why? Didn't they pay you?'

'To be honest, George, I didn't ask for it.'

'Why not?'

'One hundred and twenty-five quid? They'd have told me to fuck off.'

'Oh,' said George. The phone clicked dead.

Four hours later, there was a knock on my flat door. It was George. 'Here's your cheque,' he said.

'What's that?'

'It's your cheque.'

George had driven sixty miles from Chester-le-Street to Wallsend to Redcar to give me my money. When I saw him do that, I knew that going with George had been the right decision.

'What's the matter?' said George.

'I haven't got a bank account.'

'Well, get somebody to cash it for you.'

'I don't know anybody who'd have a hundred and twenty-five pounds.'

'Oh fucking hell,' George said. 'Give it here.' He disappeared down the corridor. Ten minutes later he was back, having cashed it nearby. 'You're going to have to open a bank account because most of my work will be with cheques. That's the way you'll get paid from now on.'

From that day, my fee shot up to £125 or £150. If I was asked for personally, it was two hundred quid. And also from that day, a whispering campaign started among my show-business pals. You can't trust George, they'd claim. But I always had an easy answer. I thought George's ruthlessness, aggression and wheeling and dealing worked for me rather than against me. I'd rather have had George fighting my corner – even if he was as hard-headed as alleged – than a spineless agent who was as honest as Brian Findlay.

George and I soon discovered that we were very alike in many ways, and maybe that was what held us together. When we stayed in hotels or pro digs, we folded the towels the same way – even George's wife remarked on it – and we'd both straighten the bed as soon as we got out of it. George liked HP Sauce on his food; so did I. We both married women whose birthdays were in June and we were both Aquarians. Silly little details, perhaps, but often it's the little things that make the difference and George and I soon became very close friends.

One of the things I liked about George was that things had to be absolutely right or there'd be trouble. George wouldn't accept second-best. He was the governor and you did things his way or else, particularly as he had a very quick temper. I once saw him lose his temper on the A1 with a van driver. He grabbed the driver by his shirt and tried to drag him through the side window of his van, he was that angry and that determined to do something about it.

But George wasn't all aggression. If it suited him, he could be very charming, particularly with the ladies. But to George, seducing a woman was like securing a business deal. I lost count of the number of times George would be in a hotel bar sweet-talking a woman, and then he'd go missing. The girl would ask where George had gone and I'd always have to shrug and say he'd gone to bed. He lost interest once he knew he could have them.

George's and my business dealings were sealed by a close friendship. I thought he was a great fella and he thought the world of me. He was the brother I never had – albeit a brother to whom I paid a percentage and gave generous Christmas presents but got little of material value in return. George's house was full of pictures and ornaments that I had bought him. I didn't resent it – I'd bought them because I was so grateful for what he'd done – but I was lucky if I got a Christmas present at all from George. Nevertheless, I wouldn't have anybody say owt against him. Other people would be surprised when I said I worked with George Forster and ask if he was still a cunt. I'd always leap to his defence. George was a wonderful fella, I'd say, and the only reason they thought otherwise was because they'd never got to know him.

As soon as I signed with George, my fortunes changed. At last I had someone who fought my corner. He was just as loyal to me and wouldn't stand anyone saying owt against me.

'How much is Chubby Brown?' a club concert chairman would ask.

'I want £250 for him,' George would answer straight back.

'Two hundred and fifty quid? I can remember when I paid fifteen.'

'Yes, I can remember when you paid him fifteen quid, too – and you robbed him blind. He was worth a lot more than fifteen pounds but you got him for that and you exploited him and you never ever gave him what he was worth. He packs places out now. You put his name on the board and people flock to see him and you still want to pay fifteen quid? He's £250. If you don't like it, lump it.'

'Yeah, but he's foul-mouthed . . .'

'He's not foul-mouthed. He's clever, very clever at what he does. How many people do you know who can stand on stage for an hour and have them in hysterics by saying "fuck"? It's not just a word. It's where you put the "fuck". If you put it at the beginning of a joke or at the end of a joke, it's got to be there for a purpose. He doesn't just say "fuck" for the sake of it. You want to sit and observe him and see how hard he works at what he does. You people come on the phone and you offer fifteen quid for him. You won't give me fuck-all for him. I'll give you him for what he is worth and I think he's worth £250 for an hour spot and I want . . .'

That was George. He always made sure I got my dues. And if it was New Year's Eve, he'd treble my price. I'd go to the highest bidder, like at a cattle market. I trusted George implicitly. I never asked to see a breakdown. He looked after me, I looked after him and I believed I could rely on him a hundred per cent. It was like a marriage.

George once booked me at a nightclub in Whitehaven, a journey that from my home took me across the Pennines, passing through Brough, one of the highest towns in England. One thing was for sure: if the weather was bad in Middlesbrough, it would be a nightmare in Brough. And that day it was snowing in Middlesbrough.

George and I arranged to meet in Whitehaven, but coming over the Pennines I got stuck in the snow along with about thirty wagons, vans and cars. Arriving at a hotel in Brough, I found a queue of eight people waiting to use a single payphone. Eventually I got through to the club in Whitehaven. George was having a drink at the bar, so I asked the club management to get him to come to the phone.

'George, it's Roy,' I said. 'I'm stuck in a snowdrift on the A66. I can't go forward and I can't go back. Everybody's waiting for a snowplough.'

'Don't worry,' said George. 'I'll ring my mate at Newcastle airport and get a helicopter to come and pick you up.'

There was no way I was going in a helicopter, especially in snow so thick that I could hardly see the tip of my nose.

'If I was you, George, I'd make a sharp exit.'

'Aye, right,' he said. George found the club owner and told him what had happened.

'George, you'll have to go on the stage and tell them,' the club owner said. His club was packed to the seams with punters who wanted to see Chubby Brown. There wasn't enough room for oxygen in the place.

'Aye, right . . .' George said. It was the manager's job to explain my non-appearance to the audience, but I knew George well enough to know he'd be petrified at the thought of walking on stage. '. . . I better have a ciggy first. I'll just get my fags out the car.'

George went out to his car, jumped in and drove off. The club owner rang him the next day. 'You crafty bastard, George!' he said. 'You knew what you were doing. You just didn't want to go on stage and face the music.'

After a year together, George suggested that instead of being an agent of twenty-odd acts, he would be a manager of just one: me. I was very happy with the arrangement.

'I'll concentrate on you because I think me and you could go a long way,' George said. 'You're the talented one. I'm the businessman. You leave the money side to me and I won't tell you what to do on stage.'

Not long after we formed the partnership, George and I were sitting in a hotel when he made a suggestion. 'I've been thinking about your act, Roy,' he said. 'There's a lot of television work coming up, but you need to decide what you want to do.

'You've got a gift for saying "fuck" without being too offensive . . .' he said. 'Well, you haven't, but this disgusting character you've invented seems to be able to say "fuck" without causing offence. I think you should stop arsing about doing blue gigs and clean gigs. I think you should go full-time blue. Because if you do, you could become one of the most successful comedians in the country.'

Put like that, it was an easy decision. Whenever I could, I'd do a blue gig even if there was only an extra tenner in it. Going full-time blue would mean more money at a time when I was struggling to make ends meet.

However, there was a sting in the tail. 'If you go full-time blue,' George said, 'you can kiss goodbye to any dreams of appearing on television. No television company will touch you.'

Regular television appearances were seen as one of the few sure-fire routes to wealth and fame for comedians. Just about every successful comedian working in the 1970s and 1980s got their big break on television – Russ Abbot, Billy Connolly, Victoria Wood, Bob Monkhouse and many others. If I went full-time blue, I realised, the crucial stepping stone of television would be out of bounds to me.

However, I also had to face the facts. I was never going to be Mr Clean, tap-dancing, singing, playing the drums and cracking jokes on my very own TV show. It wasn't going to happen that way for me because I was simply too rough for the rarefied world of television. I was no good at sucking up to the concert chairmen in clubs, so what chance would I have in television where the recipe for success was one part talent and two parts arse-licking influential producers?

So I decided to become blue because it meant I could earn up to five hundred pounds for a show. In the end everything comes down to getting paid and paying your bills, and I went for it. I decided to go right over the top and be the rudest man in the country.

As soon as it got around that I was full-time blue, many clubs that I'd played for years rang George up to say I was no longer welcome. When I became well known, they offered me fortunes to go back just because they knew I put arses on seats, but in those days they didn't want to know me.

The list of clubs that would have me got shorter and shorter. When I looked at my material, I was baffled. The only real difference between my old clean act and my new blue act was that there were more swear words. But back then, the number of comedians who had the guts to go on stage and say 'Are you cunts having a fucking good time?' instead of the same sentence without the expletives was small and the number of clubs who were prepared to tolerate such language was tiny.

At times I wondered if I hadn't made the wrong decision. In quiet moments, I'd worry about what would happen when I wanted to settle down, get married and have children. Did I want my children living with a man known as Britain's foulest mouth? I already knew that some audiences couldn't tell the difference between the bloke on stage in the multicoloured suit and flying helmet and the bloke at home with his kids. They were the kind of people who'd think I went home to my wife and said: 'Get the fucking kettle on, you fat twat. Are the fucking kids in fucking bed yet?' They were the types who would later think nothing of shouting 'All right, Chubby, you fat fucking cunt!' down supermarket aisles. I worried about all these things, but I never back-pedalled.

Instead, I placed all my trust in George. And George trod very carefully. There was no longer any point booking me to play a Catholic club. He worked hard to place me in the right clubs. Good agents are like good second-hand car salesmen. They have to be good liars. In the office, I'd overhear George on the phone – 'Yes, he's fantastic . . . comic of the year . . . sells out everywhere . . . in huge demand . . . don't know if I can squeeze you in, he's that busy . . .' – and when he put down the receiver,

I'd ask him who he was talking about. 'Oh, I was just selling you,' George would say.

'Selling *me*? I didn't recognise myself in all that, George!'

'Just leave it to me, Roy. You tell the jokes and I'll do the business.'

Gradually my notoriety started to work for me. The slamming in my face of many clubs' doors was a form of censorship. And like anything that's prohibited – booze, fags, drugs, pornography – the more I was driven underground, the greater the demand for my act. George started getting calls from punters asking where they could see me because their local club wouldn't have me on stage. Word got around that I was *the* comic to book for stag nights. So George put up my price, which made people think I must be something really special, which drove demand up even further.

My act got better because I was more comfortable telling blue jokes than the Paddy and Mick gags that were the staple of most comedians' acts in those days. I'd always thought that when an Irishman told an Irish story it was a damn sight funnier than when an Englishman told the same tale. Told by an Irishman, it looked like he was laughing at himself. From an Englishman, it looked like he was taking the piss. It was the same with blue jokes. My laughs came from ridiculing my exploits with women. 'Have you heard?' I'd say. 'J-Lo's pregnant. God, am I in the shit.' The audience would laugh because it was preposterous. They knew I was taking the piss out of myself. The same joke from a slim, good-looking comedian wouldn't have been half as funny as from a fat, balding lump, dressed in a multicoloured suit and flying helmet like a clown's outfit.

But my rise wasn't without setbacks. After playing a club in Sunderland, one of the punters came into my dressing room. 'Nobody – and I mean *nobody* – swears in front of my wife,' he said. Then he spat in my face. I lamped him and he leaped on me. 'I'll get you outside, you fucking twat!' he snarled when the club security broke us apart. I came out of the club to find my car on bricks.

I did a tour of Scottish clubs. The first night I played Penicuik Working Men's Club, as rough a club as any. I lasted two minutes. The next night I was in Lesmahagow. Paid off after ten minutes. On the Tuesday, I played Rosyth Naval Yard. Tore 'em apart. They were standing on the tables and the wives loved me even more than the sailors did. When I got a standing ovation, that big, draughty hangar felt like a little club. The following night I was paid off at Kilmarnock, at which point George suggested I came home. 'Fuck 'em,' he said. 'They don't know talent when they see it.'

I played the Pile Bar, a social club in Bradford. On the poster outside it just said 'comedian'.

'You do know what I do?' I said to the club chairman.

'All the lads have seen you at a club along the road. They said you're fantastic, so we booked you.'

'But that's not the question. Do you know what I do?'

'You're a comic, aren't you?'

'Yes, but I'm a blue comedian.'

'As long as you're not too bad, we don't mind.'

Walking on stage, I opened with 'Good evening, ladies and gentleman. My wife's got two cunts. I'm one of them.' I looked at the audience. They were just gobsmacked. All I could see was row upon row of white, ashen faces.

'Has he just said . . . ?' a woman said, breaking the silence. 'Has he just said . . . ?'

Ten minutes later, the club chairman marched up to the stage. 'I demand you get off immediately.'

'That's OK, mate.' I said, 'I told you what I was like and it's like the moon's surface up here. No atmosphere.'

I walked off, got me gear, and walked across the road from the club to a pub. I'd just got myself a pint of lager when people started arriving from the club. 'Chubby, I thought you were really funny,' one of the lads said. 'But you were in the wrong place . . .'

'I know, I know,' I said. So I started telling them a few gags at the bar in the pub. Within minutes, I had sixty or seventy people around me, so I started my act. At the end, I said goodnight. They all clapped as I walked out of the pub, got in my van and drove off. I knew I was doing something right. And it wasn't just the need to earn a living that kept me going. When I was on stage, I was on show. Every breath, every move, every hand gesture counted. The audience laughed at my movements and my actions just as much as at my patter. And when they laughed at what I did, rather than at what I said, they were laughing because they liked me. No matter how hilarious the gags, no audience laughs if they don't warm to the person telling them. And when I was on stage in front of several hundred, or even several thousand people rolling in their seats, I felt fantastic. Like heroin, no one can describe the feeling or explain the addiction you feel for that high of excitement. You need to experience it to know what it's like. And that experience was why I didn't pack in. That's why I didn't let a bad night, when I would go home crying, get to me. That's why I never stopped working. I needed and craved those nights when I had that audience wrapped around my finger, when everything I did made them laugh, when standing up on stage with them was comic ecstasy.

The turning point came in late 1986 after playing a stag night at the Viking Hotel in Blackpool. In the dressing room after the show, Eric, the manager of the hotel, came up to me.

'We had several people in the audience from the company that own the South Pier Theatre,' he said. 'They were asking: who's this lad?'

'What did you say?' I asked.

'I said he's Chubby Brown. They asked how many times you'd played here and if it was always as packed as this.'

The next morning the phone rang. It was George. 'I've just come off the phone to the management of the South Pier Theatre. They want you to do a season of Saturdays and Sundays, but you won't be on until eleven o'clock after the family show.'

I was fearless in those days and the thought of 1,600 punters didn't frighten me. It excited me. 'Aye,' I said. 'I'll have a go.'

Even in the mid-1980s, British seaside resorts were still packed, especially Blackpool. The worst thing they ever did at Blackpool was build the M55 motorway. Before that, it was twisted A-roads, traffic lights and little villages all the way to Blackpool. Once you got there, you were that glad, you'd stay for the week. Nowadays people just go in for the day and come straight out. But back then, there'd be thousands of people walking the Golden Mile every evening and the theatres would be packed with merry holidaymakers looking for a laugh. That was where I came in. The only problem with playing at eleven p.m. was that for every hour I waited to go on stage, my audience would have sunk another three pints of beer. When I walked on stage, around a thousand lads and six hundred women were waiting, more than half of them completely pissed. Some were asleep in the front row, snoring. Faced with a drunken audience, most of my act involved dealing with hecklers or telling simple jokes about Blackpool that the audience would immediately understand. Jokes like: 'A sign in my hotel room said: "For turn-down service, ring 336." So I rang it. A woman said: "I wouldn't fuck you if you were the last comic in Blackpool."' It was a tough gig, but I handled it and the word got around, especially among comics, that my show was harder and more vulgar than anything else seen in a theatre in the mid-1980s.

Occasionally we'd have a complaint that my act was too crude. And because I was known for tackling controversial topics, I'd be blamed for anything offensive said by just about any comic in the land. I learned early on never to apologise for my material and to laugh it off when I was blamed for some other comedian's offensive remark. Once you start apologising, you'll never stop and you'll get a hiding. Just look at Boris Johnson when he offended Scousers. If he'd brushed it off, he wouldn't have got half as much stick as he did when he went to Liverpool to apologise. Or look at Billy Connolly when he made the joke about Ken Bigley. It was a bit insensitive, but it wasn't Connolly who murdered Bigley, nor did he start the war that put Bigley's life in danger. Everyone in the theatre that night knew it was a comedy show and that it was meant as a joke, so Connolly was right not to apologise. No comedian sets out to frighten or offend an audience – the show's supposed to be funny. My character might say 'fuck', but so does everyone in the audience. My character might make jokes about oral sex and lighting farts, but that's only because oral sex is popular and lighting farts can be funny. If you get offended by a joke, you're taking offence at real life.

George started putting up signs outside the shows. 'If Easily Offended, Stay Away,' they said. But that just attracted even more people. By the late 1980s, I was firmly established as Britain's bluest comedian and I could name my price. A few years earlier, shortly before Brian Findlay died, I considered seventy-five quid good money for a gig. Now I was getting two grand or more a night. And my audience was changing too. When I first went blue, it was nearly all men – bus trips from building sites, industrial estates and factories, all male. Suddenly, the audience was half female. Times had changed and telling dirty jokes was in fashion with everyone. When I came on stage and said 'Good evening, my wife's got two cunts and I'm one of them', I could see them sat there thinking 'Eeee, I wish I'd thought of that!' When I said 'Girls, keep your gob shut when you're fucking . . . you know what it's like, lads – tongue down her throat, fingers in her minge, cock up her arse, you're looking for somewhere to put your foot,' they all laughed. It was different from anything they'd heard before and they loved it.

CHAPTER FIFTEEN

FRUITS OF SUCCESS

'THIS WILL TAKE TIME,' she said. 'We are going to learn how to speak. We are going to start from A, B and C and it *will* take a long time.'

The physiotherapist, a lovely woman who looked like Victoria Wood, rested her hand on my chest. 'Let's start at the beginning. You need to learn how to breathe. From *here*,' Jane said, pressing the top of my stomach. I'd always thought breathing was something that I knew perfectly well how to do but, given that I was struggling to turn hisses into audible language, it appeared she had a point.

Several times a week I would turn up at Jane Deakin's office to relearn the gift of the gab. 'Hold your stomach in and say "Ahhh",' she said at our first meeting. I tried and nothing came out. I practised my breathing with her. 'That's better,' she said. 'Let's try to say chair.'

'. . . Huh . . . cheeeer,' I said with a windy whoosh.

'Breathe right in, breathe right out again. Get as much oxygen as you can into your lungs, then try again,' she said.

'Um . . . cher', I said.

Was I ever going to speak? I wondered. Your stage career is over, I thought, kiss your hopes of being a comic goodbye, Chubby. 'There are no guarantees, Roy,' said Jane. 'I don't know if your voice will come back. It's all up to you.'

Regaining my voice seemed so unlikely that I seriously entertained thoughts of what to do instead. I made plans to go into management and started to scout around for young comics with promise and potential – younger versions of me. I'd been in the business long enough to know when someone was funny and I'd seen hundreds of comics who weren't funny at all but were still earning a living. If I could find a young lad who *was* funny, then surely I could earn more than a living by showing him the ropes.

After six weeks' intensive therapy, Jane said there was nothing more she could do for me. 'If you keep doing the exercises and practise the techniques I've taught you,' she said, 'then your voice will come back. It's all a matter of patience and time.'

Sitting on the side of my bed every morning, I'd warm up my last remaining vocal cord with a few 'ahs' and 'ums'. Slowly, I heard my voice get better, the wavering and hissing becoming less all the time. Drinking litres of water every day and eating sensibly, I was starting to feel stronger and regain confidence. Maybe I'd manage it after all.

Then George phoned. It didn't take him long to pop the question. 'Are you ready yet?' he asked. When I said no, he didn't hesitate with the follow-up. 'So when do you reckon you'll be OK?'

I felt pressured. I was the man on the microphone and from the moment I put that microphone down George's wages had slowed to a trickle. 'Just give me time, George,' I said.

Six months after I started the speech therapy, Jane called me. 'You sound much better,' she said. 'Now you need to learn how to use a microphone.'

As a visual comic, I'd always held my microphone at my stomach so the audience could see my face clearly. I didn't want anything to get in the way of the body language upon which my brand of innuendo often depended. Nowadays I hold the microphone just below my mouth – any further away and my voice would fail after fifteen minutes.

Middlesbrough was playing a big game, so I went to the football with Peter Richardson. 'How's your throat, Chubbs?' a Middlesbrough supporter asked as he barged past me in the stand.

'Fine, thanks,' I hissed. 'Getting better all the time.'

'It comes back, you know.'

'What do you mean, "It comes back"?' Peter cut in.

'I've got it. Cancer, y'know,' the bloke said, a gormless smile creasing his podgy face. 'I had it a few years ago and thought I'd got rid of it, but it comes back.'

I looked at the gormless bloke and my heart sank. It was lucky for him that my voice was still shot to pieces, otherwise I'd have called him all the names under the sun. 'What a tactless fucking arsehole,' said Peter when the cretin had moved on. 'I just wanted to pick him up and throw him two hundred yards.'

●

'If they want you, they'll pay what you want,' said George. He was right. After years of struggling, the money was pouring in and I couldn't play enough gigs to meet demand. Whenever George put up my fee, we got more bookings. And all because I was filthier than any comedian had ever dared to be.

I bought a house, the first proper home after a string of rented flats and rooms. George moved out of his run-down semi into a big, detached pile. We both started taking holidays abroad, but the best thing about my success began with a phone call from George. 'Who's your hero?' he said.

'You know who my hero is.'

'Doddy, isn't it?'

'That's right.'

'Well, he wants you on his radio show.'

My heart nearly stopped. 'You're joking. This a wind-up.'

'No, you've got to drive down to London to the BBC studios. Doddy's doing a radio show and he wants you on it.'

A few days later I was in a studio near the Haymarket in London. The door opened and in he walked. My idol, my comedy god, my definition of comic perfection – Ken Dodd. I was in total awe of the bloke. I always had been and probably always will be. For me, Bob Monkhouse had the best comedy brain of his generation, Bernard Manning was the warmest, most caring and thoughtful comic I'd met on the circuit, and Doddy was the most talented stand-up comic this country had ever produced. Face to face with my idol, I didn't know what to say.

'Hello, my hero – Chubby Brown,' Doddy said.

'Eh, you're taking the piss now,' I said as we shook hands.

'I hear you're doing very well. I follow you round the theatres and the clubs. Everyone tells me what a nice fella you are . . .' He was just like I'd expected, only better. Somehow more 'Doddy' in the flesh than on stage or on television. And his compliments were embarrassing me. This is *Doddy*, I kept reminding myself, and he is complimenting *me*. 'You've got a lovely reputation and you are a gentleman . . .'

'They say the same about you, Doddy . . .' I said, wishing he'd stop the compliments. It was too much.

'I've written this script', he said. It was for his Sunday show on Radio 2. 'We're going to turn the tables. I'm going to be blue and you are going to be dead clean. That's the sketch. People won't believe this, that Ken Dodd's been blue.'

I read the script. Doddy's lines were full of 'Knickers, knackers, knockers' and 'Up yours, missus' – hardly blue, but racy enough for Doddy.

'You need to say all your lines in a very posh accent,' Doddy said, reading my lines from the script. 'Like this: "Ken, Ken, Ken, dear boy. This is all poppycock" – that kind of voice, do you think you can do it? – "one doesn't want to start using that sort of language. There's really no need at all."'

I thought I could manage it. And I was helped in every way by Doddy's commitment to perfection. He was the ultimate professional, making me repeat my lines five or six times until I said them just the way he wanted. I've never been good at reading or writing, and I was struggling to get the lines right. There were loads of words I'd rarely seen written down before – words such as 'tampering' or 'material'. 'Mat . . . errr . . . eeee . . . all,' I said, looking around at Doddy laughing. 'What you laughing at?'

'You don't say it like that,' he said. 'You say it like this: *material*.' I felt a bit stupid, but I loved the bloke. He could do no wrong; I just thought he was fantastic.

We finished the sketch, shook hands and I left, exhilarated at meeting Doddy but disappointed it was over so soon. Travelling down to Brighton, where I was appearing that evening, I couldn't stop thinking about meeting him. I told everybody at the club that night about it. 'I've been on *The Ken Dodd Show*, you know,' I said. 'Guess what I was doing this afternoon? Recording a sketch on *The Ken Dodd Show*. That's right . . .'

For me, it was the ultimate accolade. A real sign that I'd arrived, a star in the comedy firmament. I listened to the show when it was broadcast a few weeks later and still couldn't get my head round it.

I was hungry for confirmation of my success. Being invited onto Ken Dodd's radio show was one indication. The other was how much I was worth. Other comedians would tell me that the big stars, such as Freddie Starr at that time, would routinely earn five grand a night – much more than the amount I was being paid.

'Don't listen to that bullshit,' George would snap in reply to any question from me about my fee. 'It's just artists exaggerating their value. I can tell you what Starr's getting because I'm a theatrical agent and I can book him over the phone. You get exactly the same as he does. Nobody gets a penny more than you.'

'Oh right, so . . .'

'If you want more money we can do it, but we'll have to move into theatres,' George said. 'You won't get a wage. You'll get paid according to how many tickets you sell. If you sell only one ticket, you'll lose a lot of money. If you sell out, you'll make a fortune. It's more risky, but that's how it works.'

Playing theatres meant we'd have to do all our own promotion and publicity, hire lights and fit out the stage ourselves – all added costs that we'd previously avoided. George's response was typical. 'I want thirty per cent if I'm putting you on in theatres,' he said. 'I'll need more staff, we'll have to deal with cheques, credit cards, phones, security . . .'

In a venturesome spirit, I decided to take a chance on theatre gigs, but minimised the risk by playing several club nights each week for a standard fee. We charged two pounds a ticket, twice as much as club audiences were paying to see me, and doubled the ticket price in London because we thought Londoners had more disposable cash.

Theatres were a whole new ball game. It wasn't just the fancy curtains, proper backdrop and bright lights. Everything was different. In clubland, I was nobody. Often the audience came for the bingo, the pie and peas, the raffle and to gossip with their mates. The artists were bottom of the pile. I'd arrive at a club to find a single word on a blackboard announcing my appearance: *Comic*. You knew you were a star if it was written in coloured chalk.

In the theatre, I was the star attraction and instead of a tetchy committee chairman on my case, the theatre manager would greet me pleasantly just because my name was on the poster. I was the client and he was there to make my life comfortable – a blissful turnaround. 'Is there anything you would like, Mr Brown? A drink? Anything? Can we get you a sandwich?' he'd say. The office would ring ahead when I was booked into a theatre. 'When Roy arrives, he'd like a cup of tea and a corned-beef sandwich,' they'd say. And sure enough, they'd be waiting when I walked into the dressing room.

Not all the theatres were great – you wouldn't believe the state of the dressing rooms behind some of the plushest stages and auditoria in the country, places where rats passed by, wiping their feet, and cockroaches held their noses, places where millions were spent refitting the seats and only a coat of undercoat was slapped on in the dressing rooms – but at least the staff treated the entertainers with respect. In clubland, the committee couldn't even spell 'entertainer'.

The first time I played a London theatre, George aimed high and put me on at the Dominion in Tottenham Court Road. Eighty-six people turned up in a theatre that could seat an audience of more than two thousand. It didn't bother me. I lost a lot of money that night, but I was capped to be playing a major West End venue.

George had a simple response to the Dominion fiasco: carpet bomb the towns and cities surrounding London. I played anywhere that would have me – Guildford, Hayes, Sunbury, Tunbridge Wells, Dagenham, Croydon, Gillingham and many more. Then, with the groundwork laid, George placed one massive advert in the papers. Two years after I'd had eighty-six people in the Dominion, I sold out three nights. More than seven thousand punters passed through the doors, many of them clutching tickets they'd bought from touts for two or three times their face value. When we pulled up outside the Dominion and my name was up in neon lights – *Tonight: Roy Chubby Brown SOLD OUT* – I couldn't believe it. I was a bag of nerves in the dressing room. Billy Connolly was in the audience. Afterwards he said he couldn't believe what I'd said on stage. Central London had never heard anything like it. But the punters didn't care. I tore 'em apart.

After that, barely a night passed when I didn't sell out. I played two nights at the Royalty in London, two nights at the Hammersmith Apollo, a season every summer in Blackpool, and more than two hundred theatre and large club gigs a year up and down the country. Each and every one was rammed to the rafters. After nearly twenty years of slogging my act around the clubs, suddenly I was a national overnight success, a big name who could do no wrong. Doors that had been closed to me suddenly opened. Everyone wanted a part of me.

I was invited onto *TV-am* to be interviewed by Frank Bough and Anne Diamond. I knew that Frank had lived in Great Ayton, a village outside Middlesbrough, when he worked for Tyne Tees Television. Sitting on the sofa beside Frank and Anne, my mind working overtime trying to avoid saying anything rude, I answered Frank's questions like a good schoolboy.

'Have you any plans to go to America?' Frank said.

'You know, I'm really an English comedian. I'm tea and biscuits and Yorkshire puddings,' I said as Frank smiled. 'You've been to the USA, haven't you?'

Frank looked confused. 'Have I?' he said. I think he was worried about where I was heading.

'The Uther Side of Ayton,' I said. Frank burst out laughing. Turning to the camera, he said: 'That's an in-joke, by the way.'

'How do you know I lived in Ayton?' he said. I explained. 'I'm very pleased,' Frank said. 'You're completely different from the person I thought you'd be. I've heard your tapes and you're really funny, but you're not how I expected you to be. Do you write all your own material?'

'Yeah, I write all the time,' I said.

'Where do you get your inspiration?'

'From the newspapers and what's going on around me.'

'Can we put you on the spot?'

'Yeah. Of course,' I said. Frank handed me a copy of the *Daily Mirror*. A picture of a fella who was claiming to be the new Houdini was on the front. With his bald head, rotten teeth and wrapped in chains, he looked a fright. 'Well, he looks like a ball biter, doesn't he?' I said.

For just a fraction of a second, the whole studio froze. Nobody said anything. Nothing moved. After all, nobody said 'ball biter' on breakfast television. Then Frank asked another question, brushing over it as if I'd said nothing. I'd got away with it, but for weeks afterwards people stopped me in the street.

'Eh, I laughed when you said he looks like an arsehole, a ball biter,' they'd say.

'I didn't say "arsehole",' I'd reply.

'Ah, but you might as well have done.'

After the show, I walked into the green room, sat down and took a sip of a cup of coffee. Looking around the room, my eyes nearly burst out of their sockets. Sitting opposite me was Charlton Heston.

'Morning,' he said.

'Good morning,' I replied.

'I hate doing these things.'

'So do I,' I said nonchalantly, as if breakfast TV was a regular occurrence for me. 'Why?'

'I'm doing the rounds to promote something.'

'You're Charlton Heston, aren't you?'

'That's right, and who are you?'

'Roy Chubby Brown. I'm an English comedian.'

'Do you make movies?'

'No, I'm just an English comedian. I'm on here because I talk about sex, violence, drugs and rock and roll.'

Sat on a lumpy sofa, I explained my act to Charlton Heston, who I was convinced was wearing a wig. He was the first internationally famous person I'd met. All I wanted was to ask him about *Ben-Hur*, but he wanted to talk about working men's clubs. It was bizarre.

Meanwhile, my love life, which had been in the doldrums after I'd been dumped simultaneously by Beryl, Pat and Maureen, had taken a turn for the better. While playing at a northern club, a very attractive receptionist called Shirley caught my eye. Whenever I got the chance, I'd give her a bit of patter. Nothing too strong, just subtle stuff like 'How are you doing?' and 'Boy, I would like to see you with no clothes on' and 'Do you want to go halves on a baby?'

Three months later, I was back at the same club.

'That Shirley took a shine to you,' one of the doormen said as I arrived. 'She hasn't stopped talking about you since you left.'

'What's she like?' I said.

'You're all right there.'

I went straight to the reception. Shirley was waiting. 'What are you doing later, then?' I said.

'Nothing.'

'Do you fancy going for a bite to eat?'

'Yeah.'

I took Shirley to a Chinese restaurant. She liked her drink and she clearly liked men because she dragged me home that night. She was a hell of a shag. The best I'd had until then.

I fell big time for Shirley. I didn't love her, but I was deeply besotted with her. And although she was as rough as rats, I'd come to like her. After three or four months screwing Shirley, I was booked again at the same club. When I arrived, John, the manager of the club, took me aside. 'Chubby, I believe you and Shirley are getting a bit warm,' he said. 'I would be careful if I was you.'

John and I had been friends for a couple of years and I felt I could trust him. 'Is there something you should be telling me? Is she married with kids?' I said.

'She's been married a few times,' John said. 'She's got about five kids.'

'That's funny. She's never mentioned them.'

'Well, there's a lot that Shirley doesn't mention,' he said. 'I think you'd better come and look at this.'

I followed John into his office. He opened a drawer of his desk and took out an envelope. Inside the envelope were about thirty photographs of Shirley sucking John off, being shagged by another fella and carrying on with other blokes.

'She's anybody's,' John said. 'Anybody who has money. She'll get her claws into you and she's very hard to shake loose. It took me a long time to get rid of her.'

But I was too blinded by the mind-blowing sex I was having with Shirley to take much notice. And anyway, my thoughts were occupied with something much bigger.

Late one night, after playing a big show in Leeds, my tour manager Richie knocked at my dressing-room door. 'There's a girl outside who wants to meet you,' he said. 'And I think you should. She's an absolute stunna.'

As the girl walked in, my heart stopped. Fucking hell, I thought. With perfect eyes and teeth and a cute nose, she was absolutely beautiful. 'I've got to say you are one of the—' I started.

But the girl interrupted me before I made a fool of myself. 'Hi, Roy,' she said. 'You used to be engaged to me mother.'

I stared at her. Surely it was some mistake? 'What's your name?' I said.

'Greenwood.'

'Greenwood? I've never been engaged to a Greenwood.'

'My mam married Geoff Greenwood. Her name was Sandra Pallent.'

Sandra Pallent? The penny suddenly dropped. Big-breasted Sandra from school in Grangetown. Sandra who I was in love with when I was seventeen. It was a good job I hadn't said owt. 'You're Sandra's daughter?' I said.

'Yes.'

'How is she?'

'She's just split from my dad. He's an accountant here in Leeds and he's just left Mum.'

'Where's she working?'

'At the hospital. She nearly came to this show tonight.'

The next day, I spoke to Sandra. She filled me in on her news. 'What is this about you and your husband?' I said.

'I don't want to talk about it,' she said.

'That's all right – I was only being polite. If you're ever lonely and you want a night out, give us a ring.'

A few days later Sandra rang me and came to see the show. Afterwards she joined me in my dressing room. 'What do you think of the show, pet?' I said.

'Roy . . .' she said. 'It's absolutely filthy.'

I took her out for a meal. She had aged well, but she wasn't quite the same Sandra I'd known when I was a kid. She was tougher and sharper. Life had knocked some of the softness out of her.

Slowly Sandra and I drifted together over the next few months. I was still seeing Shirley the super-slapper, but I was starting to think that Sandra might be a better long-term bet. After about a year together, I took Sandra to visit my mother, with whom my frosty relationship had recently thawed slightly after she split from Norman Trevethick. I would visit Mam more regularly than previously, taking her cakes and scones, paying her phone bill and television licence. I'd recently moved her to sheltered housing in a bungalow. 'Mother, this is Sandra,' I said. I made them a cup of tea while they chatted. The next day I visited my mother again, this time on my own.

'Is that the same girl that you went to school with?' Mam said.

'Yeah.'

'I thought I didn't like her.'

'Why?'

'As soon as she walked in the room, I took an instant dislike to her.'

'What's she done to you?'

'Not my type. Watch her. She's evil, her. She's got devil eyes. And she's full of herself.'

I ignored my mother's warnings. What with Shirley on the side and Sandra back on the scene, I didn't care what my mother had to say. And I was preoccupied with something else: a third woman. After the Beryl–Maureen–Pat farce, I'd vowed never again to get involved with three women simultaneously. But my success in the theatres had gone to my head, I thought I was invincible and for the second time I'd got myself into a three-sided mess.

The first I heard of Linda was shortly after I arrived at the Royal Theatre at St Helens with Ronnie, my driver at the time. 'Have you seen the manageress here?' he said. 'She is stunning.' A few minutes later, there was a knock at my dressing-room door and I clapped my eyes on Linda for the first time. Ronnie wasn't wrong. With long dark hair, olive skin and a beautiful face, Linda was dazzling. She told me that her real name was

Loretta but everyone called her Linda, and that she did a bit of singing in a duo.

'Are you married?' I said. There seemed little point in beating about the bush.

'No,' she said. 'I was living with a bloke, but we recently parted. I'd had enough of him.'

She told me she was Miss St Helens. Looking at her, I could well believe it. She kept talking and from what she said there was very little that she hadn't done.

She could have been a big star, she told me, but she'd turned it down. She'd been lead singer with a band, she said, but they'd dumped her in the middle of nowhere when she'd refused to sleep with any of them. Then, apparently, a West Indian fella had picked her up, so she'd started living with him. I wondered if everything she told me was true, but she was so gorgeous that I didn't care. Thinking she was way out of my league, I told her I thought she was beautiful. She smiled and kept talking.

A couple of evenings later, I was playing at the Pleasuredome in Birkenhead. Ronnie stuck his head around the dressing-room door. 'You know that bird you were talking to on Tuesday night?' he said. 'She's here with two friends.'

'Really? Is she?'

'Wait till you see her.'

I'll never forget the moment Linda walked into the dressing room. Wrapped in a low-cut black dress that flaunted a top pair of cheps and which was slit up the side to show off her fish-net-stockinged legs, she was totally fuckable. 'Hi, I hope you don't mind I came over to see you,' she said.

'No, no, no,' I said, lost for words and hoping I wouldn't blush. 'No, no, no. You're all right. No, no, no.'

Ronnie and I went back to her mate's flat in Liverpool. Linda cracked open a bottle of whisky and one of her friends made herself scarce, leaving the four of us drinking and laughing until the early hours, when Linda and I went to bed.

After about four weeks of meeting up whenever we could – mainly when I didn't have an appointment with Sandra or Shirley – Linda and I became a regular thing. Once or twice a week I'd drive from Redcar to St Helens to see Linda, sometimes stopping off in Leeds to see Sandra and often making a detour to Aintree to drop in on Shirley. It was exhausting. I was shagging myself to death. Desperately in need of a holiday, I suggested to Sandra that we took a week off.

The day before Sandra and I jetted off to Tenerife, I acted on the qualms I had about Shirley and rang her up. 'I'm sorry, Shirley,' I said. 'It's over.'

'It isn't.'

'It is.'

'You're not dropping me like that.'

'Shirley, we are just fun. It's just friends having a good time, but there's nothing serious.' But Shirley wouldn't accept being jilted, so I told her about Sandra, thinking it would convince her that our affair was over. 'I've got somebody else,' I said.

'You haven't.'

'I have.'

'You haven't.'

'Shirley . . . I don't want to see you any more. You're a lovely girl, but you deserve better.' Everyone always say things like that, don't they? And everyone who hears it knows it's bullshit. 'Get somebody who will really appreciate you,' I said.

Sandra and I had a great holiday in Tenerife. Tanned and relaxed, we returned. We pulled up outside my house in Redcar to find Shirley sitting on my step with three suitcases beside her. Fortunately she had left her kids with her sister in Liverpool. That really would have been the trump card.

'Who's that?' Sandra said.

'Er . . . that's the woman next door,' I said. 'She must be looking for someone.' Talk about thinking on your feet.

'What're you going to do?'

'Erm . . . we'll drop these presents off at me mother's,' I said, pointing at a stack of souvenirs on the back seat. 'Then we'll come back.'

My mam lived about a mile away. As soon as we got round there and Sandra had put the kettle on, I made my move. 'Me mam wants something from the shop,' I said. 'She'd like some scones.'

I jumped in the car and flew back round to my house. Shirley was still sitting there.

'What the fuck do you want?' I said.

'I am coming to live with you.'

'No, you're not. You can fuck off now. My wife's here.'

'You're not married.'

'I *am* married,' I said. 'We got married on holiday.' Quick thinking again. 'Shirley, you'd better go. I can't do owt about it now.'

'You fucking bastard' she said, starting to cry.

'Come on, I'll pick the cases up. I'll take you to the railway station.'

Shirley stood up. Swinging round, she kicked her foot through my glass front door. 'You can fuck off,' she snarled straight into my face.

I grabbed the cases and threw them on the pavement. 'I am going to pick up my wife now,' I said. 'I'll be coming back then and if you are here . . . woe betide you.'

It was all too much. I'd had enough of Shirley and her drinking and the photographs that John had shown me and her lies and her kids who she pretended didn't exist and everything else. I had Sandra and Linda. That was enough for any man. It was certainly plenty for me and I knew I had to get rid of Shirley once and for all.

By the time I returned home with Sandra, Shirley had gone. 'Eh, that Marion next door, she's a one,' I said to Sandra. 'She couldn't get in, but it's all sorted now.'

But it wasn't sorted. Shirley started sending me poison-pen letters, full of bile and hate and bitterness. I'd made the mistake of introducing Shirley to my mam, so she asked my mam if I'd got married. And my mam told her the truth: Sandra was an old flame from school and we weren't married.

A few weeks later, Sandra opened an envelope over breakfast. 'What the hell's this?' she said, her face turning white. She held out a letter and a sheaf of photographs. There in all her glory was Shirley, legs apart for the lads, sitting in a jacuzzi.

Look what you're missing, Shirley had written on the photos. I was in the deepest shit.

'Why's this girl sending you pictures of herself naked?' Sandra demanded.

'This was long before I met you,' I said, fearing my luck was about to run out.

'According to this girl, you've been going out with the pair of us at the same time.'

'She's saying that because she wants me back.' I needed to pull out all the stops to rescue the situation. 'Sandra, you know I take you everywhere and buy you jewellery and clothes. When I went out with Shirley, I did the same thing. Shirley is a bit rough. She's got nothing and she comes from the worst part of Liverpool. She dumped me before we met, but now she wants me back because nobody is spoiling her any more. She misses her sugar daddy.'

'Oh . . . right.'

'Be honest, Sandra, I didn't know you still existed until your daughter walked in that dressing room. Shirley was before you, so . . .' I was running out of words and excuses.

'I'll have to think about this,' Sandra said before leaving. A couple of weeks later, we met up for dinner. We talked about our holiday and I eventually persuaded her that Shirley belonged to the distant past. But I could sense that it would take one final grand gesture to convince Sandra that I hadn't two-timed her with Shirley.

'Get in the car,' I said. 'We'll go to Liverpool now and I will prove to you that I am telling the truth. We'll go to Shirley's house and she can tell you herself.'

'You're a liar.'

'I'm not,' I pleaded. 'Get in that car, we'll go to Liverpool,' I said, knowing that if she said yes, I was up the creek.

'All right – I believe you,' Sandra said. Phew!

My love life returned to relative normality – Sandra as the main dish with Linda on the side – and the comedy went from strength to strength. Shortly after appearing on *TV-am*, George suggested that I should stop playing clubs. 'There's no money in it,' he said. George was right, but what he really meant was there was no money in clubs for *him*. He took twenty per cent of my earnings in a club, but thirty per cent when I played a theatre.

I didn't really care how much George was taking from me. I had more than enough in the bank and in 1987 bought Sunnycross House, a large detached property in Nunthorpe with a couple of acres of garden. Very well-to-do, Nunthorpe was where anyone from Middlesbrough moved if they'd made a decent bit of money. I put down a deposit, and employed joiners and decorators to renovate it before I moved in. I also applied for membership of the local golf club, which was about a mile down Brass Castle Lane from Sunnycross House. Walking into the bar, I was stopped by a bloke in a blazer. 'You'll need a tie if you want to come in here,' he said. 'And would you mind removing your hat?'

It wasn't what he'd said that riled me. It was the pompous manner in which he'd said it. I was sure he wouldn't have spoken to anyone else in the same way. 'Excuse me,' I said. 'It's a hat, not a hand grenade.'

'If you don't remove your hat, I won't ask you again, you'll be asked to leave.'

'If I remove my hat, mate, I will stick it so far up your arse the peak will stick out of your mouth,' I said and left the club. Two weeks later, I got a letter. They'd refused my application for membership. Once again, I'd been judged by the reputation of my Chubby stage persona rather than as plain old Royston Vasey, something that was becoming increasingly the case as I became well known.

A short while later, I was in a fish shop in Hemlington. 'Oi, Chubby, you fat cunt,' one of the customers said.

'Eh, do you mind? This is the fish shop,' I said.

'Ah . . . you fucking fat cunt.'

'Hey! I told you once, there's women in here. Do you mind?'

'Chubby Brown's just told me to stop fucking swearing!' the lad shouted to everyone in the shop.

'If you want to swear at me, go outside and swear,' I said. The lad mouthed off a bit more, but I ignored him as I waited for my fish supper. As I left, he muttered something. 'What did you say?' I said.

He muttered another obnoxious insult. Putting down my wrap of fish and chips, I grabbed him by the throat and pushed him towards the door. The lad tried to swing at me, so I raised a plastic lemonade bottle I was holding. Hitting the lemonade bottle, he looked at me slightly shocked that he'd not made contact with my face, then ran off. As I drove off, I spotted him loitering in the street with two other lads. 'You fucking cunts,' I shouted from the car window. It wasn't like me, but he had me riled.

I'd just finished my fish supper when there was a knock at the door. The police were outside. 'I have reason to believe you caused a disturbance in the fish shop,' the constable said.

'Who's told you that?'

'The woman said you were effing and blinding.'

'Who?'

'The woman behind the counter.'

I saw red. 'The bitch. It was for her benefit that I pushed that lad out of the shop,' I said.

The policeman accepted my explanation and let me off with a warning. But the lesson was clear. My success wouldn't buy me an escape from my background – in fact, it would make things worse. I'd grown up and started to put my house in order but, like anyone, I still had faults. And my failing was that I could take only so much abuse or aggression or conflict. Inside I'd be boiling, but most of the time I could keep a lid on it. But if it went too far, I'd snap and then whoever was in my way would-n't know what was coming.

About a year after I'd dumped Shirley, both Sandra and Linda made it clear that they wanted to marry me. I couldn't believe my luck, but I also knew it meant facing a difficult choice. Linda was more beautiful and a better shag, but she was wayward, whereas Sandra was relatively calm and relaxed.

I was becoming increasingly well known and I knew it would take an understanding woman to put up with me. I thought of it as a simple contract – I'd spoil rotten any woman who was with me (I bought Linda jewellery, dresses and a car) but in return I expected them to give me a loose rein. Being very busy and living in the public eye, I needed a woman who wouldn't get jealous or possessive or uptight if I wasn't in the right place at the right time. Linda certainly wasn't that type of woman. And it didn't help that whenever she walked into a room, every pair of male eyes turned to her and every male mouth drooled. I didn't like that.

Although not as glamorous or as attractive as Linda, Sandra was clean, smart, attractive and good company. She was a typical housewife, which was what I needed. I thought Sandra was the better bet, but put off a final decision until, passing Leeds one day, I thought I'd drop in on her. My car parked, I knocked on the back door and walked in to find a bloke sitting on the sofa. Sandra's face went bright red and he left as soon as I'd said hello.

'Who was that?' I said.

'Just a fella.'

'What do you mean, "just a fella"?'

'I put an advert in the lonely-hearts column for companionship.'

'You are fucking joking. What about me?'

'I'm just a bit of fun to you. You've got women all over the place.'

'I haven't. I packed them all in for you.'

'I know you. You're having affairs all the time.'

I was jealous. It surprised me, but it also made up my mind. I now knew which woman I really wanted. 'Look, to prove my point,' I said to Sandra, 'let's get married.'

Sandra accepted immediately, but first I needed to deal with Linda. I decided to drop her gently by taking her on a week's holiday to Cyprus. We stayed at the Grecian Bay Hotel in Ayia Napa. We went out every night and Linda always looked stunning. One night, she was asked to dance by two German lads. When she accepted the invitation, I saw my chance. 'You're right out of order,' I said. 'I brought you to Cyprus, you're on holiday with me and you get up and dance with another lad. When we get back, you can take your bags and fuck off. I don't want to see you again because you are nowt but a fucking cow.'

Sandra moved into Sunnycross House when I got back to

Nunthorpe. And straight away Linda's phone calls started. 'Who's that woman ringing up all the time?' Sandra said.

'She's just a friend.'

'She said you took her on holiday.'

'She's lying.' Once again, I was ducking and diving with a piece of skirt. I knew I might as well come clean because in the end I'd get caught out simply because women are not daft.

Fortunately Sandra knew what I was like, so the wedding still went ahead. Maybe she liked a bit of rough. A lot of women have told me that it makes them feel protected.

As for my wedding day, even now a shudder goes down my back when I think of it. 28 July 1988 – it pissed down all day. How appropriate.

Sandra and I didn't stand on tradition or ceremony. Sandra spent the night before the wedding with me and I didn't have a stag night, mainly because I'd played too many stag nights to be able to enjoy my own. I hired a vintage car to take us to the registry office in Middlesbrough. Stopping at Sandra's mother's house to drop off some flowers for the buttonholes, I was ushered into the back kitchen by Sandra's mum, a small silver-haired chain-smoker called Gwen. I'll never forget what she said to me. 'Son, you do know what you're doing, don't you?'

'Yeah,' I said.

'It *is* our Sandra.'

'I know it is. I love her very much.'

'Well, be it on your head, then, son.'

We got to the wedding. Peter Richardson was my best man and everyone I knew from Teesside clubland was there. We had a lovely day and a party that night at the house. We went on to a club later on and somehow I couldn't get Gwen's words out of my head. She had a wise old head of her own on her.

The *Evening Gazette* was doing a cheap offer of a cruise to New

York on the *QE2* and a flight back on Concorde. I'd booked us two tickets for our honeymoon. It cost me seven grand and was worth every penny.

When the ship pulled away from the dock in Southampton, a brass band was playing on the quayside and Sandra burst into tears. 'What's the matter?' I asked.

'This is one of my dreams,' she said. 'Going away on the *QE2*. I never thought this would happen to me.'

Seeing Sandra display her emotions so openly was a rarity. As the matron of a psychiatric unit, she'd been stabbed several times and had glass thrown at her. It had made her hard and self-protective. 'You do know what you are doing, getting involved with Sandra?' one of her nurse friends once said to me when we were out having a drink.

'Yeah,' I said. 'Why?'

'She's a tough girl, you know.'

'I know. She comes from Grangetown. The same place as me. She went to school with me. I know she's a tough girl.'

I asked the nurse if she had any favourite tales about Sandra. 'The one we all laugh about,' she said, 'is the time we rang her at home one night when we were having trouble with a regular patient who came in all the time on drugs. "Sandra, Tommy's on the windowsill and he won't come in," we said. "He's going to jump."

'About twenty minutes later Sandra walked into the ward. "What do you think you're doing?" she said to Tommy. "I'm going to jump," he said. "Well, jump, then – and shut the window."'

'You can't treat people like that,' I said.

'Sandra did,' the nurse said. 'And he soon came back inside.'

The crew on the *QE2* knew we were newly-weds and gave us free chocolates and as much champagne as we could drink. We hadn't finished unpacking our cases when there was a knock on our cabin door. It was the boatswain. 'You're Chubby Brown, aren't you?' he said.

'Aye.'

'You wouldn't do a show for us, would you – in the Boatswain's Nest? It's our bar down near the engine room where all the crew drink.'

Sandra agreed to let me go. It was a tiny place and when I arrived it was heaving with sailors and crew. 'Where am I gonna stand?' I said.

'We've got a barrel in the corner,' the boatswain said. 'Will you stand on a barrel?'

Compared to playing gigs from the tops of crates or standing on sticky clubroom floors, a barrel was the Palladium. 'Yeah, all right then,' I said.

I stood on the barrel for forty minutes without a microphone, talking to the crew, cracking gags about the ship, the sea and the Navy. It was absolutely fabulous. One of my best gigs. I was on a high after the wedding, I was thrilled to be on the *QE2* and the crew were my kind of lads.

At half past five on the fifth morning, we passed the Statue of Liberty as we sailed into New York harbour. The whole ship was up to see it, Sandra in her nightie and me in my pyjamas under our overcoats because we'd been told we would arrive at seven o'clock and had to race onto the deck.

We stayed in a hotel near Grand Central Station. I couldn't get over the size of the jacuzzi and the forty channels on the television. We took in some shows on Broadway, went up the Empire State Building and shopped at Macy's and the Trump Tower on Fifth Avenue, where you could pay two hundred dollars for a tie and a flunky asked for five dollars if he carried your coffee to your table. I told him if he wanted a tip, Big Bertha in the 3.30 at Kempton Park was worth a punt.

It was a fantastic holiday. When we got on Concorde, one of

the stewardesses recognised me. 'The pilots noticed you when you got on,' she said. 'Would you like to go up front?' Sat on a little red jump seat, headphones on, I chatted with the captain through the microphone while Concorde flew twice as fast as sound over the Atlantic. Up above, the sky was inky black. Down below, the water was dark blue, speckled with the white dots of thousands of icebergs. I felt a very long way from Grangetown.

CHAPTER SIXTEEN

HOME AND AWAY

SATURDAY NIGHT IN Blackpool and every seat in the theatre is taken, all of them Chubby fans eager to see my first night back after cancer. Standing in the wings, I run through the material I rehearsed at home and peer at the audience. I know what they're whispering – 'Do you think he'll do it, do you think he'll . . .' – and I think: I can do this. I'm ready.

The music starts, I dance on stage, shuffle over to the microphone stand, open my mouth and . . .

My voice had still been hoarse a month earlier when I'd gone into my garage, locked both doors, taken a deep breath and started talking. Walking up and down, I ran through all the material I'd written in the seven months since I'd last faced an audience, just to see if I could remember it.

I'd been writing all the time I'd been convalescing. It felt good to have built up all that material, but when you write 'fuck' on a piece of paper it's not as funny as when you say it in front of 1,500 people. And by the time I was ready to go back on the road, the news had changed. Things that had happened to

Madonna, Sting and Elton John were yesterday's news and I had to start afresh. I looked through my back catalogue of gags for the jokes that had always got a laugh. After all, the first night's important.

. . . And it all goes brilliantly until twenty-five minutes into the show my throat switches off, just like a candle being blown out. One moment it's there; the next moment, nothing. After thirty minutes on stage there's only one thing for me to say.

'Ladies and gentlemen,' I whisper. 'As you can see, I've got a problem.'

Walking off to a standing ovation, I can't meet anyone's eyes as I come off stage. I keep my head down and make straight for my dressing room. The door shut and locked behind me, I burst into tears and think the unthinkable: oh fucking hell, I am finished.

Afterwards, everyone says the same thing – don't worry about it; at least you got through half an hour – but their words sound hollow and false. I thought I could do it. My mind had been willing, it was just that my throat wouldn't play along. And then I pull myself together. Don't be a defeatist, you arsehole, I tell myself. Get up and get on with it.

There's no speaking to me after that. I don't want to talk to anyone. All week I steam my throat and do my exercises. I phone Jane Deakin. 'I told you it would be difficult,' she says. 'But hey, congratulations. Half an hour is a good start. It will only get stronger.

'When we started,' Jane says, 'I told you there was no guarantee that your voice would come back. But you've done much better than I expected and from here on, it's all up to you.'

George phones, wanting to know if I still want to play the Blackpool gig booked for next Saturday. 'Are you sure you can do it?' he says. 'Because I can't ask people for seventeen quid a ticket if you're not gonna get through it.' He's right to be worried – if the press hears of it, they'll accuse us of conning my audience – but I know that George is more worried about himself than about me. He wants to get in his last couple of bob before he retires.

The next Saturday, I return to Blackpool. I play an hour. A full fucking hour. It's fantastic and the crowd is great. I still can't sing, so the audience gets a bumper show of gags, more in an hour than I've told in that time for years.

That night I go back to the hotel with the management, the crew and some friends and get completely and utterly legless. The champagne is out and everyone is celebrating, singing 'Welcome back, welcome back' until *their* voices are hoarse.

'Let's do two nights a week,' I tell George. Then we increase it to three nights a week and I go to see Jane Deakin and Dr Martin.

'You're doing too much,' Dr Martin says.

'Two nights is sufficient,' Jane says.

Feeling I could do more than two, I nevertheless stick to their advice. I tell George not to exceed two bookings a week.

'No problem,' he says. 'But is two enough?'

Six months later, I'm back up to three nights a week.

●

Of the eight years that Sandra and I were married, seven years and ten months were pure purgatory. I put up with it because I was away working most of the time and because I thought better the devil you know, but to this day I really don't know how I didn't lose my mind.

Within a month of returning home from our New York honeymoon, all the warnings I'd had about Sandra started to come true. She turned what should have been the happiest years of my life into a misery. I could tell some horror stories, but the last thing I want to do is relive the intimate details of that marriage, the worst mistake I ever made.

I've never been able to work out why I stayed with Sandra for so long when it was obvious to everyone around us that our relationship was rotten to the core. Someone once suggested that my mother's desertion of me when I was a kid left me unable to form intimate relationships with women. By 1990 my mother was in a nursing home, still banging on about my father. He was a bastard, he was a pig, he was a bully, he was an alcoholic, he was . . . she always had sommat to say about him and she never forgave him for whatever it was that pulled them apart. Although she wouldn't tell me, I was starting to get an insight into what it might have been. Looking out of a window at a bit of parkland one day, Mam snorted and pointed at two dogs. 'Look at that there,' she said with disgust.

I looked closer. The dogs were having it away. 'You shouldn't be looking at things like that, Mother,' I said.

'Bloody homosexuals.'

'You've got good eyesight, haven't you?' I said. The dogs were about two hundred yards away.

'That's because they're just like your father.'

'Now hang on, Mother, I'm getting a little bit sick of this now. Every day you have a go, but my father was not a homosexual. Of all the things he was, he was not a poofter.'

'Yeah, but he was a dirty dog.'

'C'mon, Mother, you must have loved my father at some time.'

'*He* threw our love away,' she said. '*I* didn't.'

'What do you mean by that?'

'Your dad would get into bed and I would go to cuddle him and he'd say get off and push me to one side.'

'Really?'

'I felt unwanted,' said Mam.

It was the only time Mam mentioned anything to do with her break-up from Dad and I was left wondering whether maybe my auld fella had been seeing a barmaid at the club or whether it was something else. I never found out and my mam wasn't one for revealing much. She'd been in the nursing home about six months when she needed to go to hospital, so I offered to pick her up after she'd been seen by the doctor. When I arrived she was sitting on a bed, waiting for me and bossing the nurses around. I carried her bags to my car, Mam stopping nurses she knew to show me off to them. 'He's that comedian, you know,' she said as if I wasn't there. 'That Chubby Brown.'

Driving in the car towards Redcar, I asked her how she felt.

'I'm fine, I'm fine,' she said. 'Lovely, but I can't wait to get back to my own bed. I'm more comfortable in it.'

'Well, you know we love you,' I said. 'Me and Barbara.'

'Yes,' she said. 'I know that and I know you'd do owt for me and I love you too. You know that, don't you?'

'Of course I do, Mother.'

'I do. I love you and our Barbara and I miss you terribly . . .'

Mam had never talked like that before. It was the first time I'd heard her say that she loved me or my sister.

I dropped Mam off at the nursing home at four o'clock. At half past six, I was sitting in my house when the phone rang. 'Is that you, Roy?' a woman's voice said. I could hear someone crying hysterically in the background.

'Yeah.'

'It's the matron, Roy. I've got some terrible news for you. Your mother passed away at six o'clock this evening. Your sister's here. I think you should come down.'

I was stunned. I went down to the nursing home. My sister was in a terrible state. I comforted her. I didn't know what to say. For once, I was lost for words. We took Mam to the morgue, then I went home, opened a bottle of whisky and sat thinking about all the things I wished I'd said to Mam before it was too late and why my life with Sandra had become such a mess.

Maybe I had hung on to Sandra because when we were teenagers she'd been the first woman I'd got close to after my mother left home. Maybe that's why I was still putting up with Sandra and her criticisms of George, who was her public enemy number two after me.

George had helped me rise from the relative obscurity of the clubs to national notoriety and selling out theatres from Penzance to Aberdeen. It's something for which I'll always be thankful. But when I told Sandra that George was taking thirty per cent of my theatre income, she was outraged.

I knew that for George I was the goose that laid the golden eggs, but I also knew that George was the farmer without whom that goose wouldn't prosper. Whenever someone criticised George, I said exactly what I'd always said: 'You don't know George like I do' and 'I'd rather have him working for me than against me.'

With such a miserable home life, I'd come to rely heavily on George's friendship and support. Thanks to his guidance, I'd become a household name, selling out every theatre months in advance. At last I was getting the recognition that I'd always wanted. I was spotting my name all over the place. *Viz* started featuring a comic strip called *Chubby the Foul-Mouthed Fish* for which I'd been the inspiration. I was reading the *New Musical Express* when I saw that one famous guitar hero cited me as the best medicine for a guitarist who had become very big for his boots after becoming a star. 'What he wants to do is lock himself in a room with a Chubby Brown tape for half an hour and get back in touch with reality,' the guitar hero said.

A while later, I went to a Simply Red concert. Standing about twenty yards from the front with all the young girls dancing around me, I was approached by a bouncer. 'Are you Chubby Brown?' he said.

'Yeah,' I said.

'Mick wants a word.'

'Mick who?'

'Mick Hucknall.'

'He wants to speak to me?'

'Yeah, he spotted you.'

'Ah, fuck off!'

'No, really. He did.'

After the show I went backstage. Mick Hucknall came over with a glass of champagne. 'I'm a big fan,' he said. I couldn't believe my ears.

And while trying to pass time on an afternoon before a gig, I picked up a book called *Vile Filth* in a bookshop. It had sections on the most vile kings, politicians and celebrities. One section was headed 'comedians', so I immediately turned to it. 'Britain's most vile comedian is Roy Chubby Brown,' it said at the top of a whole page about my act. When I saw that, I thought: Wow! I've made it at last.

It was a real buzz to sell out a theatre and then, on the night, to see touts selling ten-quid tickets for fifty pounds. Although I'd get my bouncers to move the touts on, I was fascinated, finding it hard to believe that I was responsible for that. Things were going so well for me from the late 1980s to the late 1990s that at times it seemed like it was happening to someone else. I'd stand on stage, watching the entire audience rocking in their seats, whole blocks of people rolling forwards as they laughed, and I'd wonder what the hell they were laughing at. I would have told the joke sixty times before and could no longer hear the humour in it. Here we go again, I'd think to myself as I started telling the joke once more. However, for the audience it was the first time they'd heard it and as long as I didn't fluff it and as long as I got the timing right, they'd all laugh so precisely on cue that it was like pushing a button. It made me feel like God.

I had watched my ticket prices rise like a meteor from a quid to two pounds to two pounds fifty to a fiver to ten quid and on up to seventeen or eighteen pounds. And the higher the ticket price, the more control I had over the audience. If I was persistently heckled or if the audience was really rowdy I'd simply walk off stage, go to my dressing room, sit down and have a cup of tea. I'd give them ten minutes, then I'd walk back on stage and it would be like a different audience. They calmed down simply because they were worried that I wouldn't come back on stage and they had paid good money for a ticket. It always worked.

I produced some of the best material of my career in that golden era. After years of fighting to be heard in clubs, at last the audiences were listening attentively, hanging on every word. I was working seven nights a week and squeezing in two Saturday shows during three-month summer seasons in Blackpool. When I wasn't on stage, I was working on the material. And like a body that needs exercise to stay fit, I was writing better gags simply because I was working my comedy muscle all the time.

The demand for new material stepped up a gear in 1990, when George suggested that we should make a video. For many years I'd produced audio-cassette tapes and records of my performances that I'd sold after shows. Television executives had picked up on my nationwide popularity and invited me onto late-night shows with the proviso that I tamed my act for a television audience. I appeared on *The Danny Baker Show*, which I enjoyed because Danny Baker had the guts to bring on guests that other shows wouldn't touch with a bargepole and because he was a very nice fella.

I appeared with Barbara Windsor (who said she was a big

fan – 'I love him! I love him!' she kept on saying) on *The Word*, a late-night cult programme for teenagers and twenty-year-olds. They interviewed me in Tenerife, asking me about political correctness while I lay beside a pool at the Palace Hotel.

But mostly I turned down any television offers, partly because I didn't really enjoy it but mainly because I was reluctant to give away some of my best material for a pittance. With fans clamouring to see me on television, the obvious answer was a video of a stage performance. The first in what would become an annual production was *From Inside the Helmet*. 'The BBC is here tonight,' I told the fans, pointing at the cameras around the stage. 'This is Bill, that's Bob and Colin's at the back.'

Filmed live in Blackpool, it remains one of my favourite videos. With no fancy camera angles, it's raw and pure. Just me and a camera. My voice was in good shape and the material had been extensively tried and tested over the previous three or four years, so it was very strong. It was a solid sixty-minute set with no mistakes and it sold like hot cakes.

Videos lifted my earnings to another level. Within a few years of releasing my first one, I was among the bestselling video artists in Britain, my tapes often at the top of the charts, outselling big names such as U2 or the Rolling Stones. What with the shows and the tapes, the money was rolling in and I could buy the kind of things I'd never dreamed of twenty years earlier when I'd been a labourer in Middlesbrough – cars costing more than I'd previously paid for houses and artworks to put on my walls. Meanwhile, George moved house again, inviting us to his house-warming party.

George had done well out of me – something that Sandra never failed to mention, but then she wasn't the only one who failed to understand the symbiotic relationship between artists and their agents and managers. Convinced that all agents were

thieving bastards, Johnny Hammond had taken out an advertisement saying as much in a Sunderland local paper. Johnny
had always been very outspoken and very honest. He believed
that playing the clubs was no different from working at a ship-
yard. If you worked at Dorman, Long all week, you expected to
walk home with your pay packet on a Friday evening. And when
Johnny played a gig, he'd go straight to the club chairman. 'I've
just done an hour's work,' he'd say. 'I want paying.' He would-
n't let the club get away with delaying payment by saying they'd
pay the agent. And he wouldn't accept an agent's excuse that he
hadn't been paid yet by a club. As far as he was concerned, he
deserved payment as soon as he'd performed the service for
which he'd been booked.

Johnny's advert didn't pull any punches. He accused agents
and managers of robbing him of his rightful earnings and called
on all club artistes to band together to ensure that they got paid
on the night.

About a month after the advert was printed I took a phone
call from Johnny. 'I can't get any work,' he said. 'Nobody will
employ me.'

'Johnny,' I said, 'you cut your own fucking throat.'

But in my heart I thought Johnny was right. No matter how
successful the artiste, there was always a manager or agent who
was not paying them promptly and treating them with contempt. Still, that was how the system worked. And as with any
system, you had to abide by the rules. It was no different from
working on a building site and having to do what the foreman
said. You'd take on the shitty jobs he handed out because if
you got on the wrong side of him he'd fire you.

George was always there for me. Most days I'd see him at the
theatre in the evenings and he'd check that everything suited
me. After the show, he'd offer constructive criticism, which was
a great help. With his encouragement, I changed the way I told

jokes. My philosophy about telling gags had always been like my thinking on the bus service: don't worry if you don't like the joke I'm cracking because there's another one coming along in a minute. But I started to put jokes together to tell stories instead of one-liners. It meant learning how to paint pictures in words for the audience.

George also got me out of a lot of trouble and got me paid when my fee should have been cut. I'd been booked to play at a very smart place in the Channel Islands, the kind of venue that wouldn't let you in unless you were wearing a dicky bow and dinner jacket, but the audience had been drinking for three hours by the time I came on stage at eleven o'clock. A fight soon broke out. When I shouted 'Give over!' from the stage, a barrage of ashtrays and insults came hurtling towards me, so I ran back to my dressing room. George was there.

'I've just been paid – the boss gave me your money,' he said.

'Well, quick, we'll fuck off, then,' I said. With our belongings stuffed in our bags, we climbed out of the back window into the car park and ran back to our hotel. We'd finished a couple of drinks in the hotel bar when we spotted a black limousine drawing up in front of the hotel. Four blokes got out.

'Fucking hell,' George said. 'Quick, Roy, get back to your room!'

The nightclub owner's henchmen had come for their money and George had no intention of giving them it. I ran straight to the lift and went up to my room. Forty-five minutes later the phone rang in my room. 'You can come back down,' George said. 'They've gone.'

Arguing that I'd played most of my set and done very well, George had refused to refund my fee – something I'd probably not have had the nerve to do myself. When the heavies hadn't accepted no for answer, George had told them that I was unwell and had gone to bed with the money in my pocket.

He'd promised them I'd give them the money after breakfast the next morning. After all, he told them, this was a Channel Island and there were few places for us to go.

At six o'clock the following morning, my phone rang. It was George. 'Get your gear now – I've got us an early flight back out,' he said. We raced to the airport, glancing over our shoulders as if we were being chased by the Keystone Cops. We got on the plane without being intercepted. When the stewardess came round with breakfast, I asked her what time we'd arrive in Birmingham, where we'd parked our cars.

'Birmingham?' the stewardess said. 'This plane's going to East Midlands.' Somehow we'd managed to get on the wrong plane. The boarding staff hadn't checked our tickets, so George started complaining.

'George, it's our fault. We can't possibly blame the airline for this,' I said.

'Rubbish,' George said. 'I'll get them to provide us with a free car to take us to Birmingham.' And he did, even though it was clearly our mistake. So whenever Sandra complained about George, I'd think of incidents such as the flight back from the Channel Islands and ignore her. Without George, I wouldn't have been paid my full fee and I would have been stranded at East Midlands airport. As far as I was concerned, he was worth every penny of his commission.

George also supported me when I said that I wanted to have a go at playing a New York comedy club. I was an established name in Britain and for years I hadn't played a theatre that wasn't sold out, but I'd always wondered whether I could cut it in America.

We stayed in a fabulous hotel in New York. Outside my room on the thirty-sixth floor, a veranda looked straight down Fifth Avenue. We were all jet-lagged and in need of sleep, but I was so excited that we dumped our bags as soon as we arrived and took in five different comedy clubs that first night. First stop was Dangerfield's, one of the world's longest-running comedy clubs, on First Avenue. I couldn't believe how bad the acts were. A guy in a checked shirt came on, sat on a stool and tried to tell jokes, but it just didn't work. He was too good-looking – often funniness and ugliness go hand in hand – and his material was poor. Most of his act was about where he came from. 'I come from Baltimore, yeah!' he'd shout and a handful of the audience would whoop. 'Baltimore, yeah.' More whoops. It was mindless. Home-town recognition is a big thing in America. When the next guy walked on and said he was a New Yorker, he got a standing ovation. What for? Just for coming from New York?

We also went to the Comedy Club, to Caroline's and the Comedy Cellar. They were all similarly scruffy places with dirty red curtains hanging in one corner, pictures of comics you've never heard of on the walls and a dozen little tables. In most of them you had to have at least three drinks. With the ten-dollar entrance charge on the door it was an expensive night out. No wonder they were half empty and the atmosphere was lousy. At the Comedy Cellar, six comics did about ten minutes each. Some of them didn't get a single laugh. They could have taped the show and called it *Where's the Laughter Gone?*. Some of them were working their socks off, but they just couldn't make people laugh.

Effing and blinding at the front of the audience at the Comedy Cellar was a bloke in a green anorak, heckling throughout. On stage, the poor American comic was lost. He didn't have any ad libs or answerbacks. I wished I was up there instead of him. After a while, the bloke in the green anorak gave up and came to the bar. It was Bobby Davro, carrying a notepad and a big bag with a load of wires in it. 'What's that?' I said, pointing at his notepad.

'A couple of ideas for my TV show,' he said.

'What's that mean?' I said, pointing at a picture he'd drawn on his pad of a little cow with a mushroom, some grass and a tree.

'It's more or less . . .' Bobby said, tailing off.

The next night I played a shop-window spot at Caroline's in front of the cream of New York's comedy agents. I slightly tailored my act to the locals, but otherwise it was material I'd been using for years. 'I'm from a little village called England,' I said as I came on. 'It's a lovely place. We have sewers but we never thought to put trains in them!' I got a laugh.

'The only thing I know about New York, boys and girls, is that John Lennon lived here, and of course I was a Beatles fan and like Ringo, I was a drummer with a pop group . . .'

'What Beatles numbers did you do?' shouted a woman in the audience.

A few days before we'd left for New York I'd been sitting at home, panicking. I knew the Americans had a different sense of humour and I didn't have a clue what to say on stage. Then I had an idea. I knew Lennon was revered in New York, so I thought I'd surely get a good reaction as long as I didn't take the piss. Sitting at my piano, I wrote out a list of Lennon song titles, hoping it would inspire me to think of some good gags.

As I looked at the list, I realised that I could use the titles to tell a story. Using a few Beatles lyrics to link the song titles, I took twenty minutes to write it. So when the heckler in New York asked what Beatles numbers I played, I took a deep breath and launched into the premiere performance of my Beatles medley.

'Michelle, imagine if yesterday I was a fool on a hill or a real nowhere man,' I started. 'Living in a yellow submarine on Penny Lane, I can't buy me love. I picture myself on a boat on a river on a good day of sunshine with lovely Rita meter maid. She'd be a day-tripper and I'd be a paperback writer.

'Listen, do you want to know a secret? I once had a girl or

should I say she once had me. She was just seventeen, a Lady Madonna, eight days a week. But boy, she could carry that weight. She was good to me, you know, and I feel fine, like Lucy in the sky with diamonds on a magical mystery tour.

'See, if I fell on the bang, bang, bang, Maxwell silver hammer and was buried in strawberry fields for ever, would you help Eleanor Rigby to pick up the rice in the church where the wedding's been?

'Would my baby be in black and just get up and dance to a song that was a hit before your mother was born? Oh you'll get by with a little help from your friends.

'Help, I need somebody. From your friends, I've had no reply. We'll get back, back to the USSR where there's a revolution.

'See, I'm a loser, I know a place along the long and winding road, it's an octopus's garden. You've a ticket to ride with the taxman, saying please, please me and wrapped up in chains, getting the taste of honey, he'll be fixing a hole to stop his mind from wandering.

'You come together because she'll have been treating me bad. Misery? I'd have been happy just to dance with you. So tell me why, Doctor Robert, I'm a walrus. Tell me what you see as my guitar gently weeps. It won't be long, run for your life. You can either do that or twist or shout.

'The things we said today, dizzy Miss Lizzy – I mean Mister Mustard 'cos she's a woman and I love her. How can she laugh when she knows I'm down?

'Hey Jude, it's been a hard day's night. Will you still feed me? Will you still need me when I'm sixty-four? You say yes. I say no. I say I don't know. Take all my lovin' here and there and everywhere. Don't hide your love away, it's getting better all the time.

'I've got to get you into my life for the benefit of Mr Kite because I've just seen her face on the tip of my tongue. Obla-di Obla-da, let it be, I don't want to be your man. I should have known better with a girl like you but we could work it out, honey-pie.

'Baby, you can drive my car. Give peace a chance, don't write to Sergeant Pepper's Lonely Hearts' Club band in a Norwegian wood on another day across the universe, through the bathroom window. With love from me to you.'

When I finished the whole room stood up and applauded. For at least a minute, I couldn't talk but I'd cracked it. I told three more jokes, leaving in all the 'fucks' and 'cunts'. The audience didn't bat an eyelid. After the Beatles medley, I could do no wrong. I walked off. My ten minutes was over and it couldn't have gone better.

George came up to me when I'd changed and was standing at the bar. 'You've been asked to do—' he said.

I cut him off straight away. I knew what was coming. 'George, to be honest with you, I'm too long in the tooth to change anything now. It's taken me all these years to get established in England. For what would I now want to come over here?'

'But every agent in the room wants you,' George said. 'They're offering you six-month tours of America.'

I was married to Sandra and I had other ties to home. 'I can't,' I said. 'I've spent thirty years playing shit-holes in Britain. Why would I now want to go around America in a bus?'

We went out to a restaurant. *The biggest steaks in New York*, it said outside. Then we went back to our hotel, slept the night, packed our bags and got the first plane out of JFK bound for England. All the way home, George pestered me. 'You know, it's there for you,' he said. 'If you want it, it's there for you. It's up to you. It's your decision.'

'How much work have you got me in England?' I said.

'You're booked for ever. For the next five years at least – everybody wants you.'

'You've just answered my question. Why would I need America?'

I was worried that if I crossed the Pond and returned to the UK five years later, my audience would have moved on and I would have lost my touch. Thirty years' hard slog would be wasted.

I'm what I call a one-type comedian. Audiences come to theatres and see my act. That's it. I don't do television. I don't do after-dinner speaking. I don't do corporate conferences at fancy hotels in London, playing to pissed-up businessmen with cigars and bow ties, waiting to show off how much money they've got by bidding fifteen grand for a signed Manchester United ball in the auction. I don't do any of that.

I've seen what happens when British comics branch out into pantomimes and game shows and corporate gigs. They lose touch with their core audience. And when the game-show producers and the businessmen no longer want them, they think they can go back to their roots. They book a season of theatre gigs and no one turns up because the public has forgotten what they do. It happened to Les Dennis and it's happened to other British comics. And once that starts and the newspapers get hold of the story and follow you around, waiting to see you fail, it's all over.

CHAPTER SEVENTEEN

MARITAL MELTDOWN

MY MIND'S GOING ten to the dozen from the minute I get into my car for the drive to the hospital. Buzz buzz buzz buzz buzz. Every six weeks it happens. A visit to Dr Martin and a camera down my throat. Two days before it's due, I start to panic. What if he says it's come back? What if he says he's got to remove my last vocal cord?

As I drive through the gates my hands start to sweat. My back is sticky and my heart pounds in my ears. I tell myself it's no worse than going to the dentist; that it will be fine. But I can't help it – the fear takes over.

Entering the hospital is like stepping into *Alice in Wonderland*. Real life is left behind and I walk into a strange dream. In the long grass, I'm relying on other people to tell me I'm all right. 'Everything's OK,' I want them to say. 'Come on in and sit down.' I watch the nurses scuttling around with clipboards under their arms. 'Mr Robinson: room three, please,' a nurse announces. 'Mr Thompson: room five. Mr Vasey – ha ha ha. We've conned ya!'

My stomach's rumbling and my head's light – no eating for twenty-four hours before the investigation, only a needle in the arm to make me even more woozy as the camera goes down.

It's the uncertainty that gets to me, the heart-stopping moments when there seems to be trouble. 'Say aaah,' Dr Martin says, his voice slow and echoing through the fog of the sedative.

'Ahhhhh,' I say.

'Say it again, please. Aaahhh . . .' he says.

Why? I scream inside. Surely once was enough? What on Earth could be so wrong that you couldn't see it the first time? 'Aaaaaaaaahhhhhh,' I say, hoping it'll do.

'I'm going to have another look,' he says. My heart nearly stops.

'Ahhh,' I say.

'Aye, that's fine' he says. 'That's fine . . . I'm very pleased. *Excellent progress.* Well done.'

Suddenly I want to fuck all the nurses and buy them all champagne. Music! Wine! Song! Let's all have a wank! I'm that excited. I walked in the hospital five foot ten; now I'm six foot six. I want to shout out to every passer-by: 'There's fuck-all wrong with me, you know!'

When I arrive home, a letter is waiting. It's about Dessy, a friend from Guisborough, a great lad who taught the kids to box and to play football. He's dead, the letter says. Lung and bowel cancer. He lasted eight weeks.

A few days later I go to the funeral. I know everyone there. 'How are you doing?' they say. 'Are you OK?'

'Yeah, I'm OK . . . so far.' It's a fact. How long will I live? How long is a piece of string? It depends how long you cut it. There are no answers. You might as well ask if there's another planet in the universe just like Earth with human beings, televisions, Hoovers and cars. We just don't know where or when it finishes.

●

I knew I'd made the right decision not to try to break America almost as soon as we arrived back in Britain. George rang me to say I'd been voted the Club Star Awards Comedy Entertainer of 1992. It was a clubland award, voted for by all the club secretaries and organised by *The Stage*, the main British show-business journal. I was told that I'd won it mainly for my ad libs and put-downs. I was made up. It was another poke in the eye for those carping critics who dismissed my act without ever having seen a Chubby Brown show, saying that because it was crude and offensive it couldn't possibly be funny.

The more videos and theatre tickets I sold, the more the critics wanted to knock me. They were delighted when I was run off stage in Gateshead in the opening minutes of a show in the early 1990s when, at the height of the child-abuse scandal in the North-East, I opened my show by saying, 'I'm surprised that there are so many of you here – I thought you'd all be at home fucking the kids.' And they loved it when lefty do-gooder councillors in Middlesbrough banned me from playing at the local town hall. I thought it was ridiculous. After all, which was more offensive? A council that let a comic tell crude jokes at its town hall? Or a council that presided over thousands of kids still growing up dirt poor in run-down Grangetown and Slaggy Island estates with little chance of a decent education or a proper job?

What those po-faced councillors didn't realise was that every attempt to push me underground directly boosted my video and ticket sales. The more my bawdy, vulgar end-of-the-pier humour was outlawed or denigrated as offensive or unfashionable, the more the public wanted to see it, simply because we all like what's naughty. Like drugs or Prohibition alcohol, my tapes had an anti-PC under-the-counter word-of-mouth cachet about them that made *Jingle Bollocks* the sixth-biggest seller in 1994, just behind *Snow White* and *Jurassic Park* and far ahead of popular 'alternative' comedians such as Steve Coogan.

The videos were selling so well that Polydor, the company that distributed them, tried to persuade me to release two a year. They'd awarded me a statuette for outselling all the other videos they distributed, although they hadn't invited me along to the dinner at which it was handed out even though I was netting them about five million quid a year. Worried that I'd swear in front of their guest Princess Anne, one of the Polydor top brass accepted the statuette on my behalf and told me about it after the event. I was told that they thought I'd say 'Thank you, you fucking cunts' and not have the brains to know how to be polite. Nevertheless, they recognised a cash cow when they saw one and pestered me to release more videos each year. When I said it was asking too much of me to give away another sixty minutes of my material without spending a year preparing it and bedding it in on stage, Polydor suggested that I should make a movie.

I'd written a story about a band, like *Spinal Tap* but more down to earth. Based on my experiences in The Pipeline and the Four Man Band, it started with a band auditioning for members in a council house and assembling a motley crew including a drug addict, a ladies' man and a drummer who was very ambitious. The idea was to show how bands are often made up of very different types of people and how that can lead to some very funny escapades. No sooner had I presented the idea to Polydor than *The Commitments* came out. The film was just as I had envisaged my film and immediately killed off that idea, so Polydor sent two writers up from London. We spent several days sitting around a table trying to come up with jokes, but Londoners just don't seem to have the same sense of humour.

Polydor sent me several scripts, but in the end I had to tell them that although some of the ideas were good, they just weren't funny. It was off-the-wall college humour, funny to students but too avant-garde for my audience. 'I know it's about me,' I told the executives at Polydor, 'but I don't want my name on it. It's just not common enough. It's not about ordinary people.'

In the end, we took the two writers' plot, I added some humour and the result was *UFO*, a science-fiction spoof in which UFO stood not for Unidentified Flying Object but You Fuck Off.

The plot involved a bloke who was kidnapped to another planet where he became the first man to have a baby. Quite excited by the project, I spent six weeks at Pinewood Studios and on location in Blackpool, working from seven in the morning until eleven at night to shoot the film – a rush job by film standards and a record according to Tony Dow, the director.

Tony had planned scenes on the beach at Blackpool, on the Golden Mile, up the Tower and outside the South Pier Theatre. I was all for it, but I warned him that I'd be on my home turf and we would be regularly interrupted by Jack the lads shouting 'Chubby! You fat bastard!' or flashing their arses out of windows in the background.

'Don't worry,' Tony said. 'We're used to it. We can handle it.'

On the first day in Blackpool, I was just getting into shooting a scene with Jackie Downey, who played my wife, when a lad in the street shouted out a typical comment. 'Chubby!' he said. 'Kiss me ring-piece!'

'Cut!' shouted an assistant director and we had to start again.

Jackie looked at me. 'Aye, you're dead popular, aren't you?' she said.

'I told you. I did say . . .' I said.

It was great to work with proper actors. Sara Stockbridge, a trendy model-cum-actress at the time, was lovely, as was Jackie.

Sara had to run naked through a park in one scene. I hadn't realised how many blokes were on the crew until it came to shooting that scene and they all turned up. And when Shirley Anne Field walked onto the set, my mouth nearly hit the floor, even though she was in her late fifties. In common with many lads of my generation, Shirley had been adolescent fantasy material and was still a beautiful woman. Sue Lloyd from *Crossroads* and Roger Lloyd-Pack, a real character who I knew from *Only Fools and Horses*, were also working on the film.

If I was gigging in the evening I'd leave the set at six p.m., jump in a car, travel to the theatre, do a show, then travel back to Pinewood or Blackpool. If I wasn't gigging, when the shoot wrapped I'd sit in the studio until two in the morning, trying to improve the script. It was long hours and hard work. By the end, my eyes were in the back of my head.

When we watched the final edited film, I thought a lot of it was crap, but there were several parts that people talked about afterwards and fortunately they were the parts I wrote, such as a scene in which a girl asks me to record a message on a cassette for her brother who was in a coma and I said: 'Get out of bed, you lazy cunt.'

We premiered *UFO* at the Showcase in Middlesbrough. Knowing that we wouldn't attract any real celebrities, we invited all our friends and relations and hired lookalikes of the Queen, Prince Charles and Rod Stewart. I walked on stage and introduced the film, an awkward experience as by then I was becoming uncomfortable with some aspects of it and I really didn't want to watch it through. Sometimes fans come up to me and say they've watched it twenty times and that they love it, but I'd rather it was consigned to the vaults.

However, for every embarrassment there were half a dozen triumphs, one of which was selling out the London Palladium. In Middlesbrough, it even made the newspapers. 'Chubby on at

Palladium,' the local rag said. People stopped me in the street. 'Fucking hell!' they'd say. 'You've come a long way!' Then they'd add the usual punchline: 'Eeh, I remember paying six bob to see you.'

When I arrived at the Palladium and looked at the photographs of the stars on the walls, a shiver ran down my spine. Every big star had played there. Like me, many of them had skeletons in their cupboards, but I bet few could claim to have played Wallsend Labour Club, where a stripper once pissed in the dressing-room sink, the night before they were on at the London Palladium.

The dressing room was a disgrace. It was shabby and dirty. The stage manager poked his head around the door. 'You've obviously given me the pigsty,' I said. 'The dressing room you keep for people like me.'

'This is the number one dressing room,' he said. 'They've all been in here, you know. Liza Minnelli, Sammy Davis Junior, Frank Sinatra, Bing Crosby – they all sat there, where you're sitting.' That shut me up.

At eight p.m. I was in front of the footlights of the West End's most revered stage, but my mind was a mess. I was too busy wrestling with my stomach to be able to think clearly. 'Boys and girls,' I said, 'I wonder if Shirley Bassey has peed in the sink in the dressing room here. Mind you, she doesn't pop her cork for anyone.' Not the right joke for the Palladium – the audience gave a few polite grunts. 'Don't worry if you don't like the one I'm telling,' I said. 'You can always run in the gents' toilet and get another gag off the wall.'

Slowly the audience warmed up. Within seconds of hearing the first belly laughs I was in full flow. I've never concentrated as hard as I did that night on the Palladium stage. Although the house was packed with fans, I knew that some of the audience were there simply because I was playing the Palladium, rather than because they were hard-core Chubby supporters. In front of them, I couldn't afford to make a mistake. After the show I sat in the chair in my dressing room, trying to come to terms with it. When I first stood on those sticky stages in Grangetown and Redcar claggy mats and clubs, I never dreamed that I'd play the London Palladium, no matter how long or hard I worked. Detention, Borstal, prison, arsehole, cunt, fat bastard . . . and now sold out at the greatest and most famous theatre in the world.

George and I took the crew out for a celebratory dinner. 'You've done it now,' George said, but I felt it was more a case of surviving than triumphing. An accomplishment rather than a victory. I was pleased to have done it, but somehow it didn't mean as much to me as a packed-out barnstormer on my home turf.

When I got back to Teesside I bumped into Steve Purnell, a lovely fella married to Brian Findlay's sister and who in the early 1970s drove me to clubland gigs for a short while when I was in trouble for driving without tax and insurance. Steve worked as a bread man, delivering loaves of Mother's Pride to houses in Redcar. After about three or four months of driving me to Alcock & Brown gigs, he told me that he'd always wanted to play the drums, so I taught him the basics. Six months later Steve was a better drummer than I'd ever been. He was obviously a natural talent and practised until his hands bled. It wasn't long before Steve rang me to say he wouldn't be able to drive me to gigs any more. He'd got a job playing drums at a local club four nights a week, getting up at four a.m. to deliver the bread until two p.m., then having a few hours' rest before drumming until midnight. Another year or so later, I heard that Steve had landed a job with Smokie, a country-rock group that was particularly successful in Germany and which had scored a few Top Ten hits in Britain with 'Oh Carol' and 'Living Next Door To Alice'. With his hangdog moustache, long hair and cowboy hat, Steve certainly looked the part.

When I bumped into Steve in Redcar in 1995, he'd been playing with Smokie for about fifteen years. 'Have you heard the version of "Alice" that the Irish shout?' he asked me. 'At the end of every chorus, they shout "Who the fuck is Alice?" at us.'

'Really?' I said. 'Sounds great.'

'We want to record it as a spoof,' Steve said. 'But we'd never get away with saying "fuck", so we thought you, what with your reputation, would be the best man for the "Who the fuck is Alice?" bit.'

A few weeks later, I met the lads from Smokie in a recording studio in Wakefield. We recorded the track in an afternoon, with me adding all the 'fucks'. The single was released in two versions – the raw, uncensored song and a version with all the 'fucks' bleeped out so that it could be played on the radio. Shortly before it was released, Smokie's lead singer Alan Barton was killed in a car crash on a German autobahn. The band were devastated and decided to donate any royalties from the single to Alan's wife. I happily agreed to follow suit, but I didn't think the royalties for a spoof record would ever amount to much. In its first week on sale, the single entered the charts at number twenty-eight. And in those days, you had to sell a substantial number of records just to get into the Top Thirty.

When it rose to number twenty, we were invited onto *Top of the Pops*, where I lip-synched to the bleeped version. The next week, it went into the Top Ten and we were back on *Top of the Pops*. When the record company released it internationally, 'Who The Fuck Is Alice?' went to number one in Australia and several European countries. In Britain, kept off the number-one spot by Simply Red, it reached number two and became one of the most popular parts of my theatre gigs, an eternal crowd-pleaser that I've brought out of retirement several times simply because audiences demand it.

The record earned a fortune around the world and every penny of my royalties went to Alan's wife.

In early 1995, just before I recorded 'Who The Fuck Is Alice?' with Smokie, I made Sandra a very generous financial offer. Things had got so bad between us that I just wanted out. But Sandra turned it down so I pushed the matter to the back burner, hoping to find another way of getting her off my back. But by July, when the 'Who The Fuck Is Alice?' single was ready to be released, my love life had got a whole lot more complicated.

Estelle Keogh was a barmaid at the De Vere Hotel in Blackpool, where I was staying every weekend of my summer season at the South Pier Theatre. Twenty-three years old, she was a bonny lass with a pretty face and long dark hair. I'd noticed Estelle behind the bar during the previous summer season, but had never got talking to her. One evening we started chatting and from then on I'd always drop by the bar when I was staying at the hotel, just to say hello.

Four or five weeks into the Blackpool season, I asked Estelle where was the best place to eat on a Sunday in Blackpool. 'I don't like all those fancy places,' I said. 'I just want a good roast dinner with a nice Yorkshire pudding.'

Estelle recommended a pub nearby. 'I'll take you there, if you like,' she offered.

'Really? Will you?' I said. I was surprised that a young lass like Estelle would be interested in spending her Sunday with a fat fifty-year-old like me.

'Yeah, what time do you want dinner?' she said. I told her midday. 'I'll pick you up here at twelve o'clock,' she said. The next day, she pulled up in a car with her brother and sister-in-law in the back. 'This is Roy,' she said to them.

After our Sunday dinner, she dropped me off. 'Thanks,' I said. 'It was lovely.'

Getting out of the car, I give her a little kiss on the cheek.

'I wondered when you were going to do that,' she said.

It was like a little firework went off inside me. Whoa! She fancies me, I thought. I couldn't see what she might see in a fat middle-aged comic. It had been so long since any woman had taken any notice of me and, after seven years' marriage to Sandra, I thought no woman would ever look at me again.

I couldn't wait to return to the De Vere Hotel the next weekend. 'Eh, thanks for last week,' I said as soon as I arrived in the bar.

'It was good fun,' she said. 'I enjoyed it.'

'Can I take you to dinner this week?' I asked.

'Yeah. Or why don't we have a coffee tonight?'

That evening, Estelle came to my room. After a couple of drinks, she went to the bathroom and I could guess what was happening. Brace yourself, Chubby, I thought, she's going to let you fuck her.

When the Blackpool season finished, Estelle and I kept in touch by phone. About two months later, while working in North Wales, I phoned her. 'I'm at Rhyl,' I said. 'Do you want to come up for a couple of days?'

I'd told Estelle I was married and that I was unhappy. By the time she arrived at Rhyl, she knew the score. Holed up in a log cabin, which was part of the hotel, we had a wild weekend. After the show on the Sunday evening, I waved her off to Blackpool before heading home.

A week later a letter arrived from Estelle. 'Dear Roy,' it said, 'thanks for a fantastic weekend. I love you dearly and miss you every day.'

I was thrilled with the letter. Then I read on. 'I was wondering,' Estelle wrote. 'I've seen a small property in the centre of

Blackpool and I would like to open up a ladies' lingerie shop. Could you see your way clear to lending me nine thousand pounds?'

I didn't like the sound of that. How was I going to explain nine grand missing out of my bank account to my wife? I rang Estelle. 'I can't just take nine thousand quid out,' I said.

'You're leaving her, aren't you?'

'Yeah, but I don't want her solicitor to have anything on me for adultery or anything like that. I don't need any of that shit.'

'Oh, right.'

'Hang on,' I said. 'I'll think about it and write you a letter.'

That evening, I wrote the letter. 'We haven't known each other very long, but you've made me feel like a sugar daddy,' I wrote. 'It's only been a few months and now you're asking me for money. You make me feel like you see me as a gold mine. I'm sorry, but I can't give you that money.'

I sent the letter off and hoped that would be the last I heard of the subject and that it wouldn't affect our friendship.

A week later on a Sunday morning, I came down for breakfast at Sunnycross House. Sandra was making a bacon sandwich when I spotted my name on the front of the *Sunday Mirror*. What's that? I thought, grabbing the paper and turning to a double-page spread on pages twelve and thirteen.

TOO-BLUE CHUBBY KEPT HIS CAP AND SOCKS ON FOR SEX, the headline said in big thick capital letters. Fucking hell, I thought. What if Sandra saw it?

'I'm just going to the bog!' I said, quickly scooping all the newspapers into my arms.

Locked safely in the toilet, my heart pounding in my mouth, I opened the paper to look at the story. 'How Britain's crudest comedian charmed a buxom young beauty into his bed,' it said in big letters stretching below the headline. 'Roy Chubby Brown in love affair with Estelle Keogh.'

Draped across half the page was Estelle, wearing white lingerie and high heels, lying on a double bed. I had to admit she looked great. The jaw of every bloke in the country must have dropped open with amazement when they saw that picture. I could guess what many of my mates would be thinking. 'Chubby's fucked her?' they'd be saying. 'The lucky bastard.'

The story didn't pull any punches. 'The married millionaire joker wooed Estelle Keogh with silver-tongued chat-up lines a million miles from his crude £10,000-a-night act,' it said. 'But when Britain's filthiest funny man finally got her into bed he slipped back into his stage role – making love to her in fluffy white socks and an old cloth cap.

'Later, Chubby got his act together, making love to her all night in a four-poster bed, in stage dressing rooms up and down the country and in the back of his luxury Mercedes car.'

Well, some of it was true. It seemed churlish to complain that the bits about the flat cap and making love in the back of my car were pure fantasy, especially as Estelle was quoted as saying 'Roy's a really sexy guy. He's got a bit of a beer belly, but the rest of him is pure muscle.' I didn't disagree with that.

The inaccuracies in the article were irrelevant. There was enough in it for Sandra to eat my balls for breakfast, mashed up on one of those bacon sandwiches she was cooking. I thought of flushing the newspaper down the toilet, but realised that it would only block the drain.

I stuffed the newspapers down the back of my trousers. Pulling my top down over them, I sauntered out of the loo as casually as I could manage. 'Is that bacon for me?' I said. 'You know, I'm sick of it.'

'Where you going?' Sandra said, noticing me moving towards the kitchen door.

'Didn't I tell you I'm away today?'

'You said it was tomorrow.'

'Well, all the lads are travelling today, so I thought I best join them.'

'But I've bought Sunday dinner.'

'Fucking hell,' I said, pursing my lips. 'Eh, I'm sorry about this.'

Thinking that it would be the last time I saw Sandra in Sunnycross House, I gave her a kiss and got in the car. At the end of our drive, two reporters were waiting. Beside them, a photographer, camera hanging round his neck, glanced into my car. I shielded my face and turned from him as I passed.

I knew as I drove away from Sunnycross House that my marriage was over – and not a day too soon for me. Things dragged on for a few more months as we tried to patch things up. I spent a small fortune buying Sandra presents and taking her on holiday in an attempt to repair things, but it didn't work. An already bad situation turned worse and eventually our marriage collapsed. Sandra's response was to go to the newspapers. A string of allegations were trotted out, most of which I felt were blatant lies.

I phoned Sandra. 'What have you told the fucking newspapers?' I said. She denied it to the hilt, but there were too many personal details for me to believe she hadn't spoken to the press. And again there were quotes from Sandra that revealed her true motives. 'I want a good financial settlement and I want to stay in this house,' she'd told the *Daily Mirror*. 'I am prepared to stick it out until I get what I want, regardless of how long that takes.'

Exactly what that entailed – and how far Sandra was prepared to go to get it – I found out in October, when our divorce came to court. Sandra filed on the grounds of unreasonable behaviour and I didn't contest it. I would have admitted anything, even being an international terrorist, just to get rid of her. After all, they say the difference between a wife and a terrorist is that at least you can negotiate with a terrorist.

Sandra arrived with most of her family – her son and daughter, her mother, her Auntie Pat. It was a top day out for them. As I walked past her into the courtroom, I gave her my best 'I hope you die' look, but once in front of the judge *I* was the one who was murdered.

According to the terms of the divorce, I'm not allowed to say exactly what Sandra got. However, I can say that all I was left with was my pension, a small amount of money in the bank and my car. Sandra even got my beloved fifty-thousand-pound Steinway grand piano, even though she couldn't play it.

But what really hurt was losing my home. I loved Sunnycross House. I bought it a year before I met Sandra and spent a fortune renovating it. It was my pride and joy, but I was now banished to a little rented cottage beside a pub. It didn't seem right. I'd been a comedian for twenty years, working my balls off to get where I was. I'd spent eight years in purgatory, married to that woman. And after just two days in court I felt gutted like a fish. I was skint.

After the hearing, George took me out for a bite to eat and a drink. 'It's all over, son,' he said. 'Do you feel as if you've been ripped off?'

'If I'd had to give her a shilling, I'd have felt robbed blind,' I said. 'A shilling would have been too much.'

'Ah, well. What we'll do is, we'll earn it back for you over the next year or so. Don't worry. You'll get your money back. We'll do it together.'

CHAPTER EIGHTEEN

LOVE CONQUERS EVERYTHING

BORSTAL AND PRISON made me grow up. Clubland showed me an escape from a life of crime and dead-end jobs. Turning blue put enough money in my pocket for me not to have to worry too much about the future. And being diagnosed with cancer made me realise that money isn't everything and that the love of my wife and children is more important than anything.

The thing that surprised me about cancer is that once I'd recovered I didn't feel any different. It's not like I was dragging my leg or I had a lump on my head and every time I combed my hair my comb caught it. But it was living inside me and maybe because of that, it made me change the way I think.

It made me realise that comics of my generation don't live long. That might be because the job goes hand over fist with drinking, smoking and not eating well. Whatever the reason, every time I open the paper these days it seems that another comedian has died. And they all seem to be around sixty-seven or sixty-eight years old – not much older than me. Anything beyond that seems to be a bonus. Woody Allen said, 'I don't mind dying, I just don't want to be there when it happens' and I'm like that. When I first discovered that I had cancer, I wondered if it was better to die than to lose the voice that had been my fortune and my saviour. I don't believe that any more, even if it means that I'm the first comic who has to mime his gags.

I want more time to improve my piano-playing and to learn new instruments, but most of all I want it to spend with my two young children. Having come from nothing I don't want to go back to nothing, so I've always worked hard. But more than anything I don't want my kids reaching adulthood and thinking that although their dad was famous and left them a good legacy, they never really knew him – like I never really knew my mam.

●

George kept to his word, packing the calendar with gigs. I never worked as hard as in those first years after I divorced Sandra, toiling to recoup gradually everything she had taken from me. My schedule was relentless and I was in dire need of a holiday when another comedian told me about playing in South Africa. It sounded fantastic – good money and a first-class air fare to a first-class hotel in a beautiful climate. I could see myself relaxing by a cool pool all day, then playing a gig in the evening. It would be like a paid holiday. I told George that I wouldn't mind having a go and he said he'd make some enquiries.

A few days later he reported back. 'You can't go to South Africa unless we take one of their acts,' he said. Equity rules stipulated that I'd have to find an act just like mine. If I'd been a girl singer or dancer, I'd have had no trouble finding a South African counterpart, but I was a filthy, dirty, disgusting stand-up blue comedian and there was no one remotely like that in South Africa. I was snookered.

'Don't worry,' George said. He had a plan B. 'We'll go to Australia and New Zealand.'

By October 1997, I was on a flight to Australia via Hong Kong, the first stop on my maiden world tour. I spent the entire flight worrying about how I'd go down. Would they understand me? Would English working-class gags mean anything to Bondi beach bums and Hong Kong wheeler-dealers? As it turned out, Hong Kong was fine. I played a small theatre packed to the rafters with expats and army lads. It was like playing any army town in England. And when I arrived in Australia I realised they were more British than I was. They watched *EastEnders* and *Coronation Street*, and of course *Neighbours* and *Home and Away*. They drove English cars on the same side of the road as us. They had Indian takeaways, kebab shops and fish and chips. They had the same problems as us – consumer debt and immigration. And to my North Yorkshire ear there was little difference between the Australian accent and cockney. The only difference was the currency and the weather.

Riding in a limousine from Sydney airport to our hotel in the city centre, I got talking to the driver. 'So you're Chubby Brown, are you?' he said in a thick Aussie twang.

'Yeah,' I replied. 'Do you know me?'

'Oh, yeah, mate. I know you. I've got all your tapes. I had Billy Connolly in the limo last week.'

'Billy?' I said. 'He's fantastic.'

'He is, yeah, mate. He rates you!'

'Does he?' I said. The taxi driver told me how they'd passed a building site surrounded by a massive wooden fence plastered with posters advertising bands on tour.

'Then,' the limo driver said, 'Billy spotted a poster for your tour, mate. "Oh, fucking hell, Chubby's coming here," he said.

"D'you know him?" I asked. "Yeah, he's fantastic, I love him. He's a broad-church comic. He's open to everybody. He talks about things that we all laugh about."'

With Doddy, Billy Connolly has always been my comedy hero, so hearing that was just the confidence boost I needed before facing an Aussie audience. I played three nights in Sydney, the first in a comedy club beneath Sydney Harbour Bridge, the steel for which my father helped produce all those years ago when I'd wave him off to work at Dorman, Long. It was a great night, with a lot of heckling, but the Aussies had never heard anything like my brand of answerbacks and ad libs – 'Why don't you get your mind read? It'll cost you fuck-all' I shouted at one of them – and they loved my act. The next night I played the University Theatre and, on the third night, another big theatre where I was on with a band that combined rock and roll with yodelling. They called themselves the Von Trapp Family. So bad they were funny, they came on stage dressed in lederhosen and green Bavarian hunters' hats with feathers. My audience, mostly lads on the piss, didn't take to them at all. 'Fucking get off!' they shouted. 'You're shite!' When the Von Trapp Family came off stage, George met the lead singer in a backstage corridor.

'I've never known a rougher crowd than that,' the singer said.

'Well, you know who's on, don't you?' George said. 'Britain's bluest comic, Chubby Brown. You didn't stand a chance.'

We checked out of the Ritz Carlton hotel the next morning. Two days later, I was on stage in Brisbane. The news had broken that afternoon that Michael Hutchence had hanged himself in the hotel I'd just left. He must have been staying there at the same time as us. 'I stopped at the Ritz Carlton in Sydney yesterday,' I said on stage that night. 'Closed the bathroom door, there's a fucking bloke hanging there with an orange in his mouth.'

The audience gasped. Hutchence was a god in Australia. It was the equivalent of making a joke about Princess Diana just after her death. But I thought it was just a throwaway line, so I kept going. 'Paula's coming over,' I said. 'Do you know Paula Yates? She has got Fifi Trixibelle and Peaches, and I think the other one's called Cream.' I told some more gags about the kids' names. The audience fell about and I'd got them back on side, but it was a close-run thing. The Aussies have no inhibitions and nothing seems to bother them. They're very accepting and take as they find, so my brand of humour went down a storm, even better than in Britain.

We went on to Melbourne, Adelaide and Perth. Every city was wonderful and every gig sold out. The staff at the theatres told me that the tickets had gone quicker than any others for years and treated me like a superstar. In Perth, we shot a video that later became *Chubby Down Under*. I thought it was one of the best gigs I'd ever played.

Spending as much time as possible looking around each city, I loved everything I saw in Australia. It was just like the clichéd view of Oz, only better. Instead of working crazy sixty- or seventy-hour weeks, like in Britain, the Aussies had got the balance right and spent as much time as they could outdoors, on the beach, drinking lager, throwing prawns on the barbie, surfing, cycling, running and swimming. It was no wonder they were so good at sports. Everyone was tanned, beautiful and healthy – I only wished I was twenty years younger. And when I went out in the evenings, the bars were relaxed and easygoing, with girls singing and bashing tambourines and the lads joining in.

The one thing I really noticed about the Aussies was that they swore so much they made me sound like the Archbishop of Canterbury – maybe that's why they took me to their hearts. Whatever it was, they looked on me as some kind of international celebrity and I loved every minute of it.

After Australia, we flew on to New Zealand. I was expecting Maoris everywhere but, riding in the taxi to the hotel, we could have been in Middlesbrough – Marks & Spencer, Woolworths, the houses and most of the stores on the high streets were the same. I got to the hotel and switched the telly on. The first channel I turned to was showing *Coronation Street*. On a side table was a kettle with Tetley teabags and sachets of Maxwell House coffee.

I played a small theatre in Auckland. Another superb night with a cracking audience. The next morning I got a phone call asking me to come onto a radio show. 'You can say anything but "cunt",' the disc jockey said.

'What? I can say "bastard", "fuck" and "fanny"?'

'Yes, anything but "cunt",' he said. 'And we want you to take the piss out of our mayor. She's a lesbian, but she thinks nobody knows it. Of course we all do.'

It sounded like the perfect radio show for me, although I was worried that they might be setting me up. When I arrived at the studio, they poured me a coffee and sat me in front of a microphone. 'Ladies and gentlemen, we've waited a long time for this . . .' the DJ said. 'He's finally here, the fat bastard himself, Chubby Brown.'

'Don't you be so fucking ignorant, you fucking halfwit,' I said. My first sentence broadcast on New Zealand airwaves had two 'fucks' in it. I thought it was great. 'And that fucking big fat lesbian you've got here, can you imagine me and her on the job? Fart and give us a clue . . .'

I talked for about twenty minutes, running through my gags. When I got to the theatre that night, the manager stopped me. 'Were you on the radio this morning?' he said.

'Yeah.'

'We've been inundated with calls for tickets. Our phone's never stopped today, we can't get them all in.' That night I played a blinder, one of my best performances ever.

Two years later, in 1999, I toured Australia and New Zealand again, but this time we flew via Los Angeles, where I played a gig at the Henry Fonda Theatre on Hollywood Boulevard. I didn't like LA. The people were rude, George nearly got arrested for smoking in a bar, we were frequently tapped for money by beggars on Venice Beach, a Groucho Marx T-shirt cost two hundred dollars, the waiters and waitresses were all out-of-work actors full of bullshit and nobody talked to us in the street. But the show was a barnstormer.

Appearing in the middle of Hollywood, the centre of the show-business universe, I was racked with nerves before the curtain went up, but as soon as I started I realised that half the audience was British. I sat at the piano, played some ragtime, told gags about America, flying, hotels, Venice Beach with its muscle men, dieting and mother-in-laws, then finished off with a number on the ukulele-banjo. I got a standing ovation.

When we returned to Middlesbrough, George was being pestered by a bloke in Bahrain who wanted to book me to play a gig in a desert tent. Having just travelled halfway around the world, I didn't feel like getting back on a plane. I don't like flying any road and I didn't want to go all that way for one gig. 'He's offering you a small fortune plus all expenses. We can take the whole crew,' said George.

'I don't want to go,' I said. 'Tell him to double it and I'll think about it. That'll shut him up.'

The bloke phoned back 'He'll pay double plus all the crew and expenses,' George said.

'Fucking hell, George,' I said. 'I don't want to go. What are we going to do now?'

George, as usual, had a plan. 'I'll tell him you're pencilled in to do a TV show and the only way you'll cancel is if he'll pay three times his original offer and provide first-class accommodation and air fares.'

The bloke phoned back again. A fee of three times his original offer of a small fortune was not a problem. It was the most I'd ever been offered for one night's work, so I reluctantly flew out to Bahrain.

Once I got there, I realised it was the best decision I'd made in a long time. With a chandelier larger than some English houses, the hotel was amazing. I was there for only a couple of days, but I felt like I'd put on more than a stone. At least I came home with a lovely tan.

Because it was illegal to drink in Bahrain, the bloke who'd hired me had erected a marquee near an expats' tennis club. We drove out into the desert until, in the middle of nothing but sand, we arrived at a wire-fenced compound like an army camp. Passing through a checkpoint, we drove on until our little convoy pulled up beside a big white tent. Inside it was carpeted, with a stage at one end, an excellent PA system that sounded better than most theatre sound systems, and a grand piano. Outside it was hot, the temperature in the high eighties even at night, but they'd air-conditioned the tent and inside it I could have been anywhere.

I played for ninety minutes to an audience of oil workers, their families and the expats who serviced them, such as doctors, dentists and cooks. There was even a lad from Grangetown who'd been three classes below me at school.

After the show, they opened a cupboard behind the stage. It was packed to the gunwales with whisky, brandy, gin, rum, sherry, beer and wine. Invited to help ourselves and with only half an hour until a taxi arrived to take us to the airport, we ripped through the cupboard's contents, nearly emptying it. By the time we arrived at the airport, I was legless. 'How are we going to get Roy on the plane?' George said. I couldn't stand up. They dragged me into the gents' toilet and splashed cold water on my face until I pulled myself together. I took a deep breath and stumbled to the check-in.

'You're in a good mood, aren't you?' said the woman at the check-in desk.

'Yesssh,' I said, slurring and grinning inanely. 'I'm in a very good mood.' And then I let out the longest, loudest fart I've ever heard. When it was finished, I turned around. George, his son Mick, the sound engineer Aaron and our lighting technician Mick were all on the floor, weeping helplessly with laughter. None of them could stand up or speak.

'Somebody's excited about getting on the plane, aren't they?' the check-in woman said.

The fact that drinking was illegal in Bahrain just made us all feel like naughty schoolboys and, despite concerns that we might be prevented from flying, none of us could stop giggling for the next two hours. It was only when the plane was in the sky and we had a fresh round of drinks in our hands that we calmed down.

When we got home, I tried on my multicoloured suit. After the stupendous breakfasts at the hotel and the booze blow-out on the last night – something to which I was no longer accustomed – it was getting tight. But then, I'd got used to being more svelte than for many years. Before going out to Bahrain I had lost more than two stone in weight since 1997. Why? Because I was in love.

After the trauma of the divorce from Sandra in 1996, I thought I wouldn't look at another woman ever again. Life with Sandra had damaged my view of all womankind, and I thought I'd be happy to bumble through the rest of my life on my own.

'If you see me with another woman,' I used to tell my friends, 'shoot me in the back of the head and hide my body somewhere. Do whatever you like, but don't ever let me set eyes on another woman.'

Sometimes I felt lonely, but I just ploughed my energy into my work. I spent a lot more time tinkling at the piano or pounding my drums. I devised a lot of songs and wrote more poetry than I had done for years. I saw Richard and Robert, my kids from my first marriage, and got to know my grand-children a bit better. Totally uninterested in women, I just kept myself busy.

That all changed after a show at the tail-end of the 1997 summer season. Skegness was on Wednesdays, Thursdays I was in Rhyl, Fridays were Great Yarmouth, Saturday and Sunday I played Blackpool. I was always travelling and always stuck behind caravans, the curse of the road. It must have been a Wednesday because we were in Skegness when my driver Peter Richardson led me out of the stage door to where some fans were waiting. 'There's a girl here,' he said. 'She was here last week with a friend. Now she's come back with her boss and her boss's girlfriend.'

'Right,' I said – thinking, so fucking what? – as Peter brought them over. 'Hello,' I said.

'Hello,' the girl said. I hardly looked up.

'Can she have a photograph, Roy?' Peter said. I picked up a colour photograph to hand it to her, but Peter interjected. 'Can she have a photograph with you?'

'Yeah,' I said. 'Of course you can.' I stood up. 'What's your name?' I said.

'Helen.'

'Oh.'

Helen looked at me and I looked at her. I won't say it was love at first sight, but there was definitely something. She was the first woman I'd noticed for a long time. And boy was she a bonny girl. I tried to guess her age Thirty-two? Thirty-one? Maybe even younger? Whatever – she was far too gorgeous to be inter-ested in me. Long blonde hair. Perfect figure. Lovely teeth and green-blue eyes. She was wearing a pink cardie and from what I could see had a perfect pair of tits beneath it. By God, you're nice, I thought.

'Have you seen the show before?' I said.

'Yes, I was here last week with a friend.'

'Is your friend a fan too?' I said.

'Well, I converted him,' Helen said. 'I heard a couple of tapes of yours, then I saw you on video and you made me laugh so much that my sides were aching. I've always been a fan, so I persuaded my pal to come to your show last week.'

'Well, that's nice,' I said.

'And I'm coming next week as well.'

'You what? You were here last week, this week, and next week? Who's this you're with?'

Helen introduced me to John, a farmer, and Julie, who giggled a lot. I smiled and Julie grinned back. 'Will you sign this?' she said, pulling her jeans down. 'Will you sign my arse?'

I looked at Helen. Her face was redder than the ripest tomato and she was staring out the window. For Julie, who moaned in mock ecstasy as I signed her arse, it was all a big joke, but I could see that Helen wasn't like that. She watched silently. Then, as they were leaving, she said quietly, 'I'll see you next week, then?'

'That'd be nice.'

'Can I come backstage next week?'

'Come early, come a couple of hours before the show and we'll have a cup of tea and a sandwich if you want.'

'Honestly?'

'Yeah.'

I stood beside Helen while John snapped a photograph of us together. 'I'll bring the photo next week,' Helen said. Then she left and I got in my car.

On the way home, Peter didn't stop talking about Helen. 'She was a bonny girl, wasn't she?' he said.

'She was, yeah. Nice as well.'

'Oh, was she?' he said.

'She's coming again next Wednesday and I'm going to have a cup of tea with her.'

'Eh, you might be in there, mate.'

'Nah, I'm not bothered. I couldn't pull a young bit of stuff like that,' I said. 'She's lovely and all that, but what would she see in me?'

'Well, you know, women are funny,' Peter said. 'They're more canny than us blokes and I can see she doesn't half like you.'

'Listen, Peter, she's nice, but she's just another split arse. And they're all the same,' I said, remembering my marriage. But women *aren't* all the same. Some can bring out the best in you and some can bring out the worst. I didn't yet know that Helen would make me happier than I'd ever been with myself.

In my dressing room at Skegness a week later, Peter knocked on the door. 'That girl's here,' he said with a wink. 'She's stood outside the door.'

I went out into the corridor. Helen looked even more gorgeous than she had the previous week. 'Where we having this cup of tea, then?' she said. We found a café with a jukebox across the road from the theatre and walked in.

'Oooh, I love them buttered scones,' I said as we sat down, pronouncing 'scone' as 'scon'.

'It's a scone,' Helen said, pronouncing it 'scoan'.

'No, it's not. Where I come from it's a scon and it always will be.'

'No, it's a scoan,' Helen said, starting to laugh.

Refusing to let me pay, Helen bought me a cup of tea and a scone. And so over a scon, scoan – whatever – we got to know each other, flirting and giggling like two teenagers. Walking back to the theatre, she touched my arm. 'I probably won't see you after the show,' she said.

'Oh . . . no . . . why?'

'I've got to get away quick because I'm working in the morn-ing.'

'Oh, that's a shame.'

'I must apologise for Julie last week,' Helen added, explaining how she'd given Julie a dressing-down the next day. 'How dare anybody do that!' Helen didn't have to say it for me to know that she was a decent woman. I could just tell. I'd lost all confidence in my judgement of when women were telling the truth, but there was something about Helen that convinced me I could trust her.

'This is my mobile number,' Helen said. 'Will you give me a ring?'

Two days later I was in the car on the way to a theatre. I dialled her number.

'Hello?' she said.

'It's Roy.'

'Who?'

'Roy, Roy Brown.'

'Eeh, I never thought you'd ring me.' Helen chatted for a while. 'Next week you're at Blackpool, aren't you?' she said. 'I'll come over with my mate and we can catch up.'

When I put the phone down, a smile as wide as the mouth of the Tees at Redcar cracked my face. 'I don't know what that's all about,' I said to Peter. 'But she wants to see me again.'

I booked two single rooms for Helen and her friend at the hotel in Blackpool and that night we chatted long into the night before we went back to separate rooms.

From then on, I called Helen every day. She was living with her parents but they didn't know about me, so whenever I'd phone her she'd hide under her duvet. We'd speak for hours, Helen whispering under her bedclothes. Four months later, Helen came to Blackpool on her own and I booked her into the room next to mine. We'd had a couple of drinks and were on the way upstairs when I gave her a kiss.

'Is there sommat wrong with me?' she said.

'Far from it.'

'Well, you know . . . you haven't, like, even . . . you haven't even put your hand on me.'

'I might be a blue, filthy, downright dirty comedian, but I'm not an animal. I wouldn't dare . . . you know, I'm twenty-odd years older than you.'

'What does that mean? C'mon, what do you think of me?'

'I think you are wonderful.'

'And I think *you* are wonderful,' Helen said. 'So do you want to stay the night?'

She had a perfect body. I was so nervous, I was cracking jokes. 'The downstairs department's not massive, you know,' I said. 'Top floor, not bad, but downstairs in the lift . . .'

And that was the start of our relationship.

The following night on stage I ran through my material at forty miles an hour, I was that excited. I couldn't believe what had just happened to me and I wanted to tell everyone.

'I told you she liked you,' Peter said.

I couldn't get over it, but I knew I was a difficult man to live with. Over the next few months, I told Helen about my past, my kids, my hard, violent days in the clubs, what I'd been and what I hadn't been. 'You're best off just walking out the door,' I said. 'You said you loved me and you're a wonderful person, but I do have a dark past and some women would find that difficult.'

Helen said it didn't matter. 'Well, at least it gives you something to talk about when you go out for dinner with your friends,' I said. '"Still with that fat bastard, are you?" they'll say.'

Again, Helen didn't care. All that mattered to her – and to me – was that we saw each other as much as we could. Working all week and most weekends, I made sure that I snatched every available opportunity, travelling to where she lived in Grimsby whenever it was possible. And if I was on the road, playing a gig near Grimsby, Helen would travel down for the night and go back to work early the next day.

We spoiled each other rotten, buying each other flowers, cards and chocolates all the time, not just on birthdays. Helen would buy me all sorts of jumpers, ties and socks, never forgetting me when she was at the shops. But most of all we just let each other know that we loved each other – after all, it doesn't cost a penny to say those few words that let someone know you really care.

We'd been seeing each other for a year off and on when I decided to rent a little cottage in a village outside Middlesbrough. Things at Helen's workplace had got complicated and she was no longer enjoying it, so very reluctantly – because she was adamant she didn't want to be a kept woman – Helen agreed to come and live with me. Shortly after that, the most magnificent house in Helen's home village came up for sale. Situated on a hill, Maltby House had a front room, side room, back room, living room, snooker room, two kitchens, wine cellar, five en-suite bedrooms and many more rooms that we didn't know what to do with. It had three and a half acres of land, tennis courts, a lake with a thousand catfish, a two-bedroom guest cottage and a three-car garage. I paid four hundred and sixty grand for it and at last we had a proper home of our own. We renovated the entire property, planting dozens of trees and plants and reseeding all the lawns. I had an indoor swimming pool built with 'Helen' and 'Roy' inscribed in mosaic tiles on the bottom of the pool. It was housed in a Swiss log cabin and cost me about sixty thousand quid. We installed a Roman bath in the back garden and fitted electric gates with a security camera at the end of the drive. When the postman rang the bell, we could see him on a television screen in the kitchen. We'd buzz him in, then press a button and all the fountains in the Roman bath would come on as he came up the drive. It was really impressive and we loved it, but we soon found that the upkeep was enormous. It cost us a fortune to maintain Maltby House, including employing a full-time cleaner and two full-time gardeners. After two years, when Helen was pregnant with Reece, our first child, we realised it was too much and we sold it. But I still miss that house to this day.

It was while Helen and I were living at Maltby House that we switched on the television to see a signpost with 'Royston Vasey' on it appear at the beginning of a show. A few months previously, George had taken a phone call. 'We're the League of Gentlemen . . .' a voice said. Neither George nor I had ever heard of them.

'We're making a series set in a small town. Would it be all right if we named the town after Chubby?' the voice continued. 'We're all big Chubby fans. We love his stuff and when we were at college we used to watch him on video and listen to his tapes and he used to have us in hysterics . . .'

George was baffled. 'I'm sure I don't have to . . . I'm sure he'll be flattered,' he said. Then he rang me.

'What are they going to call the town? Chubby Brown?'

'No, they want to call it Royston Vasey after you.'

It sounded genuine, so we said yes and took the chance. All we knew was that it was an off-the-wall black comedy.

The first time I saw it on the telly I couldn't believe that my name was on the signpost. Royston Vasey – Helen and I looked at each other and went 'Fucking hell!' The first scene showed a hearse going by and the flowers on the coffin spelling 'bastard'. From that moment on, I thought it was great.

When the first series finished, they rang me up and asked what I thought of it. 'Some parts of it were brilliant and some parts I couldn't understand,' I said. It was the truth.

They said that was the reaction they were looking for. 'Would you like to be the mayor in the next series?' they said. I agreed immediately.

The League of Gentlemen were a bunch of young lads, Mark Gatiss, Jeremy Dyson, Steve Pemberton, Reece Shearsmith. On the first day's shooting, we spent ages in the make-up caravan, talking about humour over cups of tea and biscuits. Then they gave me a script. I read through it, took note of all the directions and then went to shoot my scene.

We lined up on the set. When an assistant director shouted 'Action!' I ran through a door, stopped, looked around and ran back through the door. That was my first take and I thought I'd done a good job. But the lads were all looking at each other as if something had gone wrong.

'You didn't deliver your lines,' Mark Gatiss said.

'There aren't any lines,' I said.

'Yes, there are about ten lines.'

'No, there aren't.' I called over to George, who was standing to one side, and asked him to go to my caravan and bring the script back. I flicked through it. 'There,' I said, pointing at the sheaf of paper. 'Look – no lines.'

'What the fucking hell's happened here?' Mark said, grabbing the script. He flicked through the pages. 'He hasn't got fucking page three.'

I hadn't noticed that the page numbers jumped from two to four. All my lines were on page three. No wonder my scene had been so easy.

They gave me half an hour to learn my ten lines, then we shot the scene again. Over the next couple of days, while shooting all the rest of my scenes, we talked more about comedy. They asked me how I came up with gags. I explained how I would scan through the newspapers for ideas, writing things down and trying to play on words. Whereas I had to use my patter to paint a picture for the audience, much of their comedy involved thinking of things that would look funny or absurd on screen. While the others were acting, one of them was always writing and adjusting things to make them look better.

In my biggest scene, something that caused nosebleeds had broken out in Royston Vasey and the press wanted to interview me, as the mayor, about it. As I was being interviewed, a van pulled up with 'Mobile Swimming Pool' painted on the side and a bloke in his trunks got out of it, drying himself with a towel. I thought that was really funny – you'd never see a mobile swimming pool. As I walked past the swimming pool, the bloke in the trunks spoke to me, asking me to talk to the press but insisting that I didn't swear. 'You know me,' I said. 'I don't swear in front of the camera. Never swear on camera.' Then, with the press hounding me and onlookers pestering me, I answered questions about the nosebleeds. I was asked if there was an epidemic in Royston Vasey, if it was true that there was poison in the drains, whether an axe murderer was on the loose, and so on. At the end, I said: 'Hold it, hold it. It's a beautiful day. There's nothing wrong with Royston Vasey. We have a small problem and as far as I am concerned . . .'

'Thank you, Mr Mayor,' the press said.

'It's a fucking pleasure,' I said and then the scene ends.

The mayor was one of the first to get the disease and I had to lie on a cobbled street for an hour and a half with fake blood coming out of my ears and nose, shivering as I got colder and colder. Two days later I was in bed with the flu, but I'd really enjoyed shooting my two episodes.

While recuperating from the flu I opened the *Sun* to discover that 'the son of blue comic Roy "Chubby" Brown shot at a driver in a road-rage attack' and was now appearing in court. This was news to me. I knew that my two sons Richard and Robert were happily getting on with their lives in Redcar. They'd never cause trouble, let alone fire a gun at someone. I read on: 'Martin Reilly, 26, allegedly fired a pistol into Trevor Finn's car at Billingham, Teesside, after having to give way. The shot just missed Mr Finn and smashed a passenger window, Teesside Crown Court was told yesterday.' Now it made sense.

I'd been playing a gig a few years previously when my sister took me aside. 'There's a lad at the door who says you're his father,' she said.

'Honestly?'

'Yeah, he says his name's Martin Reilly or sommat.'

'Right?'

'He *is* your son.'

'How do you know?'

'He's the spitting image of you. He's got your eyes, your nose, your mouth, your teeth.'

'Well, you better let him in.'

I met the lad and Barbara was right. He really was a mini me. He said that his parents had recently divorced and his mother had told him that I was his biological father. I was baffled. The visual evidence was overwhelming, but other than that I couldn't figure out how I could be his dad. Gradually we pieced it together and I realised that he was the son of the girl who worked at Tesco's who I'd knocked off for a short time while seeing Beryl when I was about twenty years old.

We met again a few weeks later at the library and exchanged a few photos. I didn't see him again, but occasionally I'd hear from someone else what Martin was doing. He had a bad reputation around Stockton and had got in with some nasty company, eventually landing up in court, where he admitted firing a single cartridge from a double-barrelled shotgun pistol because he believed they thought he had access to my money. He claimed in court that he had received death threats and demands for ten thousand pounds. I thought it was a load of bollocks and that he pulled the gun for the simple reason that he thought the two other lads in the other car were going to kill him.

I was outraged that he'd been portrayed as my son when we'd had contact for no more than a couple of hours, so I rang up the paper. 'What are you fucking doing? I don't even know the lad,' I said. They didn't have an answer.

Martin wasn't the only child who came crawling out of the woodwork around that time. A year later, a letter dropped on the doormat. 'Dear Roy,' it said. 'I don't really know where to start, I've tried to write this letter a million times and still don't know what to say.

'We've never met each other although I've got to know quite a bit about you. This is very difficult for me and I've no idea how you are going to respond to this letter.

'I was born in January 1972 at Middlesbrough Hospital and was named Lisa Audrey, although that is not my name now as I was adopted at six weeks old by fantastic parents.' The letter went on to explain how its writer had traced her true parents through adoption agencies and the Salvation Army and that, although my name wasn't on her birth certificate, there was a note saying that the father was believed to be a drummer from Redcar.

I spoke to George. 'If it was me I would want to meet her,' he said. 'I would want to know.' So I made contact.

We chatted for a short while on the phone, then I told her I'd just started a new family. 'We've got a new baby. His name is Reece,' I said. I'd recently rushed from Birmingham, where I'd been playing a gig, to Grimsby Maternity Hospital, where Helen had gone into labour. Running from the car park into the hospital, I was stopped by Helen's mother.

'It's a boy! It's a boy!' she shouted, somewhat spoiling the surprise I was anticipating with Helen. 'He's eight pounds six ounces . . .' I'd hoped to have been there with Helen when the baby was born, but the price of living on the road was often missing out on this kind of precious moment.

Now I was talking to another supposed child of mine and discovering that my brood was much larger than I'd thought. This time there appeared to be a germ of truth in the story. I had known Audrey and I had slept with her shortly after splitting up with Judith, my first wife. I looked at my arm. Tattooed there, somewhat faded now but just about legible, was Audrey's name alongside Judy, Pat (who claimed that her daughter Michelle was mine), Beryl, Lana (who also claimed she was carrying my child), Sandra and a few others whose names I'd forgotten. It seemed like a fair cop.

'I did sleep with your mam,' I told the girl on the phone. 'But I didn't know you existed. Maybe we should meet.'

Sitting in the bar of the Copthorne Hotel at Newcastle, my heart almost stopped when the girl walked in the room. She was the spitting image of Audrey. I gave her a kiss and we sat down. We started talking about the old days. She wanted to know how it had ended up that she'd been put up for adoption.

'We were kids, young and immature,' I said. 'Nobody I knew had heard of condoms, but we were still at it like rabbits.' The girl looked at me.

She was lovely. Bright, intelligent, well-dressed and pretty, I would have been proud to have called her my daughter.

'You know, the jigsaw is starting to come together as we sit here,' I said. 'It's all coming back. About the time you were born, my mother told me that a girl had dropped by her house with a baby she claimed was mine. I'd assumed the girl was Lana, another girl I'd been seeing, but she must have been your mam, Audrey.'

We'd all assumed that Audrey had returned with her family to Sicily, but I'd just heard from Joan Boothby, the wife of Mick, my old mate and bass player from Jason and Everard and the first incarnation of Alcock & Brown, that she wasn't in Sicily at all. She was in Redcar, collecting her pension every Thursday at the post office, where Joan bumped into her.

'I got an anonymous letter about a year ago,' the girl said. 'It said "Roy Vasey is your father" and that's what started me looking for you. I tracked down my mother and wrote to her, but didn't get a reply. I wrote to her brothers, but they said she was in Sicily. Obviously she just doesn't want to know.'

I put myself in the girl's shoes. She'd spent ages tracking down her biological parents, then found out that she was the product of little more than a bit of fun, and now her mum didn't want to know. I felt responsible.

'I can see you are a lovely person,' I told her. 'And I wished I had loved you as a daughter, but I don't know you. I have a family and I love my kids. That's where my life belongs. But if you want anything, I'll help you.'

We kept in contact after that, exchanging birthday cards, meeting up at Christmas and speaking on the phone. One of the times we met, she brought along some photos of her adoptive parents on holiday with her.

'I'm going to tell my mum and dad that I've met you,' she said.

'Do me a favour,' I said. 'Don't do it.' The girl looked at me surprised. 'Your mum and dad have been looking after you for more than thirty years. You love them, don't you?'

'I love them very much.'

'Well, don't even think of telling them,' I said. 'After they've devoted their lives to giving you love and affection, it would just hurt them and it wouldn't make any real difference to you. Please don't tell them.' For that reason, I've not mentioned this young woman's adoptive name, only the name that Audrey gave her at birth. We still keep in touch, but I've had to recognise that she belonged to a past life far away from my current circumstances.

As I approached my sixtieth birthday, I had a sense that at last I was coming to terms with my past, putting old demons to rest. Most of it was due to the love and contentment I'd found with Helen. We married in Las Vegas in 2001, not long after my daughter with Audrey made contact with me. Six months later, I discovered that I had throat cancer and underwent treatment. A year later, in the summer of 2003, I was fined for battering a recovering heroin addict with an umbrella in Blackpool after he repeatedly insulted me and goaded me into taking him on. In November 2004, my cancer specialist gave me the all-clear to go back on the road. After surgery, radiotherapy, physiotherapy and rest, the cancer was gone and the one vocal cord remaining in my throat was strong enough for me to play three gigs a week.

Early in 2005, just as I was writing the first chapters of this book, I summoned the courage to remove George Forster. I now felt he had been quietly squeezing the soul out of our relationship until the only way for me to survive was to cut him out of my life.

When I started to write this book, I thought I'd dedicate it to George, finishing with a chapter thanking him for everything he'd done for me. It would have been a testimonial to our long career and close friendship. But I realised our partnership – the longest relationship of my adult life – would have to come to an end. I felt that George was treating me like a thoroughbred racehorse that won every race for him, but every race wasn't enough.

Instead this book is dedicated to my third wife Helen, who taught me to accept myself in the way she has accepted me since the day we met. When I realised that Helen was the one for me, I sat her down and explained how my life worked. 'I love you very much, darling, but I'm Chubby Brown and I've got to give him a hundred per cent,' I said. 'That means in most cases you will come second. I'm sorry but that's how it is.'

Without Chubby, I told Helen, I couldn't earn a living. Before Chubby, I was nobody, just another stupid arsehole with no future and a dodgy past, like many of the kids with whom I grew up.

Edmond Saul, who'd been my best friend in Grangetown, whose tin soldiers I nicked as a kid and whose leg I injured when we went camping as teenagers, came to one of my shows shortly before my sixtieth birthday. 'In our class,' he said, 'there were twenty-two girls and fourteen boys. Out of those fourteen boys, eight have died.' If I hadn't got out of Grangetown, it might well have been nine dead. I've watched dozens of Grangetown lads who were just like me when I was younger – always stealing, lying, fighting and drinking, constantly in and out of prison – drop like flies, cut down in their prime by cancer, heart attacks or violence. That was their miserable life. I was part of that brigade, part of that shitty existence, but Chubby showed me a way out. He taught me that until the music started and you walked on stage, you didn't know what the audience would be like or what the night would bring. That's how I look at my life – don't make assumptions about anything until you've been there. And think on your feet if you want to succeed.

Chubby made me something. Call it schizophrenia if you want, call it two people in one suit, call it what you like, but I owe him everything. He saved me from myself and brought me the kind of success and riches no Grangetown lad could ever reasonably expect. There's some people who say money's not everything, but you try and get something without it. We all know how it works.

I said my bit to Helen and she accepted it all. We got on with our strange life and, over time, Chubby stopped taking first place. One evening, when I was getting ready to go on stage, I took a phone call from Helen saying that Amy, our two-year-old ray of sunshine, was not very well. My immediate impulse was to cancel the gig and rush home to be with my family.

Helen persuaded me that it could wait until I'd done the show. Another ninety minutes wouldn't make a difference, she said. She was right, but I realised something that night. Helen and the kids had replaced Chubby. Nothing had ever made me think of cancelling a gig before. Chubby had always been more important to me than anything, but not any more. He used to rule my life because I felt I owed him everything. Those days were over. Chubby had become just a bloke with a mucky mouth and a silly suit. A bloke in a flying hat and goggles, a clown who goes on stage every night and tells rude jokes, but who gets packed away when I go back to my dressing room, take off the suit and the helmet, get under the shower and wash off the greasepaint before I step out into the night. And that's all.

ACKNOWLEDGEMENTS

Thanks to my perfect wife, Helen, and my beautiful children, Amy and Reece.

To Richard, Robert and your families – so proud of you all: 'Our dad was an arsehole in his younger days but we wouldn't change a minute.'

A big thank you to the 'team' who accompany me on the road: Ritchie, Scottie, Ian, John, Keith, Jeff and Steve and the fantastic band Hooper. Also the 'team' at my management company Handshake Ltd: Craig, Jean, Bob, Todd, Kate, David, Carla and Nicola for organising my life so well, and an extra special thanks to my accountant Philip Steele and my manager Stuart Littlewood.

To Eddie, Helen, AJ, Chris, Stuart and all at Universal for everything they have done for me during the past fifteen years.

To Robert Uhlig for his brilliant contribution in writing this book with me and to Robert Kirby (PFD) and Antonia, Viv and all at Little, Brown for believing.

Since I started to write this book, some very good things have happened. My children are one year older, and even more wonderful. I have changed my management and I am now happy in that department; my latest DVD *King Kong* has gone double platinum; Middlesbrough Football Club has had a great season and has supplied the new England manager; and you, the great British public, have continued to support me. My only sadness is that Mam and Dad never witnessed their son at the peak of his success. I have enjoyed recalling the highs and lows of my life and I do hope you have enjoyed sharing them with me.

LOOK OUT FOR THE LATEST LIVE DVD:
KICK ARSE CHUBBS
COMING IN NOVEMBER 2006
VISIT WWW.CHUBBYBROWN.BIZ FOR MORE INFORMATION